Solutions Journalism

Solutions Journalism

News at the Intersection of Hope, Leadership, and Expertise

Bill Dodd

LEXINGTON BOOKS
Lanham • Boulder • New York • London

Published by Lexington Books
An imprint of The Rowman & Littlefield Publishing Group, Inc.
4501 Forbes Boulevard, Suite 200, Lanham, Maryland 20706
www.rowman.com

6 Tinworth Street, London SE11 5AL, United Kingdom

British Library Cataloguing in Publication Information Available

Library of Congress Cataloging-in-Publication Data

Names: Dodd, Bill (College teacher), author.
Title: Solutions journalism : news at the intersection of hope, leadership, and expertise / Bill Dodd.
Description: Lanham : Lexington Books, 2021. | Includes bibliographical references and index.
Identifiers: LCCN 2020051609 (print) | LCCN 2020051610 (ebook) |
    ISBN 9781793618719 (cloth) | ISBN 9781793618733 (pbk)
    ISBN 9781793618726 (epub)
Subjects: LCSH: Journalism—Social aspects.
Classification: LCC PN4749 .D63 2021 (print) | LCC PN4749 (ebook) |
    DDC 302.23—dc23
LC record available at https://lccn.loc.gov/2020051609
LC ebook record available at https://lccn.loc.gov/2020051610

Contents

Acknowledgments

This book is in many ways about realistic optimism, its importance for audiences and journalists, and how individual hopes are reliant upon, and distributed through, communication and attentiveness. This is a lesson I have learned both through research and in the process of writing itself. I have been the extremely fortunate beneficiary of support, encouragement, and advice without which my naive hopes of writing this book would never have been converted into realistic optimism and ultimately the book you now read. Katrina Clifford steered me firstly through my honors dissertation and into the world of academic rigor before again supervising the doctoral research that underpins this book. Her kindness, precision, and pragmatism were indispensable and I am very thankful for her support over the years. Libby Lester's work and reputation drew me to the University of Tasmania and I was beyond thrilled to be able to draw upon her wisdom and expertise in the process of crafting this research and book. Her encouragement and insights have been revelatory and I thank her for her support over the years. I would also like to thank Kathleen Williams who saw my doctoral thesis over the line and found me excellent reviewers to assess the work. Thank you to Craig Norris who both trained me in media scholarship when I first arrived at the University of Tasmania and, by chance, prescribed a reading by David Beers that inspired the next four years of research. I would also like to thank Claire Konkes who has been a great ally and friend at the University of Tasmania Media School during difficult times.

A book such as this passes through many hands and benefits from the collective wisdom and suggestions of a global community of scholars and professionals. I am extremely thankful to reviewers of this work who provided excellent suggestions. In particular, I would like to thank Rodney Benson who offered friendly support beyond his initial role as an assessor of my doctoral thesis. His research has been a particular inspiration for me and his advice regarding this manuscript was very valuable. I would also like to thank the editors at Lexington Books, Jessie Tepper and Nicolette Amstutz, who, during the pandemic, remained highly professional and offered excellent support throughout.

Thank you to my family and friends for their love, generosity, and patience. Thank you to the wonderful and talented Ivett Dodd. Your turn.

Introduction

One week after the World Health Organization (WHO) declared the COVID-19 virus a global pandemic, and amid the ensuing global disruption and uncertainty, the WHO released a second advisory regarding the psychological effects of the outbreak. It included the explicit warning for audiences isolating at home to "minimize watching, reading or listening to news about COVID-19 that causes you to feel anxious or distressed; seek information only from trusted sources and mainly so that you can take practical steps to prepare your plans and protect yourself and loved ones" (World Health Organization 2020, 1). The urgent caution was reaffirmed by psychologists from the American Psychological Association (APA) who recommended that the public "avoid speculative stories and limit repetitious exposure to media stories that provide little new information, while staying abreast of critical updates" (Garfin et al. 2020, 2). The safest source of information, even in moderation, they recommended, was from the WHO, the Centers for Disease Control and Prevention, or otherwise, from Apple updates, Instagram, or Twitter. Thus, their advice corresponded with that given by associate professor of communication, Sheila Murphy, that, ultimately, the best practice would be for you to turn the news off entirely and watch a happy movie, read a book, or do something you truly enjoy (Murphy in Polakovic 2020).

Likewise, politicians, who at other times might have problematized the mass disengagement from journalism and public affairs, also supported the call for moderation if not outright avoidance of news media. The prime minister of New Zealand, Jacinda Ardern, was joined remotely by a prominent psychologist to discuss coping strategies for the prescribed social isolation. In the social media broadcast of the video, which received three times as many views as the size of New Zealand's population, Nigel Latta's advice was simple: "I don't watch the news all the time because it's bad for me . . . the more of that stuff that you consume, the worse you will feel, and it will make you just want to sit on the couch and look at that stuff, and it's pretty much the worst thing that you can do" (Ardern and Latta 2020). The advice was put more bluntly, still, by the premier of Tasmania in Australia, Peter Gutwein, albeit in relation to social isolation: "Tasmanians have parents and grandparents that went to war, put their lives at risk; I'm asking people to sit on the couch and watch Netflix. Surely that message can get through" (James 2020).

As might be expected, news organizations were fairly mute on this point, and perhaps remiss in suppressing what were very direct public health warnings. Understandably, journalism too was facing a sharp contraction in revenue with many local newspapers suspending operations. This led prominent commentators to reaffirm the value of journalism in a crisis. According to Peter Greste (2020), formerly a political prisoner of the Egyptian regime and now the founding director for the Alliance for Journalists' Freedom, these times should serve as a reminder that high-qualify information saves lives:

> It alerts those at risk of a looming emergency; it tells us of escape routes and strategies likely to keep us safe. It keeps us abreast of the latest science, the judgments of experts and the experience of others. It informs policy and alerts us to the plans and strategies of government, and when we use it to measure the decisions of our political leaders, it helps us hold them to account. (Greste 2020)

In Australia, news had provided this vital service with rolling coverage of the catastrophic bushfire season preceding the 2020 pandemic. Bushfire alerts were regularly accompanied by advice to keep the radio tuned to the public broadcaster at all times for important safety announcements. Survival instincts have long been tied to information salience. The fight-or-flight stress response makes humans evolutionarily fixated on information about risk (Holman et al. 2020) and explains why crisis coverage is such compelling and compulsive viewing. Yet, overconsumption of risk information can cause acute anxiety, trauma, and mental illness when crises are protracted and uncertain. As has already been observed in relation to COVID-19, news consumption may produce disproportionate or ill-directed responses such as hoarding of safety equipment or unnecessary hospital visitation (Garfin et al. 2020, 2; Park et al. 2020). However, with countries such as Australia closing their Parliaments, postponing elections or, as in Hungary, descending altogether into authoritarianism (Dam 2020), Peter Greste's arguments remain urgent and correct. For institutions to emerge from these crises with their democratic institutions intact, journalism must continue to do its crucial work of freely gathering and verifying information, asking difficult questions and broadcasting their reports. Yet, if serious journalism becomes widely understood as unhealthy, anxiety-inducing and emotionally exhausting, then the crowded "attention economy" (Marwick 2015) may prove adept at shifting audiences toward easier content; a possibility foreshadowed by new lifestyle, entertainment, and advice columns in the *New York Times* and the *Guardian* for self-isolating audiences (Sifton 2020).

Even prior to this latest crisis, awareness of journalism's effects on mood and mental health have been increasing, as has news avoidance generally. In a survey of Australian digital news consumers, news avoidance rose from 57 percent to 62 percent between the years 2017 and 2019 (Fisher et al. 2019). While Australians were satisfied with the news media's provision of up to date information relative to the global average (66 percent compared to 62 percent, respectively), they were more likely to think the news is too negative (44 percent compared to 39 percent). The Reuters Institute's Digital News Report has found a similarly inverse relationship globally between journalism's core functions and public perceptions of negativity, noting that, statistically, a " 'negative' press is often the flip side of robust scrutiny" (Newman et al. 2019, 28). However, it would appear that mood preservation may be a stronger motivation than scrutiny for audiences, with news avoiders in Britain overwhelmingly citing news' negative impact on mood (58 percent and the perception they were powerless to influence events (40 percent) as the reasons for their avoidance, rather than trust in the veracity of its information (34 percent) (Newman et al. 2019, 26). These trends present a serious difficulty for journalism, raising a number of existential questions: How can journalism maintain its normative democratic functions of scrutiny, accountability, and transparency, while offering a product that does not promote unsustainable emotions of anxiety, cynicism, and fear? How can it decouple the relationship between negativity and rigorous scrutiny? Or, inversely, the perceived association between positivity and laxity?

While lifestyle and advice columns have been a successful journalistic response, providing welcome respite for anxious audiences—journalists have also sought to adapt serious journalism by reporting rigorous, realistic, and optimistic solutions. The *New York Times*, having already established the solutions journalism column "Fixes" (Bornstein 2011; Bornstein and Rosenberg 2016), released a new long-form and interactive assemblage of opinion columns titled "The America We Need." Adopting a literary structure, the first chapter was titled "A Nation Tested" in which the *New York Times* editorial board argued that that the virus had revealed the fundamental weakness of America's market-lead, racially segregated and vastly unequal society, providing an opportunity to radically revise the social contract, end segregation, and (noting pointedly that an election was due in November) restore a proactive style of government. The series of essays would, the editors explained, "envision how to turn the America we have into the America we need" (Editorial Board 2020). However, in so doing, the *New York Times* was also contributing to the ongoing revision of its own profession: transitioning journalism—that everchanging, borderless yet crucial profession—from the journalism we have into the journalism we need.

SOLUTIONS JOURNALISM

In a period of social, economic, and ecological precarity, journalism is increasingly being called upon to tell engaging and optimistic stories about the future. As audiences increasingly avoid negative news content (Newman et al. 2019) and perceptions of future risk are fragmented by polarized media ecologies and audiences (Kahan 2012), advocates of solutions journalism argue that it is more constructive to report "what might go right tomorrow and who is showing the way" than endlessly answer the question "what went wrong yesterday and who is to blame?" (Beers 2006, 121). Proponents of solutions journalism at the Solutions Journalism Network and the Constructive Institute, and practitioners at the *New York Times*, *Quartz*, the *Huffington Post*, and the *Guardian* urge journalists to report effective responses rather than the problems alone (Bornstein 2012; McIntyre and Lough 2019; Haagerup 2017). Many news organizations and journalism education institutions have taken up this challenge and, increasingly, there are now regular columns, programs, podcasts, and segments that specialize in solutions reporting. Moreover, there are entire media organizations, such as Quartz, Positive News and Good Media Group that "help audiences see around corners [and] navigate disruption in their industries" ("Global News and Insights for a New Generation of Business Leaders" 2020).

Nonetheless, these emerging solutions-based practices remain controversial. While advocates characterize solutions journalism as simply 'good journalism' and as telling a fuller story (Huffington 2015), many professional journalists express reservations (see Haagerup 2017, 88–91). Reporting solutions, some argue, "blurs the distinction between impartial reporting and political advocacy, forces them to take sides in political conflicts and gloss over complex problems for which no simple solutions exist" (Haas 2006, 248). Often these criticisms point to departures from journalism's core normative and temporal commitments. Whereas news traditionally offered a chronicle of immediate events—"operating at the cutting edge of the present as distinct from the past or future" (Nash 2016, 137)—the reporting of solutions may require journalists to cover (and even advance) hypothetical and utopian futures. Speculating about "what might go right tomorrow and who is showing the way" (Beers 2006, 121), it would seem, sits uncomfortably with journalism's temporal focus in the here and now.

Due to these misgivings, the project of normalizing the reporting of solutions in journalism has proceeded with extensive normative and empirical justification, as well as a minimalist conception of what counts as acceptable reporting of solutions. The Solutions Journalism Network begins its training manual with five points that distinguish solutions journalism from the "seven types of solutions journalism imposters we've all seen in the media before" (The Solutions Journalism Network 2020). Stories that exhibit flaws such as "hero worship," "silver bullet," or "think tank" are discounted from the properly rigorous reporting of solutions that the Solutions Journalism Network endorses, thereby providing a smaller target for would-be critics.

The tendency to police these boundaries reflects a cultural logic of distinction identified by Pierre Bourdieu who found that fields of cultural production, from poetry to pulp fiction, are characterized by a tension between "incumbents and pretenders," between protectors of orthodox values and purveyors of new practices (Bourdieu 1996a, 126). The importance of cultural distinction is especially relevant in journalistic meta-discourses (Carlson 2016) with reporting practice splintering into multiple subgenres and normative innovations such as slow journalism, peace journalism, constructive journalism, public journalism, and interpretive journalism, each with its own imperatives, practices, proponents, purists, and innovators (Aitamurto and Varma 2018). Yet the overriding imperative for the actors who have invested the most in these sub-disciplines—whose careers the discipline has defined—is toward distinction, standardization, and refinement. Likewise, research of solutions reporting has tended to follow the Constructive Institute (Haagerup 2017; Gyldensted 2015) or the Solutions Journalism Network (Bornstein 2004) in developing and testing a standardized best practice for reporting solutions. By interviewing members of the Solutions Journalism Network, Karen Elizabeth McIntyre and Kyser Lough condensed the established ten qualities of a good solutions journalism into a six-point "guide for how to operationalize a solutions journalism news story" (2019, 11). Likewise, Powers and Curry conducted both a textual analysis of the Solutions Journalism Network's materials and guides and a survey of its members to formulate "clearer objectives, metrics used to measure its impact, and guidelines for when and how to share impact" (2019, 3). Establishing professional consensus for a singular standardized practice has enabled empirical testing of the effects and impacts of solutions journalism, so defined, in order to test solutions journalism against its claims. However, standardization does tend to ossify solutions journalism, crystallizing the practice as it exists at this historical juncture and thereby narrowing its scope for change and adaptation.

While the carefully delineated categories of "solutions journalism" and "constructive journalism" serve the exigencies of the journalistic field by providing a shield of legitimacy and professionalism, these normative categories are of limited value for analysis of the reporting of solutions. Historically, solutions reporting has featured in a range of journalistic genres, including public journalism, development journalism, constructive journalism, and, most explicitly, solutions journalism. In each iteration, the normative value of solutions stories and the proper method for reporting them has varied. Public journalism endorsed localized deliberative democracy as a means of identifying public solutions (Merritt 1996; Woodstock 2002), constructive journalism mobilized prospection theory and positive psychology as a rationale and method for reporting solutions (McIntyre and Gyldensted 2018, 668), whereas solutions journalism has foregrounded empirical rigor in the identification and reporting of scalable solutions (The Solutions Journalism Network 2020). Yet most reporting of solutions globally proceeds without awareness of these conventions and boundaries, and an analysis of the reporting of solutions according to these normative models would be a rather arbitrary exercise in scholasticism. As such, while the title of this book may give the impression that it endorses or seeks to develop the solutions journalism model of reporting, in fact the book is agnostic in this respect and is concerned, more broadly, with firstly developing a generalizable framework for analyzing how journalists report solutions before considering normative lessons that can be derived from this analysis. It does so by identifying three common denominators that can be applied universally since they are invariably present (albeit in different ways) whenever journalists report solutions: these, I will argue, are hope, leadership, and expertise.

Understanding how journalists report solutions matters because, as risk communication scholarship has shown, news media assist audiences to anticipate the future and make good decisions in the present (Boykoff and Roberts 2007). Risk communication scholarship has been the most extensive research effort in progressing understanding of how journalists mediate the future for their audiences and, consequently, inform how that future takes shape. However, reflecting journalism's own preference for negative news content, media scholarship has been preoccupied with issues of risk communication, problem definition, and issue framing (Gamson and Modigliani 1989; Entman 1993). This body of research has examined the media's role in constructing public perceptions of intangible risks, visualizing invisible future consequences, and thereby helping communities navigate uncertain futures (Lester and Cottle 2009; Beck 2009; Nisbet 2009). Less studied has been the role of media in constructing positive futures, fostering realistic optimism, and communicating successes and strengths (Seligman 2002; McIntyre and Gyldensted 2018; McIntyre and Lough 2019) despite risks sharing many common features with solutions. Like risks, prospective solutions are intangible, have consequences that are difficult to anticipate, and are open to contestation and vulnerable to the public relations campaigns of powerful interests. With journalism under pressure to engage the public in with more optimistic content, media scholarship should take seriously the reporting of solutions and the role that this has in shaping public perceptions of agency and optimism. In seeking to establish a framework suitable for analysis of solution reporting as an extension of risk communication scholarship, this book explores the full range of solution-oriented journalistic practices that are necessarily shaped by competing professional priorities. By foregrounding the analysis of solutions, this approach nonetheless opens up new normative possibilities that extend and complement existing journalistic attitudes and practices rather than requiring wholesale conversion to a particular normative model.

Solutions reporting involves and is shaped by a range of social actors outside of journalism. Rather than examining solutions journalism as a purely journalistic practice, the book argues that solutions journalism occurs at the intersection of fields: the academic field, the market field, the journalistic field, and "the governmental field" (Hage 1996, 2000). I explore this interdisciplinarity through the prism of field theory: a sociological approach founded by Pierre Bourdieu that foregrounds the dynamic interrelations between fields of professional practice (Benson 1999; Bourdieu 1990). Like all fields of cultural production, solutions journalism is a field of practice: a site of struggle and distinction where individuals occupy unique social locations between a heteronomous, market-oriented pole and an autonomous, intellectually consecrated pole (Benson 1999). A strong autonomous pole is formed by universities that teach solutions journalism and through the standardizing and consecrating functions of solutions journalism networks like the Constructive Institute and the Solutions Journalism Network. Here, solutions journalism in prestigious newspapers such as the *New York Times* is typical of intellectually consecrated and autonomous solutions journalism. On the other hand, many news organizations report propositions for the future without awareness of solutions journalism. This heteronomous reporting of solutions has been described as more susceptible to, and characterized by, the engagement campaigns of political and business sources (Beers 2010, 121).

Thus, solutions journalism can be considered a relatively autonomous practice. Solutions journalism has been adopted by the most culturally legitimate members of the journalistic field in the United States and Europe, popularized through prestigious publications, such as the BBC and the *New York Times*, and refined through the research of journalism scholars who, in turn, educate emerging journalists in solutions journalism. Interestingly, some scholars have made the reverse conclusion. Amiel and Powers described solutions journalism as essentially heteronomous: a "Trojan horse" for public relations that erodes traditional journalistic practices with new marketing-oriented practices, and only admissible when "journalists experience employment insecurity and receive limited recognition for their work" (Amiel and Powers 2019, 236). This generalization mistakes autonomy for journalism's professional inertia and resistance to change when, in fact, autonomy (etymologically self-rule) is precisely the mechanism by which a field such as journalism governs itself and whereby practices are progressed, refined, and improved as consented by its leading practitioners. I understand solutions journalism, then, as a concerted and relatively autonomous effort within the journalistic field to improve best practice journalism.

Yet, solutions journalism, like most cultural products and especially journalism (Champagne 2005), is nonetheless shaped through a tacit negotiation of myriad external economic and political necessities, resulting in a practice that is simultaneously marketable and professionally acceptable. This compromise reflects the relatively heteronomous location of journalism more generally (Benson 1998, 466) where, according to Bourdieu, "much more than the scientific, artistic, literary, or judicial fields, the journalistic field is permanently subject to trial by market, whether directly, through advertisers, or indirectly, through audience ratings" (Bourdieu 1998, 71). Thus, in terms of field theory, solutions journalism can be understood as an internal effort by journalism to report solutions in ways that go beyond the demands of market pressure and political expediency, in the interests of democracy and "good journalism" (The Solutions Journalism Network 2020), while still producing a viable journalistic product.

THE ARGUMENT AND STRUCTURE OF THE BOOK

The book's argument begins with the observation that reporting solutions is neither a new nor rare phenomenon. From the earliest "news letters" traded between European merchants (Conboy 2004, 11) to coverage of President George W. Bush's justification for the "War on Terror" (Dunmire 2005), journalism has reported the ideas, proposals, and solutions of powerful leaders, politicians, and business sources. However, the voices that are routinely relied upon to articulate solutions and "frame our collective future," according to David Beers (2006, 121), tend to be "corporate-funded think tanks, public relations experts paid by corporations, advertising experts selling us the shape of the new, and government officials beholden to corporate lobbyists," What distinguishes more standardized models of solutions journalism from traditional reporting practices, I argue, is a democratized and autonomous conception of effective leadership and expertise. Whereas news access in traditional (heteronomous) solutions reporting tends to reflect existing power structures, autonomous solutions journalism is more proactive, rigorous, and democratic in evaluating whose leadership is legitimate and whose expertise is effective. Thus, solutions journalism's distinctive feature is "rigorous, compelling coverage of responses to social problems" (The Solutions Journalism Network 2020), with the emphasis on rigor indicated greater investigative autonomy on the part of journalists in interrogating the effectiveness of solutions and leaders. For David Bornstein, cofounder of the Solutions Journalism Network, social entrepreneurs are central protagonists in solutions journalism: "people with new ideas to address major problems who are relentless in the pursuit of their visions" (Bornstein 2007, 1). Such local success stories can be broadcast globally to "give citizens data and real life experiences from which to make judgments about how to respond to injustices and, collectively, choose a different path" (Beers 2010, 122). In its more rigorous and reflexive practice, solutions journalism is nonetheless interdisciplinary and cannot be understood without, as constructive journalists have argued (McIntyre and Gyldensted 2018), accounting for its basis in positive psychology, or, as public journalism scholars have argued (Woodstock 2002), deliberative democratic politics.

Across this complex intersection of sources and professions, this book identifies three common denominators—hope, leadership, and expertise—that are subjective and variable in their construction in relation to the reporting of solutions. As such, these three concepts, I argue, are central to solutions journalism and form the basic structure of the book. As I will argue in chapter 1, hope is a central concept for solutions journalism. Its normative mission, and legitimizing meta-discourse, is to restore faith in journalism and public institutions by reporting goals, pathways and success stories that restore social hope. Such stories are routinely excluded as un-newsworthy, they argue, with the result that audiences receive a fundamentally inaccurate picture of the world, a picture of disorder, decay, dishonesty, and disaster without hope of improvement (Bornstein and Rosenberg 2016). However, in pursuit of a marketable and rigorous journalism—distinct from soft news, advocacy or boosterism—hope is often suppressed as a feel-good emotion. As David Bornstein explained in the *New York Times*, reporting solutions "doesn't mean that the media's job is to soothe people or provide hope" (2012). However, recent findings from positive psychology have found that hope is not merely an emotion, it is cognitive—involving goal-directed thoughts about pathways and perceived agency in accessing those pathways (Snyder, Shane, et al. 2002). This chapter seeks to clarify and add nuance to the role of hope in shaping solutions journalism, with reference both to positive psychology (Seligman 1991; Seligman and Csikszentmihalyi 2012; Schneider 2001) and to a "boom" in hope scholarship in anthropology and sociology (Hage 2003; Miyazaki 2006; Kleist and Jansen 2016).

Chapter 2 presents a second distinguishing concept for solutions journalism: leadership. Public journalism, a democratic forebear of solutions journalism, shared many of its concerns and ambitions, even using solutions reporting a mechanism to reengage the public in the democratic process (Merritt 1996, 23). However, whereas public journalism maintained a strong deliberative democratic methodology in sourcing its solutions, most characteristically by face-to-face townhall meetings and focus groups, solutions journalism has departed markedly from this practice. Solutions journalism is uniquely focused on a certain type of pragmatic community leadership, with the "social entrepreneur" constituting something of an ideal source of solutions (Bornstein 1998, 2004; Bansal and Martin 2015). This prompts a more general discussion about the centrality of leadership for solutions reporting, both in orthodox and heterodox practice. In establishing the theoretical structure for the subsequent case study analysis, building on work by Ghassan Hage (2000), Walter Lippman (1922), and Nancy Fraser (1990), it is argued that solutions reporting relies on a "governmental field" (Hage 2000) of leaders whose pronouncements form the basis of solutions reporting.

Having established hope and leadership as central interdisciplinary concepts for solutions journalism, chapter 3 introduces the case study of "New Tasmania" where these ideas and arguments can be tested. Despite its remoteness, the challenges facing Tasmanian are globally resonant. Like many communities in the developed world that have historically relied upon primary industry and manufacturing, Australia's southernmost island province is facing challenges and negotiating fiercely contested visions of the state's future, often through the local Tasmanian news media. Its small and mostly rural population has experienced a profound economic transformation since emerging from the 2012 financial crisis. In 2014, the period chosen for this case study, Tasmania was engaged in vigorous debate concerning prospective solutions and visions of "New Tasmania" across several news platforms. This chapter contextualizes the case study by charting Tasmania's history of contested solutions and development conflict, conflicts that have shaped not only Tasmania but also global ecological politics. In this rugged, heart-shaped island, hydroelectric schemes led to the flooding of the iconic Lake Pedder—a mountain-hemmed, rose quartz beach set in the cool temperate rainforests of South West Tasmania—and, subsequently, the formation of the world's first environmental political party. Environmental conflict over contentious development proposals have since galvanized politics in Tasmania, yet the common dichotomization between pro- and anti-development politics tends to overlook who is privileged in proposing development solutions, and how their leadership was legitimized through the local news media. While "New Tasmania" represented a new spirit of bipartisanship in pursuing diversified economic development—oriented around tourism, the arts, real estate and quality produce—old disputes over protected areas remained (Lester 2019) providing a useful opportunity to gauge whether New Tasmania corresponded with new forms of mediated hope and leadership. The chapter presents the results of the content analysis of solutions reporting from 2014, which aimed to determine, firstly, the range of news sources relied upon to propose solutions and, secondly (through interviews with editors and frame analysis of news content), the evaluative frames that journalists and editors routinely deployed to select their news sources and report the act of proposing a solution. This latter step identified patterns and asymmetries in the range of news sources in the sample: most notably the high prevalence of business and political news sources, the low profile of female leaders, and the relative scarcity of expert sources.

Chapter 4 presents the ethnographic and interview findings from newsroom observation and discussions with the editors of Tasmania's two major newspapers, Matthew Deighton of the *Mercury* and Simon Tennant of the *Examiner*. Both representing "one-paper towns," these editors detailed the political considerations in catering for such a politically diverse audience. A central finding from this research was that leadership quality was a ready subject of discussion while evaluation of specific proposals appeared to be a more delicate topic. In particular, both editors appeared to endorse what I term, borrowing from Deighton, an "entrepreneurial spirit" of leadership in "New Tasmania." In describing valuable leadership, editors were specifically in favor of the innovation and energy of entrepreneurialism—leaders with "an entrepreneurial spirit" (Deighton, 28 September, 2014) who could achieve change "without a cent of government money" (Tennant, 4 November, 2015): innovative start-ups, companies that are unsupported by government largess, and entrepreneurs with international experience. This idealization of new governmental field with new voice and a democratized range of sources, however, stood in some contrast to the asymmetries in news access observed in chapter 4; however, this finding nonetheless supports the book's argument that leadership valorization is central in the reporting of solutions.

Chapter 5 extends this research through a close textual analysis of metaphors by employing George Lakoff and Mark Johnson's theory of framing and conceptual metaphor (Lakoff and Johnson 2003; Lakoff 2016). While the act of proposing a prospective solution is often an unremarkable "pseudo-event" (Boorstin 1992), journalists dramatized these press conferences and acts of governmental leadership by deploying three dominant conceptual metaphors: navigation, construction, and nurturance. The quality of leadership, especially in daily editorials, was evaluated and tested according to whether it corresponded with some basic virtues implied by each of these metaphors. For example, in proposing a solution, leaders were, metaphorically: lost, on track, behind or taking steps in the right direction; nation building, securing the foundations or repairing the damage; or helping a child find its feet, administering medicine or performing life-saving surgery. These metaphorical constructions, pervasive throughout the sample, provided a constellation of leadership virtues and vices, conditions of success and failure, and seemingly objective grounds for celebration or condemnation—thus forming crucial frames in the mediatization of the governmental field, and legitimation of the dominant sources within it.

Chapter 6 explores in detail the scarcity of expert sources—scientists, researchers, analyst, and other specialist knowledge professions in "New Tasmania." Despite the metaphors regularly playing upon different forms of expertise and their associated virtues, only 7 percent of the commentary was provided by actual experts. This provokes a discussion of expertise in democracy and, more specifically, its centrality and interdisciplinarity for solutions journalism. Whereas solutions journalism is characteristically utilitarian in its rigorous assessment of effectiveness, the case study found that the heteronomous reporting of solutions followed a virtue ethics of legitimate leadership. This represents, I argue, a point at which there are mutual lessons for both traditions of solutions reporting and where I defend a virtue ethics of expertise as an especially useful and generative method for autonomous solutions journalism in its ongoing revisioning of journalistic practice.

The book concludes by reflecting on journalistic autonomy in the context of the interdisciplinary nature of solutions reporting, four years after the 2014 case study. It returns to the questions posed earlier: How can journalism reconcile the dual imperatives of rigorous scrutiny with emotional sustainability? Ultimately, this question falls to journalists themselves. While rapid change in journalism's form and function appear inevitable in the current climate of uncertainty and anxiety, journalism will be variously proactive or reactive, autonomous or heteronomous, in reconciling these seemingly irreconcilable aims. This chapter positions this book and its findings as one external resource upon which journalism may draw, while reiterating that the necessary expertise for journalism's revisioning is essentially internal, and will rely upon an autonomous reconfiguration of external expertise: from psychology, politics, academia, and economics. As in solutions journalism itself, much will depend on who journalists speak to and how they navigate the interdisciplinarity at the intersection of hope, leadership, and expertise.

Part I

Chapter 1

Hope

With emerging solutions and constructive journalism practices, news outlets have increasingly sought to moderate negative news reports by centralizing more positive content: solutions, success stories, innovations, alternatives, and even utopian re-imaginings of society. An important motivation for solutions journalism is the idea of optimism, both as a psychological and democratic good in times of increasing cynicism and disengagement. However, as solutions journalism has become more recognized as a journalistic practice, the concept of hope has become, arguably, implicit and even suppressed as an ideal. While early solutions-based innovations explicitly centralized hope in their titles and marketing, contemporary iterations of solutions journalism eschew hope as too soft, saccharine or un-journalistic. However, with a "hope boom" in sociological thinking (Kleist and Jansen 2016), and the continuing importance of hope for positive psychology (Seligman 2019; Rand and Touza 2016; Snyder, Shane, et al. 2002), there is a new impetus and evidence base from which to salvage a properly journalistic concept of public hope.

The former centrality of hope for early solutions journalists was hard to miss. In a prescient essay for the *Columbia Journalism Review*, Susan Benesch (1998) documented the aims of emerging solutions-focused publications—their titles' exuberant expressions of optimism. These included *YES! A Journal of Positive Futures* and a magazine called, simply, *Hope*. Both founded in 1996, these publications coincided with a proliferation of new columns in daily newspapers devoted to solutions reporting. The founding editor of one such column in the San Diego Union Tribune, Karen Lin Clark, explained that "my task is to provide hope . . . not only information but help and hope" (Benesch 1998, 37). With the same commitment to optimism, French entrepreneurs and journalists founded Reporters d'Espoirs (Reporters of Hope) in 2004: an association and news network committed to spreading

hope by reporting informative solutions. Such was the importance of optimism that Jon Wilson, the founding editor of *Hope* magazine, complained
that "we're up to our ears in hope, we're mired in hope, we're surrounded by
miasma of hope" (Jon Wilson in Milbank 1997).

The idea of hope as a fundamental public good provided early innovators
with a normative mission and, publishers gambled, an audience of paying
optimists. However, as early pioneers soon discovered, these foundational
assumptions were just that. Shortly after launching *Hope*, Wilson gave a
somewhat forlorn interview for the *Wall Street Journal*:

> Here in Maine, *Hope* is losing $750,000 a year. The advertising saleswoman,
> calling her task "incredibly infuriating," has asked to be reassigned. Lesser
> men might abandon *Hope*, but Mr. Wilson continues to hope against . . . well,
> you get it. "In utter naivete I thought we could find a lot of readers real fast,
> and that was where I was wrong," he says. "It was very sobering." (Milbank
> 1997)

Wilson persisted for nine years before shutting production in 2004 without
Hope having turned a profit. He later explained to Associated Press (2004)
that stories of goodness and hope "were not dramatic enough for readers."
They were, he continued, "hard to read, not only because of the subject matter, but because they carried with them an inferred expectation of action on
the part of the reader" (2004).

In addition to the commercial challenges facing hope-based reporting, the
practice was also met with alarm by journalists in traditional mastheads—
undermining efforts to legitimize the new practice as simply "good journalism" (Huffington 2015). Relating his experiences in establishing constructive
journalism in Denmark, Ulrik Haagerup recalled his colleagues' forthright
rejection of the idea. Upon releasing a landmark essay on the subject, he was
criticized as an evangelist, crazy, a right-wing politician, a North Korean
communist and as euthanizing the journalistic watchdog (Haagerup 2017,
88–90). "Many journalists have a visceral, adverse reaction to solutions journalism," Benesch related (1998, 38). Hope-based reporting offended journalists for a number of reasons. According to Haas and Steiner, who canvassed
journalists' attitudes regarding public journalists' solution-based innovations,
journalists warned that reporting solutions "compromises their independence
and blurs the distinction between impartial reporting and political advocacy;
it forces them to take sides in political conflicts, and . . . gloss over complex
problems for which no simple solutions exist" (2006, 248). Certainly, it is one
thing to report an idea as a "solution," and quite another for a journalist to
state that the outcome is an object of hope: whether theirs or their audiences.
In either case, hoping for a certain outcome, especially in contested policy

settings, would have seemed unduly partial, and may only have exacerbated journalists' concerns regarding impartiality.

The challenges facing hope-based reporting, as both a commercial and cultural commodity, prompted practitioners to revise the practice and, to a certain extent, the brand. In contrast to the first wave of explicitly hope-based reporting, contemporary solutions journalists have sought to develop a more marketable and professionally acceptable model (Rani 2016). The Solutions Journalism Network's guidebook disavows soft news, hero stories, or inferred audience activism (Bansal and Martin 2015). Less explicitly, the language of hope, that an editor for *Hope* magazine described as emitting "a saccharin flavour" (Holmstrom 1998), was quietly replaced by more technocratic terminology. The Solutions Journalism Network now defines the practice as "rigorous, compelling coverage of responses to social problems—reporting done with the highest of journalistic standards" (The Solutions Journalism Network 2020). By focusing critically on effective responses, reporting is anchored in the recent past rather than the utopian future. Thus, rather than distributing hope, solutions journalism provides "data and real-life experiences from which to make judgements about how to respond to injustices and, collectively, choose a different path" (Beers 2006, 122). Likewise, the term "constructive journalism" represents a newly pragmatic and journalistic nomenclature, arguably eschewing the centrality of optimism in positive psychology on which constructive journalism was founded (McIntyre and Gyldensted 2018). Solutions journalists such as Bornstein, are often emphatic that it is not journalism's job "to soothe people or provide hope" (Bornstein 2012), while elsewhere justifying solutions journalism as countering "fear, learned helplessness, hopelessness, cynicism, depression, isolation, hostility, contempt and anxiety" (Bornstein and Rosenberg 2016). As the following exploration of hope psychology will argue, the hope in solutions and constructive journalism discourses rests upon a false dichotomy. Rather than hope and rationality being opposed—as emotion and thought often are—psychologists maintain that hope is cognitive: it is a rational thought process. As positive psychologists, Snyder, Rand, and Sigmon (2002) proposed, hoping involves a process of goal setting, pathway thinking and appraising one's agency in reaching making a desired future come about. This thought cycle, I will argue, contains important lessons for journalists seeking to broaden the range of perceived public options and pathways.

The second aim of this chapter is to re-politicize solutions journalism by entangling the psychological theory of optimism with, what Kleist and Jansen described as, "a veritable explosion of writings on hope in the social sciences and the humanities" (Kleist and Jansen 2016, 373). In contrast to the bipartisan appeal of hope psychology, anthropologists and sociologists such as Ghassan Hage (2003) have conceptualized hope as an unequally distributed social resource—one that is ever scarcer in an age of transnational capitalism and austerity. This chapter seeks to ground solutions journalism in both theoretical traditions: positive psychology and the sociology of hope. By triangulating these theoretical approaches, comparing recent findings from each, this chapter identifies a series of research questions and normative dilemmas for solutions reporting. While positive psychology has refined our understanding of the nature of hope and its importance for individual well-being, the sociology of hope can help identify the contingent social and political structures that have contributed to the epidemic of depression and political disengagement experienced in many countries today.

SOCIAL HOPE

The idea that having hope is a transferable social commodity—a commodity that can be possessed, traded and disseminated unequally throughout society—has become influential within sociological and anthropological research (Miyazaki 2006; Kleist and Jansen 2016; Hage 2016). In particular, the emergence of hope-based studies arose from the perceived deficit of hope in society, and the corrosive consequences of hopelessness for people, institutions, and communities. As Kleist and Jansen observed, "We find studies of hope in political and economic crisis, during or after protracted conflict, in times of rising inequality and stratified globalization" (Kleist and Jansen 2016, 373). As in solutions journalism, hope becomes most relevant when it is perceived as being in short supply.

The distributive logic of hope was an approach founded by Lebanese-Australian anthropologist, Ghassan Hage, in a study of Australia's anti-immigration discourses (2003). He proposed "that societies are mechanisms for the distribution of hope, and that the kind of affective attachment (worrying or caring) that a society creates among its citizens is intimately connected to its capacity to distribute hope" (2003, 3). For Hage, building on Slavoj Žižek (1991), social hope is intimately tied to nationalism. The nationalist cares for the imagined national community and the people within it because, in return, the nation provides hope: an implicit assurance and expectation of upward social mobility and ongoing safety. Yet, he argued, these national hopes are frequently denied to migrant communities whose position in the nation is constructed as more contingent, temporary, and exploitable (Hage 2000). This violent denial of hope to others has intensified, according to Hage, with transnational capitalism and its corresponding politics of austerity and scarcity. As governments have become preoccupied with attracting transnational capital to invest locally—by driving down wages and conditions, aestheticizing the city through gentrification and exclusion, and offshoring labor with multinational trade deals—hope is denied even to those nationalists formerly entitled to a share of hope by virtue of their whiteness or national capital (2003, 19–20). This has created communities of disenfranchised white Australians that Hage termed "refugees of the interior" who are nonetheless "mobilised in defending 'the nation' against 'the refugees of the exterior' " (2003, 21).

Hage's diagnosis of "paranoid nationalism" as a form of entitled hopelessness has only become more relevant fifteen years later with the emergence of right-wing populism, the election of Donald Trump, and the spread of organized online misogyny and racism (Scaptura and Boyle 2019). Related concerns about the corrosiveness of hopelessness and the rise of populism have also informed solutions journalists. In their critique of the social and psychological harms of pervasive negativity in news reporting, Bornstein and Rosenberg, the founders of the Solutions Journalism Network, lamented that "journalism's steady focus on problems and seemingly incurable pathologies was preparing the soil that allowed Trump's seeds of discontent and despair to take root" (Bornstein and Rosenberg 2016). In furnishing their argument about hopelessness, Bornstein and Rosenberg (2016) referenced positive psychology and, in particular, the idea of "learned helplessness and optimism" (Seligman 2019). While sociologists and anthropologists such as Ghassan Hage have studied discourses and the unequal distribution of hope throughout society, psychologists have sought to understand the cognitive mechanisms of hope, and the relationship between hopelessness and depression. Indeed, the psychology of hope and optimism has shaped solutions journalism, as psychology has shaped journalism more generally.

JOURNALISM'S PSYCHOTHERAPEUTIC TURN

In popular culture and cinema, the link between journalism and mental health is frequently dramatized. The latest batman franchise, Joker (2019), opened with a crackly radio broadcast: "The news never ends. This is 10.80 GCR. You get all the news you need, all day long." The camera slowly tracks toward Joker, hunched and applying makeup at a mirror. Meanwhile the morning bulletin begins. A hot day is forecast and the headline story is of garbage truck strikes causing a city-wide emergency in Gotham, a build-up of trash and stench. The broadcast is overlaid with other radio bulletins describing similar scenes of hopelessness, decay, and disorder while a police siren cuts through, bringing home a sense of oppressive overlapping crises. Amid this audio pastiche of journalistic negativity, the camera cuts to a close-up of Joker, frowning absurdly then grinning terrifyingly in clown's makeup. This opening sequence captured the widely perceived relationship between journalism and mental health, foreshadowing the climax of the film where the joker shoots a news anchor on live TV before leading a populist revolution of clowns to take over the city: a none-too-subtle reference to Sidney Lumet's classic critique of television journalism, Network (1976), that famously linked journalism and collective madness.

Despite this common cinematic image, journalism has accepted a psychotherapeutic imperative in conveying news to its audiences in recent decades. Rather than seeking to produce in its audience "an almost physical effect, causing fear, interest, laughter or shock" (Marr 2004), today, many journalists accept some therapeutic responsibility for preserving, or even improving, audiences' mental well-being. The most familiar of these practices are now ubiquitous, routinely appearing in news bulletins. Reporting of suicide observes strict protocols to reduce incidences of self-harm, and such stories are routinely coupled with resources for seeking help; graphic images are redacted or accompanied by prior warnings to reduce shock or trauma, while the #MeToo movement brought attention to the ubiquity of male violence against women and the role of misogynistic communication in enabling it (Our Watch 2015). Consequently, journalists have been recommended to consider how reporting may endanger mental health and perpetuate harmful assumptions regarding the causes of family violence (Simons and Khan 2018; Sutherland et al. 2015). These reforms have occurred in tandem with the emergence of mental well-being as an urgent public health issue. In many developed countries, such as Australia, suicide is the leading cause of death for people aged between fifteen and forty-four years of age (Australian Institute of Health and Welfare 2019)—a tragic statistic underlying a more general "mental health crisis" (Hall 2015). Recognition of these social ills (and the centrality of communication and journalism in constructing and reproducing them) is shaping journalism.

Collectively, these new practices are the most prominent features of a broader transformation that might be termed, to use Tomas Matza's phrase (2018), journalism's "psychotherapeutic turn." This turn, that Matza studied in post-Soviet Russia, was constituted by "new forms of psychotherapeutic work through the creation of human-resource departments, trainings for success, and psychological-education courses" (2018, 4). Journalism's psychotherapeutic turn, perhaps less individualistically, extends duties of care to its audience, vulnerable communities, and indeed to society and democracy at large. While this turn is incomplete—especially with regard to journalists' own mental well-being (Browne et al. 2012)—the significance of the transformation is sometimes overlooked in studies that seek to further shift journalism toward psychotherapeutic best practice. Indeed, it is difficult to make sense of the proliferating denominations of journalism—whether constructive, civic, public, slow, solutions, peace, strength-based or positive—without accounting for the cultural salience of psychological disorders. Journalists and editors often claim an insight into the collective mood and mindset of their audience, so it is unsurprising that an understanding of common psychological disorders should be common among journalists and media scholars, informing their journalistic practices. However, psychology has lately sought to reform its disease and disorder focus by shifting toward positive psychological states, psychological strengths, and mental well-being—a psychological trend that journalism has, perhaps, found more challenging to incorporate.

POSITIVE PSYCHOLOGY

Positive psychology refers to a refocus of therapy and research: away from psychology's preoccupation with diagnosing and curing mental disease, and toward an understanding of mental strengths and well-being (Seligman and Csikszentmihalyi 2012; Seligman 1999). As President of the American Psychological Association Martin Seligman urged his colleagues to forge "a new social and behavioural science that seeks to understand and nurture those human strengths that can prevent the tragedy of mental illness" (1999), a new research agenda was subsequently established based on the idea that "treatment is not just fixing what is wrong; it is also building what is right" (Seligman 2002, 4).

Journalism's incorporation of this burgeoning positive science has occurred, largely, under the banner of "constructive journalism." In conceptualizing constructive journalism, two leading founders of the practice, Karen McIntyre and Cathrine Gyldensted (2018, 2017), centralized positive psychology, defining constructive journalism as "journalism that involves applying positive psychology techniques to news processes and production in an effort to create productive and engaging coverage, while holding true to journalism's core functions" (2017, 20). However, the tension evident in this definition—between positivity and journalism's core functions—reflects familiar professional reservations regarding journalistic positivity.

Constructive journalism's appropriation of positive psychology was, in the first instance, by analogy. Just as positive psychology sought to correct a perceived imbalance in psychology—that Seligman (2002) argued was overly focused on disease and insufficiently attentive to well-being, virtue, and resilience—likewise, constructive journalism sought to correct journalism's "negativity bias" and offer a more realistic picture of the world (McIntyre and Gyldensted 2018). Their critique of journalism's negativity bias aligned conveniently with journalism's commitment to objectivity. As they argued, "An overfocus on conflicts, dissent, heated debate, wrongdoings, faults and weaknesses, thus result[s] in an overriding negativity bias and consequently a skewed portrayal of the world" (McIntyre and Gyldensted 2018, 662). From this basis, constructive journalists recommended greater reporting of successes, solutions, and strengths as evidence of resilience and agency. Journalists, then, should become just as vigilant against negativity bias as they are against political bias, distortion, and partiality. As well as seeking to move journalism analogously away from the "disease model" of the world, constructive journalism has also sought to incorporate specific therapeutic techniques in their reporting such as depolarization techniques and adapting interviewing techniques from family therapy into journalistic interviews (McIntyre and Gyldensted 2018, 668–669).

However, as Seligman emphasized, positive psychology is fundamentally a preventative therapy (2002). It operates by identifying and fostering human strengths that are proven to mitigate or prevent the onset of mental illness. These strengths included "future-mindedness, optimism, interpersonal skill, faith, work ethic, hope, honesty, perseverance, the capacity for flow and insight, to name several" (2002, 5). Indeed, there are more than several, as the weighty *Oxford Handbook of Positive Psychology* attests (Lopez and Snyder 2016). McIntyre and Gyldensted (2018) pick from this growing literature those findings that corresponded with the main elements of constructive journalism (see Hermans and Gyldensted 2019). This approach promoted a broad-based, albeit selective, literacy of positive psychology research among journalists, arguably at the expense of a thorough working knowledge of its founding discovery: optimism. The specific human strengths and virtues journalism should incorporate into its reporting practice was left open-ended, overlooking, perhaps, the centrality of hope and optimism as the foundational discoveries of positive psychology. This points to a potential, but often unrecognized, distinction between constructive journalism and solutions journalism. If constructive journalism is journalism that incorporates a range of positive psychological strengths (McIntyre and Gyldensted 2018), then solutions journalism might be considered, more specifically, as reporting founded on the psychology of hope. The following sections will develop this idea by considering the challenges and opportunities for centralizing the psychology of hope in news.

THE PSYCHOLOGY OF HOPE

Experiments conducted by Martin Seligman on the subject of learned helplessness, optimism, and explanatory style are credited as the founding discoveries of positive psychology—marking a historic break with behaviorism and psychology's myopic focus on pathology. While positive psychology was consecrated by Seligman's Presidency at the American Psychological

Association (Seligman 1999), by then, the findings underpinning this movement had already been popularized by his book, *Learned Optimism* (1991). The results of these experiments, from the perspective of journalism and democracy, are chillingly insightful. They originate from a chance observation of laboratory dogs for whom the usual Pavlovian conditioning was not working. Despite being exposed simultaneously to a loud noise and a mild electric shock, the dogs would not subsequently seek to escape by jumping over a low wall when exposed only to the noise, as they had been trained to. Despite the seemingly obvious escape route, the dogs lay down whimpering and enduring the loud beeps that they had learned to associate with pain. Seligman hypothesized that "accidentally, during the early part of the experiment, the dogs must have been taught to be helpless . . . they had concluded, or 'learned,' that nothing they did mattered" (1991, 20). To test this hypothesis, Seligman designed a triadic experiment to compare the behavior of dogs who were administered three types of conditioning: in one group, the dogs were given "escapable" electric shocks (shocks that they could switch off by pressing a panel); in a second group, the shocks were "yoked" to those of the first group (the dogs received the same number of shocks, but had no capacity to switch them off); and a third group received no shocks at all. Subsequently, these dogs were moved to a "shuttlebox" experiment where they could all escape shocks easily by simply jumping over a small wall.

Stunningly, and against the accepted wisdom of behaviorists, Seligman found that the dogs who had been taught helplessness would not jump over the wall to escape the shocks. While the dogs who had learned to control the shocks or had received no shocks at all both quickly escaped, the helpless dog simply endured: "pathetically, it soon gave up and lay down, though it was regularly shocked by the box. It never found out that the shock could be escaped merely by jumping to the other side" (Seligman 1991, 23). So began a decade of experiments to prove that humans, too, are routinely taught this crippling pessimism, and that the absence of optimism prevents people from seizing opportunities in life, rebounding from failure, recovering from depression and achieving their full potential in life. Like the helpless dog, sufferers of pessimism and depression will fail to take the most obvious steps to alleviate their suffering.

The learned helplessness experiment, at a society scale, is a tragic allegory of political disengagement, cynicism, and policy inertia—one that holds acute lessons for journalism. Like the dog receiving the "yoked" shocks, news audiences are routinely presented with stimuli that arouse negative emotions without offering recourse to a solution or providing the broader context in which such events take place. Societies that become helpless let slip opportunities to confront problems, act against their best interests, and withdraw into grim endurance. The phenomenon was crystallized by Susan Sontag in her book *Regarding the Pain of Others* that offered a striking criticism of war journalism:

> It is because a war, any war, doesn't seem as if it can be stopped that people become less responsive to the horrors. Compassion is an unstable emotion. It needs to be translated into action, or it withers. The question is what to do with the feelings that have been aroused, the knowledge that has been communicated. If one feels that there is nothing "we" can do . . . and nothing "they" can do either . . . then one starts to get bored, cynical, apathetic. (Sontag 2003, 101)

In addition, and perhaps of most concern for publishers, audiences that come to feel helpless often avoid reading the news altogether. The Reuters Institute for Journalism's 2019 Digital News Report found that worldwide, 32 percent of people avoid reading the news, up from 29 percent in 2017 (Newman et al. 2019). In the United States, where news avoidance was 41 percent, 57 percent of news avoiders explained their aversion with the statement: "it can have a negative effect on my mood" (Newman et al. 2019). In summarizing the findings, Joshua Benton (2019) recommended:

> The solutions journalism people should be sending this article to all potential funders, because the problem they're trying to address shows up crystal clear here: *News about big problems is depressing if I'm not presented with potential solutions.* Regular news consumption can engender a kind of learned helplessness that make clear the appeal of ideologically slanted news—which offers up a clear cast of good guys and bad guys with no moral grey—and just avoiding news entirely. [Original italics]

Fortunately, Seligman's learned helplessness model of optimism seems uniquely suited for incorporation into journalistic practice because, in his view, optimism is fundamentally discursive—it is tied to the way people talk about (and hence think about) the causes of good and bad events.

Optimistic Explanatory Style

For Abramson, Seligman, and Teasdale (1978), the cause and treatment of learned helplessness (pessimism) related to, what they termed, "explanatory (or attributional) style." In their view, people develop a habitual style of explaining good and bad events in their everyday life, and this explanatory style locates individuals on a pessimism-optimism scale. Three variables in explanatory style are decisive: permanence, pervasiveness, and personalization. The causes that pessimists routinely identify for negative events are permanent (going to last forever), pervasive (extending into other domains and situations) and personal (the fault of oneself). Correspondingly, the perceived causes of positive events for pessimists are the reverse: temporary (short in duration), specific (to a given situation), and external (not caused by oneself). Optimists tend to explain negative events in the opposite manner—as the result of temporary, specific and external causes—and positive events as caused by permanent, universal, and internal causes.

Journalism and Explanatory Style

One's explanatory style and optimism, research has found, is taught early in life by influential figures such as parents, coaches, teachers, and, later in life, employers (Seligman 2002, 1991). As such, it is not unlikely that journalism, too, as Gyldensted found, may "influence the explanatory style used by people who would read, watch, and listen" (2011, 8). Indeed, Seligman had been involved in the development of a content analysis methodology— the content analysis of verbatim explanations or CAVE analysis (Peterson et al. 1983)—that allowed explanatory style to be deduced from historical documents such as newspapers and speech transcripts (Zullow and Seligman 1990). Applying this technique to newspapers, Oettingen and Seligman explored journalism's explanatory style in East and West Germany prior to the fall of the Berlin Wall (1990). They found that West Germans exhibited a much higher rate of depressive symptoms than East Germans and that this corresponded with the explanatory style of causal statements in their respective reporting of the 1984 Winter Olympics. While both sides reported negative events in a relatively optimistic way, East Germany's reporting of good events, such as winning Gold medals, was markedly pessimistic, attributed to good fortune rather than as a result of a pervasive or permanent attribute of the athlete.

Oettingen and Seligman's study raised an important but overlooked problem in equating solutions reporting with improved optimism. Explanatory style theory implies that reporting solutions, alone, may not necessarily cultivate optimism in its audience since solutions (positive events) may still be reported and explained in a pessimistic way. Indeed, journalism about good events, as Oettingen and Seligman found in relation to sports reporting, may pessimistically fixate on their specific, temporary, and external causes. Journalists often seek to avoid hype by explaining positive events, somewhat pessimistically, in terms of their contingencies and specificities. For example, an editorial in the *Mercury* titled "The amazing MONA effect" illustrated this tendency. Like Bilbao in Spain, Tasmania's capital city of Hobart, in Australia, was also the beneficiary of a transformational contemporary art gallery: the Museum of Old and New Art (MONA). However, in explaining the recovery of Tasmania's economy after the museum (an ostensibly good event for the state), the Tasmanian editor could hardly have been more modest:

> The phenomenon known as the butterfly effect suggests the gentle flap of a butterfly's wings can reverberate and ignite a chain of events that can cause a cyclone somewhere else on the planet. It is an intriguing concept. The idea of cascading or exponentially expanding series of events—like a domino effect but with increasingly large consequences—is part of modern science's Chaos Theory and has been applied in the study of meteorology, astronomy and cosmology. It now seems to be a factor in Tasmania's incredibly buoyant tourism industry—only in Tassie it is known as the MONA effect. (*The Mercury*, 2014)

From this perspective, Tasmania was the beneficiary of a miraculous gift—a wonderful accident of chance, independent of any enduring quality of the state or its people. Indeed, there is a prevailing Australian meta-narrative that was encapsulated in Donald Horne's (1968) characterization of Australia as "the lucky county": beneficiaries of a fragile good fortune at risk of being squandered by mediocre leadership and economic foolhardiness.

Correspondingly, while journalism favors negative stories, it often seeks explanations for negative events that are relatively optimistic: temporary, specific, and external. Take, for instance, the outbreak of the coronavirus in China. An Australian Broadcast Corporation (ABC) story titled "Possible Coronavirus Case under Investigation by NSW Health after Flight from Wuhan Arrives in Sydney" reported the possible causes of a negative event: the spread of the infectious disease into mainland Australia. However, as the title indicated, journalists and public health investigators alike were seeking specific and discrete causes of the spread of the virus. The flight was the last direct flight leaving Wuhan, the source of the outbreak, prior to the city being locked down in quarantine. As such, the flight itself and its passengers represented a clear, yet manageable, cause of a possible outbreak. Australian prime minister, Scott Morrison, was quoted recommending clear causal information: "I think it's important that we continue to get good information, we go about our normal course of business, but just being aware of those risks and to the extent that they are there." Ruminating on the more pessimistic causes of the outbreak—Australia's enormous reliance on Chinese tourism, university students and exports—would presumably make this a potentially inflammatory story with serious economic consequences. Such a reading of the unmanageability of risks in a globalized world—as encapsulated in Ulrich Beck's (2009) highly pessimistic book, *World at Risk*—is an impression that government officials are keen to avoid and will contest in journalism. From these observations, it might be concluded that the learned helplessness model of optimism cannot be straightforwardly mobilized as a justification for solutions reporting. In addition, explanatory style also sits uneasily with journalistic objectivity.

Optimism and Objectivity

While solutions journalists point out the negativity bias in traditional news values, positive psychologists have found that an optimistic explanatory style is more distorting of our view of reality. The relationship between optimism and objectivity is tackled directly by Martin Seligman (1991, 108–111). In his review of the research, he is conclusive: pessimistic and depressed people are more objective than optimists. Pessimists are fairer in their appraisal of their own skills and competencies than optimists who, by comparison, tend to distort reality and inflate their competence relative to their actual performance (1991, 109). Whereas, "the pessimist seems to be at the mercy of reality . . . the optimist has a massive defence against reality that maintains good cheer in the face of a relentlessly indifferent universe" (Seligman 1991, 111). While positive psychology has tended to valorize these biases as strengths that mitigate risk of mental illness (Snyder 1989), other studies have shown that "unrealistic optimism" makes people impervious to risks when they should be more proactive (Weinstein et al. 1998). Indeed, when asked by a major CEO whether his executive staff should be taught to be more optimistic, Seligman moderated his advocacy of optimism, conceding that pessimists play an important role in a balanced leadership team. In his words, "Mild pessimists—call them professional pessimists—seem to make good use of pessimistic accuracy (it's their stock in trade) without suffering unbearably from the costs of pessimism: the bouts of depression and lack of initiative" (p. 112). Likewise, Sandra Schneider posited the idea of "realistic optimism": defined as "hoping for and working towards desired outcomes without having the expectation that particular outcomes will occur, especially with little or no effort to bring the about" (Schneider 2001, 253).

Journalists may recognize the virtues of professional pessimism in relation to their own reporting practice. It is fair to argue that journalists do and should provide this valuable, yet at times dispiriting, insight into the grim realities of human nature and the true causes of events. Investigative reporting, for instance, rests upon an ability to see beyond appearances and to hypothesize about the baser motivations of powerful people. According to Walth et al. (2019) in a comparative analysis of investigative and solutions journalism, there appeared to be limited crossover in their reporting styles. In their view, the enduring difference was primarily temporal: investigative reporting sought to uncover the past and present, whereas solutions journalism was characterized by its "forward tilt" (2019, 187). However, as pessimistic objectivity would suggest, the disjuncture may be more intrinsic with pessimism representing a constitutive feature of the embodied journalistic "gut feel" or habitus (Schultz 2007). Whereas a doe-eyed optimist might be liable to report hyperbole in a press release, an investigative journalist thinks about good news the way Homo sapiens evolved through ice ages to think about good weather: "as mere prelude to a harsh winter" (Seligman 1991, 111). This argument further explains the instinctive rejection of hope-based reporting, where optimism is easily conflated with gullibility and seen as inimical to investigative reporting: the archetype of good journalism.

The question then is how journalists might promote a healthy balance of public optimism through their reports while maintaining a professional pessimism (or realistic optimism) that enables them to do their job and report objectively. Because Seligman's model equates optimism with explanatory style, it is unclear whether this dilemma can be resolved within his model. Journalism is largely the work of seeking and writing explanations, and the style in which a journalist learns to do this is normatively objective and realistic—which is to say pessimistic, according to Seligman's model. The question, then, is how to translate journalism's pessimistic rigor into the more optimistic domain of solutions reporting?

To do so, it is necessary to stress that news sources, not journalists, are the proper vehicles for translating solutions into social hope. News sources are central in reports about uncertain futures. Gaye Tuchman studied how journalists use sources to distance themselves from controversy and critique, terming the practice a "strategic ritual of objectivity" (1972). More recently Karin Wahl-Jorgensen (2013) adapted the phrase in her study of "the strategic ritual of emotionality." Journalists rely on sources to help outsource speculation that, like emotionality, "is at odds with journalistic self-understandings" (Wahl-Jorgensen 2013). Thus, in a similar vein, it could be suggested that journalists report solutions through a strategic ritual of optimism where sources are found who can testify to the possibility, desirability, and opportunity presented by certain solutions.

While strategic outsourcing of optimistic speech serves to distance journalists and preserve their objectivity, journalists remain implicated in the construction of solutions and collective hopes. Journalists construct solutions by selecting news sources, devising questions and arranging their responses into compelling and engaging stories. Solutions journalism is therefore subject to routine framing practices that impose implicit evaluative schemas of newsworthiness to configure sources and prospective solutions into conventional journalistic products (a practice elaborated in the following chapter). The question, then, is what science of optimism can be called upon to guide these subjective deliberations to maximize the distribution of social hope through society? To answer this question, let us now consider a theory of hope that, I will suggest, is more amenable to journalistic pessimism yet provides a structure that can inform solutions journalism as a reporting practice.

HOPE THEORY

Hope theory, developed by Charles Snyder (Snyder, Shane, et al. 2002; Snyder 2002), has become a widely studied and applied model of constructive, proactive and positive thinking (Rand and Touza 2016). While both Snyder and Seligman operate within a positive psychology tradition, the main difference between their theories relates to the distinction between excuse making and hoping. For Seligman, routine excuse making for negative events is a healthy sign of an optimistic demeanor. An optimistic explanation for a negative event distances oneself as the cause of the accident by habitually attributing such events to temporary, specific, and external causes. For Snyder, hope is the opposite, or "the 'other side' of the 'excusing' process" (Snyder 2002). In his view, hopeful thoughts are goal-oriented cognitions: "Put simply, hopeful thought reflects the belief that one can find pathways to desired goals and become motivated to use those pathways. We also proposed that hope, so defined, serves to drive the emotions and well-being of people" (Snyder, Shane, et al. 2002, 256). This pivot away from excuse making and toward thinking about goals, pathways and agency is highly amenable to solutions journalism. Solutions journalism seeks to drive progress by "reporting on where and how people are doing better against a problem [thereby] removing excuses and setting a bar for what citizens should expect from institutions or government" (Solutions Journalism Network 2020). Accordingly, solutions journalism is involved in benchmarking and comparing standards of relative success to demonstrate the viability of a range of goal-directed pathways, thereby removing excuses and driving progress. For Snyder, hoping is an iterative process that cycles between three key domains of thought: goal setting, pathway thoughts and agency thoughts (Snyder 2002, 254). Journalistic interventions can effectively take place at any point in this iterative process: usefully providing a taxonomy of related solutions reporting practices.

Goal Setting

According to Snyder, all human actions are goal-oriented and these goals anchor hope cognitions. Goals can range from the very modest—aiming to cook pasta from the leftover vegetables in the fridge—to more challenging personal, family, career, or health goals. Goals can be positive (seeking or augmenting something desirable) or negative (seeking to prevent or delay something undesirable). However, in relation to her concept of "realistic optimism," Schneider (not Snyder) noted that positive goals are functionally superior to negative goals: "Positive approach motivation leads to greater persistence, greater flexibility in strategies to reach a goal, greater creativity in solutions, better outcomes, and higher subjective well-being" (2001, 256). Thus, positive goals are more apt for a solution-focused discourse compared to risk aversion goals. Goals also vary in their level of abstraction, significance, and temporal scale (Snyder 2002, 250). Suitable goals for hoping may include visual images of a desirable future or be verbally elaborated. All goals, however, are more likely to occur if they are made to be less abstract since "it is difficult to imagine pathways or motivations to pursue vague goals" (Snyder 2002, 250). This represents a clear point at which journalistic interventions would be valuable. Solutions journalists, viewing the world through a suitably critical and realistic lens, might seek to make collective goals more explicit, specific, achievable, and consonant with community values and expectations. Thus, journalism should seek to make optimism realistic by providing "regulate reality checks to update assessments of progress fine-tune one's understanding potential opportunities, refine causal models of situations and re-evaluate planned next steps" (Schneider 2001, 257). However, there is also a more pre-emptive role for journalists in holding news sources to their stated goals, for instance, by prompting leaders to articulate goals when they have not; by evaluating their stated goals against comparable goal setters in different communities of nations; or by aligning goals with community expectations and values. These types of stories may be constituted by journalists' goal-oriented, rather than problem-oriented questions (Beers 2010, 122).

Hope in Snyder's theory, like Seligman's, is dispositional: it is an enduring mindset that one brings to new goal-oriented cognitions and opportunities. This disposition is shaped by historical experiences in successful goal-oriented pursuits. A low-hope individual (or society) with a history of obstacles and dashed hopes will "tap into a reservoir of negative and passive feelings about task pursuit endeavours" (2002, 253). As such, failed goal pursuit in a news source should be taken seriously as having a potentially corrosive effect on public attitudes. Repeated public disappointments regarding collective goals are, arguably, a significant factor explaining audience's declining levels of hope, and subsequent disengagement from political processes and news consumption.

While the benefits of goal-thinking have been primarily studied in terms of individuals—often termed "high (or low) hopers" (Snyder 2002, 254)—news audiences are presumably interested in communal goal with shared benefits, rather than individual goals with private benefits. Indeed, social psychology research has found that people think about the future collectively and that images of collective futures drive social change (Bain et al. 2013, 523). Reflecting the social nature of hope, Snyder and Feldman (2000) concluded the *Handbook of Hope* with a chapter titled "Hope for the Many: An Empowering Social Agenda." Taking up this research agenda, Jin and Kim extrapolated hope theory to include "social hopes" (Jin and Kim 2019) or what Bain and colleagues termed "collective futures" (2013). They argued that high hopers tend to be invested in a plurality of individual and communal goals, rather than narcissistically pursuing their individual well-being. Thus, in their view, myopic investment in one individual goal—whether money making, physical appearance, intellectual achievement, and athletic accomplishments—is less healthy than adopting a plurality of goals that are individual and collective, such as caring for others or producing goods that have wide social benefits (Snyder and Feldman 2000, 391).

In this spirit, solutions journalists also have a role in pluralizing social hopes by canvassing a variety of collective goals. Indeed, journalists often work to make leaders accountable for their stated goals by articulating the frustrations of their audiences at the lack of progress, delays or foreseeable obstacles. However, typical lines of journalistic questioning about failed goal attainment may prompt many sources to resort to excuse making, the opposite of hoping (Snyder 1989), and further disillusion the public. Thus, journalists might investigate goal attainment by adopting David Beers's recommendation that, rather than asking "what went wrong yesterday and who is to blame?" ask "what might go right tomorrow and who is showing the way?" (Beers 2010, 121). Thus, journalists would foster a trait that Snyder observed in high-hope individuals: a tendency to have more goals at their disposal should one fail. A high hoper, Snyder found, is "a diversified 'goal investor' who has a readily available new goal should an original goal prove unreachable" (Snyder 2002, 253). So, in holding leaders accountable to their stated goals, journalists might pivot immediately to the next goal, or other comparable goals. These are all properly journalistic practices within a watchdog role, holding powerful individuals to account in the public interest, while maintaining an objective and evidence-based standard of verification.

Pathway Thinking

Hopeful thought, for Snyder, reflects the belief that one can find pathways to desired goals, and become motivated to use those pathways (2002, 257). Generalized to a social level, Jin and Kim defined social hope "as individuals' belief that their society will achieve desired social goals through people's collective efforts to find pathways to the goals" (2019, 20). Having a plurality of pathways is essential for hope cognitions, and necessary for making goals seem achievable (and worth investing hope in) rather than vague or utopian. With the same diversified investment portfolio logic, Snyder found:

> Pathways thinking in any given instantiation involves thoughts of being able to generate at least one, and often more, usable routes to a desired goal. The production of several pathways is important when encountering impediments, and high-hope persons perceive that they are facile at finding such alternate routes; moreover, high-hope people actually are very effective at producing alternative routes. (2002, 258)

There is a role for journalism in furnishing the public imagination with a range of realistic pathways that make collective goals seem eminently achievable, thereby keeping leaders accountable for their progress toward goals. Accordingly, what might be termed "pathway reporting" is a way of converting goals and visions into realistic projects: manufacturing "concrete utopias" (Bloch 1995, 197) and fostering "realistic optimism" (Schneider 2001). This journalistic role was well-encapsulated by David Beers who described the purpose of solutions reporting as giving "citizens data and real live experiences from which to make judgements about how to respond to injustices and, collectively, choose a different path" (2010, 122). The singularity of the alternative path in Beers' definition reflects, perhaps, a peculiarity in North American journalism's preferred narrative structure. In light of the importance placed on pathway plurality in hope theory, journalists and researchers might also seek to experiment with what Rodney Benson termed "debate ensemble" news formats (Benson 2013, 108). This style of reporting—typical of French outlets such as le Monde or Libération—brings together a range of different opinions and news formats regarding one pressing topic, such as immigration. While, according to Benson, American journalism has celebrated "personalized narrative journalism" as its ideal, multi-genre debate ensemble formats "helps ensure the presentation of multiple frames (and speakers)" (2013, 108); in short, it "helps make the news more multiperspectival" (2013, 153). The Solutions Journalism Network, while discouraging hero worship, emphasizes the importance of character-driven storytelling in making solutions reporting engaging (Bansal and Martin 2015, 17), an aspect of solutions journalism that has been explored by American media scholars (Thier et al. 2019). Instead, a "solution ensemble" format could also increase pathway plurality regarding a given goal or social issue, allowing the public to invest more social hope into achieving a collective goal. This is not to say that "narrative transportation" (Thier et al. 2019) is not a useful tool in engaging the public more thoroughly with other types of solutions journalism. Indeed, as the following will suggest, character-driven narrative might be especially useful in fostering a third component of hope thinking: agency.

Agency

Agency refers to the motivational thoughts that correspond with hopeful pathways thinking; "the perceived capacity to use one's pathways to reach desired goals" (Snyder 2002, 251). Beyond merely dwelling upon goals and thinking about pathways to attain them, hoping also involves agentic self-talk such as, "I can do this," and "I am not going to be stopped" (2002, 251). It is impossible to identify pathways without some level of assumed agency. Indeed, Snyder found that pathway and agency thinking are iterative and additive: "pathways thinking increases agency thinking, which, in turn, yields further pathways thinking, and so on" (Snyder, Shane, et al. 2002, 258). However, agency becomes especially important when one encounters an obstacle or when a chosen pathway proves unviable. At this point, perceptions of agency motivate one to imagine alternate pathways and apply the requisite motivation to the best alternate pathway, thereby staying on track toward the desired goal (2002, 258).

Agency thinking depends on historical conditioning—making hopefulness a disposition or trait. According to Snyder, an individual develops an "emotion set" regarding the hope process: "the residue from myriad previous goal pursuits" (Snyder 2002, 253). Low-hope individuals tend to have experienced repeated disappointments, raised expectations, and dashed hopes, whereas hopeful individuals have a history of overcoming challenges and goal attainment (Snyder 2002, 254). At a societal level, some groups (and, perhaps, generations) have achieved a range of goals or social progress collectively, or have experienced upward mobility through participation in business and commerce. These societies might therefore be expected to have a high level of agency regarding social goals and be disposed to consider a range of pathways with an ingrained belief that they will be motivated to attain those goals. Indeed, in a study of social hope in Korea, Jin and Kim found "a significant relationship between social hope and political efficacy" (2019, 24). This finding suggested that "those who believe in their abilities to influence the political process tend to be hopeful for their society" (p. 24). On the other hand, as Hage documented (2003, 23–30), decreasing faith in the ability of political and economic systems to facilitate upward social mobility produces passive and paranoid "worriers": low-hope communities who presumably have lowered perceptions of political agency regarding pathways to collective goals. The collective loss of hope and perceived agency erodes a more caring bond with the nation, that Hage described as an "active and affective participation in the nation" (2003, 30).

This democratic deficit, and loss of agency, has been explicitly targeted by solutions journalists in their reporting practice and, specifically, in the practice of reporting success stories. Successes are the central cue for solutions journalism. Identifying a successful response to a common issue is the first investigative task of the solutions journalist, often accomplished by studying data for "positive deviance": "the best performers in a dataset" (Bansal and Martin 2015, 19). Normatively, focusing on successes, according to Bornstein and Rosenberg, "provides information crucial to democracy. It shows that people care. It helps new ideas circulate. It shows that incremental system change is possible" (Bornstein and Rosenberg 2016). Thus, the best way of demonstrating the viability of a certain pathway, and thereby maximizing hope, is by showing others successfully traversing it.

Personalized narrative is an important story format for agency-based solutions journalism because it encourages audience identification with the protagonist. While solutions journalists eschew "hero worship," analysis has found that "hero" characters are a necessary and influential feature of narratives in public policy discourses (Shanahan et al. 2013; Jones 2014). In policy narratives, a hero will "offer solutions (e.g., a moral of the story) and evidence in support of the solution" (Shanahan et al. 2013, 458). While narratives require characters, a key variable in the arrangement of narrative elements is the relative salience of the hero, compared to the victims or villains (Jones and McBeth 2010). In a study of climate change policy narratives, Jones found that the relative salience of a hero corresponded with stronger persuasion of the risks of climate change and support for solutions (Jones 2014, 22). This finding is consonant with narrative transportation theory that, according to Green and Beck, describes audiences who were "transported into the world of the narrative and became involved with its protagonists" (Green and Brock 2000, 701). Personalized narrative in solutions journalism makes use of audience identification to provide tacit instruction to audiences. The Solutions Journalism Network recommended that "what matters most is not the quirks and qualities of the main character, but the transferable wisdom found in his or her actions" (Bansal and Martin 2015, 20). While there might be specific policy recommendations or ideas about how to implement an idea or pathway in solutions journalism, the implicit lesson is agency. As Bornstein explained, "If we want more people to invest themselves in smart efforts to improve society, we need to do a better job helping them to see opportunities as well as risks" (2012). Such success stories are, to use another term that borders on the saccharine, inspiring. By profiling communities and individuals pursing goals, grappling with challenges, and succeeding, it is likely journalists help their audiences see new opportunities and feel an augmented sense of agency in pursuing their goals.

CONCLUSION

Together, these three aspects of the hoping process—goals, pathways, and agency—form the triumvirate of solutions journalism. They correspond with what might be considered three types of solutions-based articles that can be delivered in a variety of formats and styles. This taxonomy shows that solutions journalism is a more diverse and evolving set of journalistic offerings than is sometimes implied in scholarly and professional efforts to standardize the practice. The Solutions Journalism Network has sought to distinguish between true solutions journalism and its "imposters" by listing ten qualities (Solutions Journalism Toolkit 2018). Media scholars have likewise sought to build consensus for a singular understanding of solutions journalism, "to ensure consistency in measuring the effects of such stories" (McIntyre and Lough 2019, 13). Accordingly, after interviewing fourteen journalists—79 percent of whom were working in America, and all recruited through The Solutions Journalism Network—McIntyre and Lough offer a condensed list of six basic requirements (2019, 5). This standardizing project (while usefully constructing a consistent unit of analysis) underplays, perhaps, the extent to which solutions journalism is subject to ongoing contestation and a product of competing professional motivations (Amiel and Powers 2019). Standardization by institutional-consecration risks solutions journalism becoming over-determined by American news values and reporting formats with, for instance, the consistent preference for personalized narrative rather than debate ensemble or multi-genre formats (Benson 2013).

This chapter identifies some contestation in the justification of solutions journalism based on hope. While hope is sometimes associated with emotion and partiality, this chapter sought to look past this familiar yet false dichotomy between emotion and reason. Solutions journalism needs a more sophisticated understanding of hope cognitions—where emotions and reason are entangled—in order to develop products that are effective in engaging the public. While Seligman's theory of learned optimism is the most culturally salient (Seligman 1991, 2019), it is founded on the concept of "optimistic explanatory style" (Abramson et al. 1978; Oettingen and Seligman 1990), which is largely incompatible with journalistic ideals of objectivity. Instead, we have posited Snyder and colleagues' hope theory as the most promising basis for solutions journalism (Rand and Touza 2016; Snyder 2002). Basing solutions journalism on a sophisticated understanding of human hope cognitions may allow journalists to experiment and tailor media products that will be effective in facilitating "realistic optimism" (Schneider 2001).

Chapter 2

Leadership

INTRODUCTION

While solutions journalism is concerned with and perhaps constituted by the democratic distribution of social hope, in practice, the solutions canvassed are typically proposed by a restricted field of news sources. Proposing a solution and having that idea be taken seriously by journalists is a marker of social status, legitimacy, and, ultimately, leadership. In articulating or enacting a solution, a proponent becomes subject to journalistic interpretations and evaluations regarding newsworthiness, reliability and character, including the speaker's legitimacy to propose something at all. Thus, how journalists assess and evaluate leadership is central to the reporting of solutions. Indeed, this chapter will suggest that solutions journalism, in its standardized form, is not only characterized by its reporting of hopeful solutions, but by the way in which it approaches the question of leadership.

Leadership is a fundamentally interdisciplinary concept, and the ideals of leadership are transferable between different professional contexts. Thus, despite its seemingly commonsense attributes, the concept of leadership is constructed and value-laden. As Ronald Heifetz argued, "There is not neutral ground from which to construct notions and theories of leadership" (Heifetz 1994, 14). Feminist scholars have demonstrated that, across various professional contexts, leadership discourses are typically gendered (Gerrits et al. 2017), and masculine leadership archetypes can form an impediment for female leadership (Eagly et al. 1992). According to Hage, the exclusion of migrants and other marginalized people from "governmental belonging," the perceived ability to have a say about how society might be otherwise, helps to explain the persistence of marginalization in multicultural societies (Hage 2000). Thus, the radical potential of solutions journalism is its tendency to democratize the governmental field through its pragmatic conception of leadership as social entrepreneurialism.

FROM PUBLIC JOURNALISM TO
SOLUTIONS JOURNALISM

While I have defined solutions journalism by its aim of distributing hope through society, as a public engagement strategy, optimistic reporting is not new. Most prominently, public journalism sought to bring the public directly back into the political process by reporting solutions to common problems, developed through a process of democratic deliberation (Rosen 2011; Merritt 1996). Public journalism was a coincidence of academic interest in the health of democracy and journalists' concerns regarding the public's apparent disengagement with current affairs and political news (Rosen 1999; Merritt 1996; Glasser 1999; Haas 2005). Originating in the United States amid great dissatisfaction with political reporting, public journalism became an umbrella term for a wide reformation movement. The media's polarized and superficial coverage of presidential campaigns—of which "the 1988 presidential campaign [was] widely considered one of the worst in modern memory" (Rosen 1999, 36)—precipitated a new discussion about journalists' reporting of politics. Public journalists pointed to historically low voter turnout and lower newspaper sales (Rosen 1999, 22), while many were alarmed by Robert Putnam's (1995) account of collapsing social capital and civic culture in *Bowling Alone*.

So concerning were Putnam's findings—encapsulated in the tragic figure of the lone ten-pin bowler—that the sociologist was summoned to Camp David to brief President Bill Clinton. In the subsequent deliberations, journalism, already innovating with public and civic innovations, was conscripted in the fight against loneliness and atomization. A reporter for *The Chronicle of Higher Education* observed that "Mr. Putnam's influence can be seen in recent series in the *Chicago Tribute* ('Nation of Strangers') and *The Washington Post* ('The Politics of Mistrust')" (Heller 1996). The responsibility was placed even more squarely on the media by Putnam himself in his subsequent book (2000, 410):

I challenge media moguls, journalists, and Internet gurus, along with viewers like you (and me): *Let us find ways to ensure that by 2010 Americans will spend less leisure time sitting passively alone in front of glowing screens and more time in active connection with our fellow citizens. Let us foster new forms of electronic entertainment and communication that reinforce community engagement rather than forestalling it.* [Original emphasis]

In reaction to this erosion of public interest and involvement, newspapers sought to reintroduce the public directly into the political conversation. As Rosen surmised, in the context of a disappearing public, the task of public journalism was "not just to inform a public that may or may not emerge, but to improve the chances that it will emerge" (1999, 19).

In seeking to forge new ties between media organizations, the public and the political process, a key strategy advanced by public journalism was reorienting journalism toward constructive solutions and positioning journalism as a medium for sourcing citizens' initiatives and ideas. In 1987, *The Ledger-Enquirer* launched a series of articles titled "Columbus: beyond 2000" to "examine the future of the city and the issues it needed to confront" (Rosen 1999, 28). Similarly, in 1992, then editor of the *Wichita Eagle* and leading public journalism advocate Davis Merritt (1996, 23) initiated "The People Project: Solving It Ourselves." According to Merritt, the series aimed to reorientate the political conversation toward solutions:

> Little space was spent describing the problems, since they were the sort that citizens knew about first hand. Rather, the reporting dealt with the potential solutions, with citizens' ideas about what should happen, with stories of people who had made some impression on the problems, no matter how small. (1996, 23)

Thus, reporting collective futures was central to public journalism yet the method for discerning public solutions was largely open-ended and experimental. Many of these experiments aimed to provide a conduit for public ideas for the future through town hall meetings, focus groups and interviewing members of the public; a tactic that Louise Woodstock (2002) characterized as public journalism's "talking cure." Public journalism, for Woodstock (2002, 39), "brings citizens together to discuss the issues they define as most pressing and to cultivate workable solutions to those problems."

A key question that emerged in prosecuting this change was the extent to which journalists could claim to know the public mind or fairly attribute a solution to community consensus, especially in contexts where the public is riven with internal divisions and inequalities (Haas and Steiner 2006; Woodstock 2002; Zelizer 1999; Schudson 1999). The assumed unity of community concerns and interests was considered deeply problematic. According to Haas and Steiner, "Public journalism scholars rarely consider how citizen deliberation may be affected by social inequality" (2001, 126). They assumed that "by virtue of inhabiting a certain geographical territory, community members are assumed to confront 'common problems' and share an overarching vision of the 'common good' that enables them to reach consensual solutions" (Haas and Steiner 2001, 126). This understanding of public journalism as oriented toward a "common good" (Christians 1999) was accused of disguising journalistic power and autonomy in setting the terms of the debate, papering over deep disagreements and constructing a false consensus. Woodstock (2002) described the approach as journalism's "talking cure." In her view, "conversation, in the public journalism sense, while aimed at problem-solving also has a social agenda. Public journalism not only wants to address political issues; it also simply wants us all to get along" (2002, 48).

Public journalism articulated no objective measure for adjudicating between rival claims between members of the public and, according to media historian Michael Schudson (1999), ultimately could not offer the public unconditional access to setting the agenda, nor could it define what the conditions of entry should be. In Schudson's (1999, 123) view, it "advances an unresolved blend of empowering the people and entrusting elites and experts with public responsibility." Journalists exercised authority in setting the topic, framing the problems, and subtly mediating the possible solutions in ways that were not dissimilar to traditional media practices. Hence, Woodstock concluded, "In current practice, the public remains disappointingly similar to the one said to result from traditional journalism – an entity invoked to maintain and obscure journalistic authority" (2002, 51). To some extent, however, public journalism was explicit in claiming a proactive and influential community role. According to Merritt (1999, 184), "It calls for purposefulness and declared intent as we go about our work." Similarly, Rosen (1996, 13) called for "proactive neutrality," where journalists should be committed to the mission of re-engaging the public without which journalism itself would not exist.

Nonetheless, with the public becoming more fragmented, with deeper political divisions and social inequalities, public journalism's mission to bring forward new constructive solutions appears to have floundered. After a decade of criticism and debate—that Schudson described as "the most impressive critique of journalistic practice inside journalism in a generation" (1999, 118)—discussion of the ideals and practices of public journalism have largely subsided. The public journalism period is thought to be bookended by the 2003 closure of the Pew Centre for Civic Journalism that, according to Haas and Steiner (2006, 239), "signall[ed] the end of public journalism." While many of public journalism's methods of public engagement have been absorbed into routine journalistic practice—the routine polling of the public to discern mood and attitude, and the spontaneous interviewing of the public about their views, ideas and concerns— most public journalism practices did not outlast the tenure of the working editors (Nip 2008, 191). In an article titled, "Last Days of Civic Journalism," Nip concluded that "the practices still in place could not achieve civic journalism's goal of engaging the community in deliberation to solve problems" (Nip 2008, 192). It is instructive to consider solutions journalism as inheriting this reform agenda and solution orientation, albeit without its deliberative methodology.

Solutions Journalism and Leadership

Rather than engaging the public directly in conversation about solutions, or deriving public solutions from town hall meetings or surveys, solutions journalism is distinguished by its emphasis on the actions of people who are already implementing solutions to common challenges. That is to say, it articulated a new brand of pragmatic leadership in the service of the public good—whose actions, individual or collective—demonstrate effective pathways, innovations, and viable alternatives. The centrality of leadership in solutions journalism is evident in its focus on "responses to social problems" (Bansal and Martin 2015, 2). Noting that journalists routinely rely upon corporate interests to source propositions and predictions, Beers urged journalists to ask "who is showing the way?" (2006, 121). This type of question in a global context requires journalists to investigate "a possible alternative future by reporting firsthand on experiments, whether local and small scale, or large and even society-wide in other nations" (2006, 122). The idea of exploiting international examples of best practice in the public interest was exaggerated to an absurd degree by the documentary film maker, Michael Moore, in "Where to Invade Next" (2015). Drawing on America's recent military failures, Moore proposed a more efficient means of exploiting the wealth of foreign nations: copying them. Standing at the helm of a gun boat draped in the American flag, Moore opens the films saying:

> Instead of sending in the marines, my suggestion, send in me. I will invade countries . . . take the things we need from them, and bring it all back home to the United States of America. For we have problems no army could solve. (Moore 2015)

The documentary showed how comparable countries, across a wide range of health, education, justice, labor rights and women's rights issues, provide basic services more efficiently and equally than the United States.

The colonial hero that Moore parodies points to an interesting tension in solutions journalism practice. Compared to public journalism, solutions journalism relies to a greater extent on effective leaders and innovators as its key sources and protagonists rather than the collective intelligence of the community, yet the Solutions Journalism Network rejects "hero worship" as a narrative device. In their guide to solutions reporting, hero worship is the first of seven solutions journalism "imposters": "stories that celebrate or glorify an individual, often at the expense of explaining the idea the individual exemplifies" (Bansal and Martin 2015, 8). While they recommend journalists adopt compelling storytelling structure—often using personalized narrative (Benson 2013, 143)—the writer should adopt a more pragmatic interest in the details of the protagonist's actions. Thus, "solutions-oriented stories tend to focus less on a character's intrinsic qualities (e.g., altruism or courage), and more on the character's work" (Bansal and Martin 2015, 21). In contrast to the traditional reliance on powerful sources who make consequential pronouncements about the future (Beers 2010, 121), solutions journalism tends to seek out community-level sources who are actively working to overcome common challenges using innovative means. Nonetheless, solutions journalism does evince a preference for a specific type of pragmatic community-minded leadership that Bornstein has termed "social entrepreneurialism."

Social Entrepreneurs

The cofounder of the *Solutions Journalism Network*, Bornstein has written extensively about a new type of social actor, the social entrepreneur (Bornstein 1998, 2004; Bornstein and Davis 2010) whose efforts and attitudes in solving problems make them ideal news sources for solutions journalism. The term designates civic-minded individuals who pursue opportunities and solutions to major social issues with the pragmatic ruthlessness of an entrepreneur: they are "people with new ideas to address major problems who are relentless in the pursuit of their visions" (Bornstein 2004, 1). For Bornstein, these actors initially filled an innovation deficit in the contemporary welfare state where government policies "remained insulated from the pressures and incentives that forced businesses to continually improve their products" (2004, 274). To remedy this, "citizens took matters into their own hands by establishing community- and church-based organizations, labor unions, women's rights organizations, specialized service groups such as the Salvation Army and Alcoholics Anonymous, and so forth" (2004, 274). These represented early examples of public problem-solving that, since the spread of democracy and the internet, have accelerated rapidly.

In particular, Bornstein has worked in close collaboration with Ashoka, a fellowship that searches for and finances social entrepreneurs worldwide and has been central in implementing leading innovations in agriculture, education, journalism, and development. Bornstein has written a number of feature profiles of, Bill Drayton, the founder of Ashoka and a leading proponent of social entrepreneurialism (Bornstein 1998, 2004; Bornstein and Davis 2010). According to Bornstein and Davis (2010), social entrepreneurs are "transformative forces": "People with new ideas to address major problems who are relentless in the pursuit of their visions, people who simply will not take 'no' for an answer, who will not give up until they have spread their ideas as far as they possibly can" (2010, 1). These actors operate with or without partnership from the government. Rather than lobbying or advocating for a change in policy or business practice, social entrepreneurs attack the problem directly. By seeking to fill gaps created by the shrinking welfare state, social entrepreneurialism does, perhaps, supplement a small government ideology. As Firmstone and Coleman reported, even while social services and support have shrunk, "governments have increasingly employed the rhetoric of 'active citizenship' and 'the Big Society' " (2015, 191). This concept is supported by new theories of social change that posit bottom-up innovation as a driver of transformation. Avelino et al. (2017) point to accelerated social innovations and transformations that have arisen in response to "game changing" events such as the Global Financial Crisis. By bringing greater media attention to social innovation and entrepreneurialism, journalism, they argue, can accelerate these transformative effects and improve bottom-up responses to complex crises.

For Ashoka, recognition of the value of an idea is inextricably linked to an assessment of character. The organization evaluates leadership quality in interviews with prospective grant recipients and Ashoka fellows (Bornstein 1998). To qualify for an Ashoka fellowship, a candidate has to meet four selection criteria: creativity, entrepreneurial quality, the social impact of the person's idea, and ethical fiber (Bornstein 1998, 38). Thus, according to Bornstein, a "social entrepreneur is a pathbreaker with a powerful new idea, who combines visionary and real-world problem-solving creativity, who has a strong ethical fiber, and who is 'totally possessed' by his or her vision for change" (1998, 37). The question of ethical fiber is essential for social entrepreneurs because they rely upon community support and trust. According to Drayton, "It is virtually impossible to get people to make big changes in their lives and in their relationships with others if they do not trust the changemaker. Society already has too many untrustworthy public leaders" (2005). The mission of Ashoka, therefore, is to direct money to individuals with the best likelihood of implementing lasting change in communities through the strength of their idea and, importantly, through their strength of character. The examples that Bornstein and Drayton give are frequently of local actors solving problems in their own countries; often developing countries in Africa, South America, and Asia. Bornstein (1998, 38) described Fabio Rosa as "an agronomist and engineer whose driving ambition is to bring electricity to tens of millions of poor people in Brazil." In this sense, solutions journalism is not dissimilar to "development journalism" where, according to Xiaoge (2009, 357), "journalism was believed and expected to play a key role in facilitating and fostering national development." However, one might ask whether American men are fit to adjudicate the suitability of social entrepreneurs globally or whether they might misunderstand what constitutes ethical fiber in local communities. Yet Drayton maintains that testing ethical fiber is a primordial and instinctual response, and recommends the following method for assessing trustworthiness:

> After an interview, imagine yourself in a situation that brings fear right up into your throat (I picture myself on the edge of a cliff) and then inject your interviewee into that picture. Your primitive brain will let you know (do you feel yourself reaching for the edge of your chair?) if there's a problem before the cerebral cortex can edit. (2005, 30)

This moral emotivism is certainly vulnerable to subconscious bias and relativism (MacIntyre 2007, 8). But what is most significant is the idea of philanthropists or journalists developing an explicit evaluative schema for assessing leadership quality prior to funding or reporting a given solution.

Like Ashoka, a solutions journalist stakes their credibility on the conduct and reputation of the social entrepreneurs that they choose to profile. Reporting a solution might be scandalous if it becomes apparent that the proponent opposes vaccination, for example. According to Bornstein, "My big fear is writing about something I think is sensible, effective and efficient only to discover that it's wrong-headed, harmful and wasteful" (2011). Thus, the Solutions Journalism Network often relies on third-party networks to verify the credential of their leaders such as "groups like Ashoka, The Aspen Institute, Echoing Green, The Skoll Foundation, The Schwab Foundation, and TED [who] have vetted thousands of entrepreneurs and innovators" (Bansal and Martin 2015, 16). However, the evaluative schema that organizations use to vet individuals is implicit in solutions journalism. In his ruminations about leadership quality, Drayton reflected that "over the last century society, to its great loss, has shied away from treating ethical fibre openly" (2005). Thus, in this view, a more explicit model of pragmatic leadership could help to standardize solutions journalism as a practice and distinguish it from traditional reporting that is vulnerable to monopolization by powerful sources and public relations campaigns.

The centrality of leadership quality in solutions journalism contrasts sharply public journalism that posited no definition of character and looked to an undifferentiated mass of local community members for its solutions to community problems. Public journalism sought to distil community opinion through a variety of deliberative methods. Like alchemists, journalists were thought to be able to help make the public "emerge" (Rosen 1999, 19), make their readers into citizens (Leonard 1999), and, on this basis, articulate a common good (Christians 1999). However, this project was widely criticized for overlooking deep ideological and material schisms within the supposedly singular community and eschewing journalists' tendency to set the terms of the debate (Woodstock 2002). In comparison, solutions journalism has largely avoided assuming or attempting to identify community opinions and ideas. While there is growing interest in the potential for solutions journalism to engage diverse or disengaged audiences (Wenzel et al. 2018), with research produced in collaboration with scholars of "engagement journalism" (Curry et al. 2016), this research has largely examined "downstream" audience engagement after the story is published rather than "upstream" public engagement (Anderson et al. 2014) by considering how audiences might help to identify solutions.

Rather than relying on the public to identify effective solutions, solutions journalists have posited a type of individual and organization in the process of implementing effective, scalable and newsworthy solutions. For Beers (2010), these news sources were people who, whether operating locally or internationally, were already experimenting with and implementing solutions and alternative practices. Bornstein (2004, 2010) and Drayton (2005) offered an even more detailed definition of a desirable source: a social entrepreneur. Observing the success of solutions journalism, it might be concluded that a schema of leadership evaluation is important for reporting ideas for the future, usefully narrowing the scope of relevant sources and ideas to those that stand the best chance of being effective and lasting. As the following section will suggest, the act of proposing change has always come with an implicit schema of leadership legitimacy that has structurally excluded marginalized groups from making propositions for change. Based on this analysis of solutions journalism, a theoretical framework is established that will inform the case study and content analysis in part II of this book.

THE PUBLIC SPHERE

The democratic reporting of solutions can be understood in relation to public sphere theory, which, as recent theorists have argued, has tended to overlook the idea of leadership and fundamental power imbalances regarding whose solutions are most worthy of becoming subjects of further discussion. In *The Structural Transformation of the Public Sphere*, Jürgen Habermas (1991) charted the emergence of an educated and literate section of bourgeois society whose discussions regarding current affairs formed a realm of discourse termed "the public sphere." Conceived as an area of free and critical discourse that could be mobilized as a rational check on government power, the emergence of the public sphere laid the foundations for the current importance placed on public opinion in democratic societies, and the rise of monitory institutions to hold power to account (Keane 2018). The rise of an informed and credible public opinion, replacing the term's former meaning as a euphemism for ill-informed (Habermas 1991, 90), was facilitated by a new trade in printed "news letters" and pamphlets in European trade cities from the year 1570 onward (Conboy 2004, 11).

Interestingly, this early trade in "news letters" was precipitated by merchants' need to be appraised of dangers and emerging opportunities in overseas markets. Such letters were exchanged through trade routes in order to transmit economic information among merchants to improve predictions about future profits and losses (Habermas 1991, 16). International trade was an expensive and risky enterprise with many variables to consider before an investment was made and shipping secured. The state of foreign markets, political news, shipwrecks, and other tidings formed the basis of early "news letters" between members of elite merchant guilds. As Beck noted, discussion of chance and danger "became an issue in the course of industrialization, starting with intercontinental shipping . . . when it is confronted with the openness, uncertainties and obstructions of a self-created future . . . no longer defined by religion, tradition or the superior power of nature" (2009, 4). Only later did printers begin to report on affairs of broader public consequence outside of merchant circles. Specifically, according to Conboy, English public interest journalism was precipitated by new wars with France in 1589, thereby producing an imagined national community "unified in the face of dangers from across the Channel" (2004, 11). Accordingly, the formation of national community and the informing of that community about their shared future was an integral part of journalism's genealogy, both in its early private iteration and subsequent public expansion.

While Habermas's theory provided a detailed account of this transformation in public discourse, it also posited a normative theory of journalism's proper function in maintaining the public sphere as an area of relatively free, open, and rational debate. The normative public sphere, as Nancy Fraser surmised, "was to be open and accessible to all; merely private interests were to be inadmissible; inequalities of status were to be bracketed; and discussants were to deliberate as peers" (1990, 59). Thus, Habermas prescribed an open and egalitarian space where everyone's ideas would be considered regardless of personage. This was interpreted by Beers as also involving a diversification of news sources when reporting ideas for the future. According to Beers, "Going back to Habermas' ideal, democracy is best served by a public sphere where competing visions for the future can be expressed and subjected to debate without skewing or censorship to fit the agendas of capitalist media owners or government officialdom." However, like Habermas (1991, 175), Beers found that today's public discourse fell short of its proper pedagogical role due to public relations strategies that suppressed alternative futures (2006, 121). Accordingly, employing public sphere theory to understand the reporting of the future necessarily involves an accounting of news sources and analysis of how their authority is constructed. This concern brings analysis back to the staging and construction of the future through the epistemic authority of news sources.

Arguably, public spheres have always been constituted by implicit leadership values that concentrate and constrain leadership legitimacy. In particular, Fraser (1990) offered an influential critique of Habermas's conception of the public sphere. Drawing on revisionist and feminist histories, Fraser argued that the democratic virtues of discourse in the public sphere—disinterestedness, rationality, solemnity—were, in fact, markers of status and class among a restricted group of wealthy men that served to exclude women and others from public deliberations. The emergence of the public sphere was, in her view, characterized by "a new, austere style of public speech and behaviour . . . a style deemed 'rational,' 'virtuous,' and 'manly' " (1990, 59). Thus, rather than a democratic institution, the bourgeois public sphere was in fact "the arena, the training ground, and eventually the power base of a stratum of bourgeois men, who were coming to see themselves as a 'universal class' and preparing to assert their fitness to govern" (1990, 60). In particular, the idea that a proposition is, regardless of its content, implicitly an assertion of one's fitness to govern brings attention to the ways that competency is euphemized in journalism about the future.

For the philosopher, Hannah Arendt (2013, 177), a proposition is an "action" in the narrative sense, which forges a new beginning and, in doing so, discloses the character of the actor. According to Arendt, "To act, in its most general sense, means to take initiative, to begin" (2013, 177). Recognizing the centrality of action for the construction of identity, Arendt argued that "with word and deed we insert ourselves into the human world" (2013, 176). Action and its accompaniment with speech (a proposition) involve a performance that reveals the unique narrative genealogy of the speaker and compels its audience to interpret the act as a reflection of character: "In acting and speaking, men show who they are, reveal actively their unique personal identities and thus make their appearance in the human world" (Arendt 2013, 179). In this Greek conception (where man is defined as *zoon politicon*, a political animal) while everybody can theoretically make propositions, it is absurd to make such pronouncements alone, and equally absurd to make them in domestic settings where they could be of no consequence. A proposition could only be adequately voiced, according to the Ancient Greeks, in a restricted sphere of men (the polis) who had freed themselves from domestic household management (ruled by mute strength and authoritarianism) enabling them to debate ideas and politics (ruled by reason and rational debate among equals) (2013, 26). Thus, Arendt concluded that "action needs for its full appearance the shining brightness we once called glory, and which is possible only in the public realm" (2013, 180).

What was once called glory might, today, be called media visibility. Within media scholarship, the importance of publicity for a proposition was articulated powerfully by John B. Thompson:

> To achieve visibility through the media is to gain a kind of presence or recognition in the public space, which can help to call attention to one's situation or to advance one's cause. But equally, the inability to achieve visibility through the media can confine one to obscurity—and, in the worst cases, can lead to a kind of death by neglect. (Thompson 2005, 49)

Being invisible is a democratic harm and, perhaps, a kind of misrecognition (Fraser and Honneth 2003). Conversely, as surmised by Benson, "media power is ultimately the power to 'consecrate,' that is, name an event, person, or idea as worthy of wider consideration" (Benson 1998, 469). Thus, journalism is also involved in the recognition and consecration of leadership, thereby creating exclusive fields of influential sources whose ideas are routinely reported, and a public of those whose propositions are routinely ignored.

GOVERNANCE AND PUBLIC OPINION

Solutions journalism marked a transition away from public journalism's deliberative method and toward reporting solutions in practice. In its shift away from deliberation, solutions journalism is nearer, perhaps, to Walter Lippman's famous skepticism regarding the efficacy of public opinion is shaping governance (Lippmann 1922). Indeed, solutions journalists are fond of quoting the following passage from Lippman's book *Public Opinion*: "The way in which the world is imagined determines at any particular moment what men will do" (Lippmann 1922, 16). Bornstein and Rosenberg use this quote to show how pervasive negativity distorts reality, making one imagine a much more dysfunctional state of affairs than may be the case and subsequently losing interest in public affairs (Bornstein and Rosenberg 2016). The world that solutions journalism seeks to construct in the public mind, by comparison, is one where individuals are empowered to tackle common problems, share their experiences and inspire others to participate more fully in solution-oriented pursuits. As they suggest, "These kinds of stories are abundant and real; they are the hidden history of our time" (Bornstein and Rosenberg 2016).

However, the usefulness of Lippman extends beyond why solutions reporting matters, to how certain solutions enter the news and who is able to place them there. In *Public Opinion*, Lippman adopted a skeptical argument regarding the capacity of the public to meaningfully engage in matters of state

(1922). His skepticism was partly justified by the public's unequal capacity to attend to ongoing issues and policy dilemmas, noting that "there are vast groups, ghettoes, enclaves and classes that hear only vaguely about much that is going on. They live in grooves, are shut in among their own affairs, barred out of larger affairs, meet few people not of their own sort, read little" (1922, 31). Lippman sketched three concentric rings of public awareness of current affairs, groups whose opinions are informed to the extent that they might shape governance. Usefully complicating the cartoonish insider-outsider dichotomy, Lippman argued that there are social sets within society: circles formed by families, cliques and acquaintances. Within these sets are, firstly, social leaders who "must combine an intimate knowledge of the anatomy of their own set with a persistent sense of its place in the hierarchy of sets" (1922, 34). Then, "there is something which might almost be called a social set of the social leaders" (1922, 34) whose opinions shape the behavior of those within certain sets. And finally, there is a highly exclusive yet strikingly interdisciplinary circle of cosmopolitans whose opinions are most informed and influential in shaping public opinion generally. Lippman described this elite circle as follows:

> The powerful, socially superior, successful, rich, urban social set is funda-mentally international throughout the western hemisphere, and in many ways, London is its center. It counts among its membership the most influential people in the world, containing as it does the diplomatic set, high finance, the upper circles of the army and the navy, some princes of the church, a few great news-paper proprietors, their wives and mothers and daughters who wield the scepter of invitation. It is at once a great circle of talk and a real social set. But its importance comes from the fact that here at last the distinction between public and private affairs practically disappears. (1922, 35)

Lippman in no way endorsed this aristocracy. Rather, as Michael Schudson usefully reminded us, Lippman maintained a commitment to representative democracy to the extent that "at election times . . . citizens make largely one decision, to keep the bums in or to throw them out" (Schudson 2008, 1035). Between elections, however, public opinion cannot, Lippman argued, be adequately mobilized or constituted by journalism to guide decision-making.

While such a concession is never made by solutions journalists, in prac-tice, solutions journalists do tap a restricted pool of leaders, whose efforts to drive change form the basis of their stories. Indeed, social entrepreneurs share some similarities with the elite leaders referenced by Lippman. They tend to be socially networked and cosmopolitan in outlook. Indeed, the Solutions Journalism Network recommend social entrepreneurs because of their net-worked nature since, "many of these networks hold social change conferences, which can be a great place to meet many of the people on this list" (Bansal and Martin 2015, 16). Their recommendation, however, came with the caveat that some entrepreneurial networks "may, consciously or not, be advancing a particular view of the world" (2015, 47), yet little advice is given regarding how journalists should judge the impartiality or ethics of the social entrepreneur networks from which they draw their solutions. Notably, the list of networks that they provide is quite different from the elite field of cosmopolitan leaders outlined by Lippman, including: Ashoka, TED Fellows, Echoing Green, Ascend Network, and the Skoll Foundation. They represent, to use Fraser's formulation, "subaltern counter-publics [that] enhance the participation of subordinate strata in stratified societies" (2007, 12). These forums represent, in effect, an alternative leadership network to elite solution-focused networks such as Davos (the World Economic Forum) or global executive leadership summits—networks whose solutions are already pervasive in solutions reporting. However, underscoring the fact that this distinction is rarely articulated by solutions journalists, Arianna Huffington launched the *Huffington Post*'s solutions initiative at the World Economic Forum, Davos 2015. With less democratic intent, Huffington explained that, "as the number-one social publisher on Facebook, we've learned these are the stories our readers are most interested in reading and sharing" (2015). While *The Huffington Post*'s "What's Working" is one of the most recognized solutions journalism outlets, it appears less inclined to distinguish between the elite circles of global leadership as opposed to bottom-up social change that solutions journalists elsewhere report exclusively.

Reflecting these apprehensions about solutions journalism, Amiel and Powers found that solutions journalism can represent a "Trojan horse" for marketing that "legitimates and valorizes marketing discourses among journalists, who use solutions journalism to describe efforts to grow audiences, boost sales and monetize content" (2019, 235). Accordingly, in practice, solutions journalism does appear at risk of blurring into amplification of brands, elites, and other powerful figures. In this, Beers's forthright condemnation of corporate monopolization of future-focused discourse remains a rare exception (2006). However, there are intersecting fault lines in the asymmetrical distribution of political recognition and news access, requiring a more nuanced distinction between corporate and community-aligned sources, an approach that is less reliant on public sphere theory and more empirically grounded than Beers' intervention. For this task, I propose field theory.

FIELD THEORY

Field theory, established by Bourdieu, is a valuable framework for examining unequal news access in solutions journalism (Bourdieu 1993, 1996b, 1991a).

As will be suggested, field theory and its associated concepts of symbolic capital usefully foreground questions of legitimacy while providing a mechanism for explaining how power is invested in certain voices and not others. As such, journalism scholars have widely adopted (and adapted) Bourdieu's theories of field, capital, and habitus (Benson 1998; Schultz 2007; Amiel and Powers 2019; Willig 2013; Benson and Neveu 2005)—yet they have less often considered these concepts in relation to news access and leadership evaluation. The following explanation of field theory as it relates to communication also provides the theoretical background for the case study analysis in the following three chapters.

Fields can be defined, using Benson's formulation (2006, 188), as "semiautonomous and increasingly specialized spheres of action (e.g., fields of politics, economics, religion, cultural production)." Fields are a distinguishing feature of modernity and a result of the rejection of "aristocratic and ecclesiastical tutelage" over cultural production (Bourdieu 1993, 14), whereby increasing intellectual freedom allowed the proliferation of specialized fields and subfields of cultural production. These are conceived as microcosms that can assert their own specific values and rules but also exist in relation to other fields that can exert power over a field's internal laws. Most notably, the dominant fields of politics (the state) and economics (capital) exert the greatest pressure over the integrity of subordinate fields and their ability to autonomously set their own standards and rules. Fields are therefore semiautonomous, each constituting "a social universe freed from a certain number of the constraints . . . without being completely independent of the external laws" (Bourdieu 2005, 33). The tension between freedom and constraint in fields is conceptualized as involving two opposing tendencies. On the one hand, there is a tendency toward greater field autonomy (literally "self-rule") where ongoing refinement and loyalty to the field's own rules and intellectual values is the highest imperative. On the other hand, there is a tendency toward heteronomy where actors in the field adopt the rules and values of external fields. Normatively, the tendency for field autonomy is considered most valuable because it provides "the conditions necessary for the production and diffusion of the highest human creations" (Bourdieu 1998, 65). In the context of commercialization (where the economic field imposes its logic of commodification and mass-market appeal on all subordinate fields) or in conditions of political authoritarianism (where the state imposes its system of hierarchy and censorship), fields cannot produce their specific cultural goods but produce, instead, a homogenous and impoverished simulacra of their former cultural good.

Taken as a whole, the modern social world comprises fields in which individuals must compete for limited positions of influence but also reconcile the contradictory imperatives of field autonomy and heteronomy.

Individuals can either resist the cultural gravity exerted by the dominant fields of politics and economics or, conversely, accept or even promote compromise with either of these powerful fields. The attitudes one can assume in this regard are determined by one's own position in the field and one's personal resources or capital, which Bourdieu divided into three kinds. Whereas capital is normally understood as an economic resource, Bourdieu understood capital, more broadly, as "accumulated labour" (1986, 15), which can take a variety of non-monetary forms and can be transferred between those forms:

> Capital can present itself in three fundamental guises: As economic capital, which is immediately and directly convertible into money and may be institutionalized in the form of property rights; as cultural capital, which is convertible, on certain conditions, into economic capital and may be institutionalized in the form of educational qualifications; and as social capital, made up of social obligations ("connections"), which is convertible, in certain conditions, into economic capital and may be institutionalized in the form of a title of nobility.

>   (Bourdieu 1986, 16–17)

Cultural capital, distributed through official consecration or educational attainment, is the resource that individuals call upon to defend the autonomy of fields. Cultural wealth entitles a limited range of actors to a legitimate opinion and judgment on that field's cultural products. Conversely, individuals with lower cultural capital but higher economic capital are comparatively less capable of evaluating cultural products but, through patronage and investment, can influence the field's rules by proxy and thereby exert a heteronomous cultural influence on cultural production. Thus, according to Thompson (1991, 14), a field is defined "as a structured space of positions in which the positions and their interrelations are determined by the distribution of different kinds of resources or 'capital.' " While cultural, economic, and social capital represent objective social facts (titles, connections, property, etc.), these possessions are also intersubjective and relational. They exist in terms of social recognition of their worth and value and are deployed euphemistically in language, conspicuous consumption, and the reception of cultural products and their "symbolic evaluation" (Thompson 1990, 154). Thus, Axel Honneth defines symbolic capital as the "sum of cultural recognition . . . acquire[d] through skillful manipulation of the system of social symbols" (1995, 187). Accordingly, it is not enough to simply possess capital. Individuals and groups struggle within fields to "valorise those forms of capital which they possess" (Benson 2006, 190). As Bourdieu argued in *Distinction* (1984), individuals subconsciously allude to their stock of capital through displays of taste and conspicuous consumption that serve to distinguish them from their peers and symbolize their social standing.

Pertinently for solutions journalism and news access, Bourdieu argued that certain pronouncements and propositions can only be made from a certain field position. Whereas linguistic analysis had tended to elide questions of power, status and legitimacy, Bourdieu sought to recentralize legitimacy in analysis of discourse:

> From a strictly linguistic point of view, anyone can say anything and the private can order his captain to "clean the latrines," but from a sociological point of view . . . it is clear that not anyone can assert anything, or else does so at his peril, as with an insult. (1991a, 74)

This somewhat obvious case presaged a broader discussion of the ways that field location constrains what can be said and by whom. The same principle can be applied to news access. As Bourdieu observed, journalistic interest an invaluable sign of social recognition. He argued that "the abundance of microphones, cameras, journalists and photographers, is . . . the visible manifestation of the hearing granted to the orator, of his credit, of the social importance of his acts and his words" (1991a, 193). For instance, a news source might have a particular solution in mind and therefore call a press conference, but unless that news sources occupies a certain position of legitimacy, journalists are unlikely to turn up. Thus, journalists are implicated in the distribution of legitimacy: both in their recognition of symbolic power and, circuitously, in the generation of that symbolic power through consecration of people, events, and ideas (Benson 1999, 469). For powerful sources such as politicians or entrepreneurs, appearances in bulletins articulating solutions and propositions are everyday occurrences. Media attention recognizes, reinforces, and in some cases, generates the symbolic capital of personal and instrumental value to a range of actors in, what Hage has termed, the governmental field (1996, 2012).

THE GOVERNMENTAL FIELD

Ghassan Hage proposed the concept of a "governmental field" in the context of his study of nationalism and multiculturalism: *White Nation: Fantasies of White Supremacy in a Multicultural Society* (2000). Nationalism, for Hage, refers to various forms of homely belonging that give meaning to the nationalist's life and a sense of ownership over their locality. These feelings of belonging, however, are unequally distributed among citizens and are bestowed according to one's "national cultural capital," including "looks, accent, demeanour, taste, nationally valued social and cultural preferences and behaviour" (Hage 1996, 466). An important part of homely belonging is the sense of legitimacy can articulate preferences, plans, and propositions regarding the domesticated space. Thus, with relevance to the idea of leadership, Hage found that migrants are often excluded from a particular form of active national belonging termed "governmental belonging" (2012, 46) which

> can merely be the feeling that one is legitimately entitled in the course of everyday life to make a governmental/managerial statement about the nation—to have a view about its foreign policy, for example, or to have a governmental/managerial attitude towards others, especially those who are perceived to be lesser nationals or non-nationals, to have a view about who they can be and where they can go. (2000, 46)

Accordingly, feeling empowered to legitimately propose and make a "governmental-type statement" is an expression of power and national belonging regardless of whether "the 'policy directive' expressed in them is not followed by the state" (Hage 1996, 468). While one's governmental belonging is irrespective of the policy action of the government, those who propose solutions cannot be indifferent to journalism, since media coverage is an important way in which legitimacy is conferred on an idea of person. In journalists' routine decisions regarding news access, the governmental field is policed and symbolic capital within the field recognized and distributed.

This application of field theory is consistent with Thompson's definition of symbolic power and symbolic action. With reference to Bourdieu's theory of capital, Thompson (1995, 16) wrote that "individuals draw on [their specific] resources to perform actions which may intervene in the course of events and have consequences of various kinds." Thus, he continued, "symbolic actions may give rise to reactions, may lead others to act or respond in certain ways, to pursue one course of action rather than another, to believe or disbelieve, to affirm their support for a state of affairs or to rise up in collective revolt" (1995, 16–17). Propositions, then, are symbolic investments and interventions within the governmental field that may alter the course of events. Yet, to be effective, they often require the recognition of journalists who govern access, in many instances, to the governmental field.

LEADERSHIP AS SYMBOLIC CAPITAL

In seeking to adapt this concept to solutions journalism, one can consider the responses that form the basis of solutions journalism as "governmental" statements: statements issued to journalists that propose an idea or initiative for the wider community. Beyond the national frame that Hage intended, governmental solutions can be considered in a more cosmopolitan sense, since social entrepreneurs offer solutions across national jurisdictions. Likewise, the perceived attributes that empower someone to come forward with a solution go beyond the national symbolic capital identified by Hage. Rather, solutions journalists are in the business of recognizing and evaluating a particular form of symbolic capital that I will term "leadership capital."

Leadership is not an objective possession but must be established and maintained semiotically with "signs of leadership" and through actions that are habitually interpreted as demonstrating leadership. Leadership, therefore, is a transposable quality (across fields) that is deeply embedded in cultural myths and class structures of prestige and privilege. One can be a leader of a field and simultaneously have their leadership qualities recognized in more general terms, abstracted from context in the forms of propositions and visions for society as a whole. Thus, "leadership capital" is the symbolic currency of the governmental field. While leadership capital can be accumulated, there is an "aristocratic logic" that implies that one is born a leader: "a self-constructed 'natural' ruler" (Hage 1996, 467). Thus, a true leader cannot be assembled by learning a range of leadership attributes.

Leadership is also a conduit between the governmental and journalistic fields. Evaluating and policing leadership quality according to taken-for-granted community expectations is core business for editors, polemicists, investigative journalists, and beat reporters (Ettema and Glasser 1998). It is a resource that is especially relevant when the future is uncertain and up for grabs (Kerr 2008). When audiences seek reassurance about the future of their locality, the media can supply a range of leaders to outline their plans and visions. Kerr (2008) examined the discourse of leadership from a Bourdieusian perspective and argued that "floating discourses of leadership are reproduced in the relatively autonomous social spaces or fields of political and corporate leadership and in turn reproduce those fields as socially stratified and hierarchical" (2008, 204). This is an important area of study because, as Kerr suggested, a discourse of leadership evaluation "plays a part socially in that reality's construction" (2008, 204). Thus, the way good leadership is evaluated shapes the decisions that can be legitimately made and, by proxy, shapes the future reality.

Considering leadership as symbolic capital is especially relevant to an analysis of solutions journalism because propositions and proponents are evaluated according to the leadership virtues that they reveal: virtues like honesty, timeliness, courage, consistency, responsibility, care, and pragmatism. Conversely, a proposition might reveal a deficit of leadership capital where a proposition is a sign of weakness, impertinence, cowardice, dishonesty, inconsistency, or irresponsibility. These evaluations, that Thompson called "the valorisation of symbolic forms" (1990, 154), are an indispensable part of journalism's celebrated role as a watchdog (Borden 2008; Borden and Tew 2007). However, they are also historically contingent and vary according to news outlet. These sensibilities are embedded in what Lakoff terms (Lakoff 2016) the "moral politics" of ideological groups. The symbolic valorization of leadership is apparent not only in whose voices and solutions are heard in news, but also how solutions are framed in news texts.

LEADERSHIP FRAMES

Journalists, like other professional communicators, must make a range of routine decisions regarding selection and salience in conveying the content and consequences of a given proposal. The quantity of journalistic decisions required to produce a news article, compounded by "the buzzing complexity of the world" (2013, 4), requires journalists, for efficiency, to habituate many of these decisions. While this habituation can be readily conceptualized within a Bourdieusian framework via the concept of habitus, an argument that I have elaborated elsewhere (forthcoming), suffice it to say that, frames refer to the structured nature of this habituation.

Frames—often defined as "persistent patterns of cognition, interpretation, and presentation, or selection, emphasis, and exclusion, by which symbol-handlers routinely organize discourse, whether verbal or visual" (Gitlin 1981, 7)—are of interest in many issue-specific contexts, both for their generative and enabling qualities as well as their limiting and even hegemonic functions. Frames have been found to both enable communication and deliberation by providing an interpretive repertoire (Lakoff and Johnson 2003) while also being responsible for cultural inertia, biases, assumptions, stereotypes, and unreflexive behaviors (Gamson 1992; Nisbet 2018; Tierney et al. 2006). By making these subconscious structures salient, frame analysis offers the promise of deeper understanding of meaning making and corresponding behaviors by uncovering the cognitive and cultural structures that underpin them.

Likewise, deciding who to interview for a particular story and how to describe their intervention is likewise subject to journalistic framing practices. Robert Entman (1993) famously argued that:

> [To] frame is to select some aspects of a perceived reality and make them more salient in a communicating text, in such a way as to promote a particular problem definition, causal interpretation, moral evaluation, and/or treatment recommendation for the item described. (1993, 52)

In particular, Entman's reference to "treatment recommendation" suggests that, even in stories that describe a negative event, a frame may implicitly point to a p remedy. Less obvious in Entman's conception is how frames imply who is legitimately entitled to articulate a solution or how a solution is to be evaluated. To guide journalists' everyday newsgathering and writing practice, frames of leadership evaluation, I will suggest, provide the evaluative structure against which sources can be selected and the act of proposing a solution described.

Legitimation, according to Barker (2001, 32), "is a claim or expression made by or on behalf of that person to assert the special and distinctive identity which that person possesses, which . . . justifies or authorises or legitimates the command by legitimating the person issuing it." Legitimacy frames, then, are different from rhetorical frames (Kuypers 2010) in that they do not persuade the audience of the value of a proposition. Rather, they are frames that allude to those attributes that justify, authorize, or legitimate the speaker's appearance in a given text. In this sense, those parts of discourse that Gamson and Modigliani referred to as "framing devices"—metaphors, exemplars, catchphrases, depictions, and images (1989, 3)—form a constellation of valorizing and legitimating symbols in solutions journalism, thereby issuing symbolic capital within the governmental field. While journalists develop their own field-specific schema and lexicon for evaluating news sources, they are also caught up in political struggles over meaning and evaluation.

METAPHOR

The most significant evaluative framing mechanism, however, may go unnoticed. For cognitive linguists, George Lakoff and Mark Johnson (1999, 2008), the key components of frames are metaphors. Rather than rhetorical flourish, metaphors are considered both pervasive and central to moral reasoning about abstract concepts such as leadership. A metaphor is defined, simply, as "understanding and experiencing one thing in terms of another" (Lakoff and Johnson 2008, 5).

In the same way that frames are habituated shortcuts that allow individuals to navigate complexity in their personal and professional lives, so too, conceptual metaphors structure and enable unconscious reasoning. The theory of cognitive unconscious holds that "most of our thought is unconscious, not in the Freudian sense of being repressed, but in the sense that it operates beneath the level of cognitive awareness, inaccessible to consciousness and operating too quickly to be focused on" (Lakoff and Johnson 1999, 10). Unconscious reasoning, Lakoff argued, is structured and it is the work of the cognitive linguist to uncover "what, exactly, our unconscious system of concepts is and how we think and talk using that system of concepts" (Lakoff 2016, 4). In this sense, the cognitive unconscious is roughly synonymous with Bourdieu's concept of habitus. Indeed, Bourdieu began his 1989 book, *The State Nobility*, by describing his sociology as "merging with psychology [where] an exploration of objective structures is at one and the same time an exploration of the cognitive structures that agents bring to bear in their practical knowledge of the social worlds thus structured" (Bourdieu 1996b, 1). Thus, both the habitus and the cognitive unconscious refer to a domain of habituated cognitive instincts that allow individuals to negotiate social life.

Like Lakoff, Bourdieu is concerned with the effects of the unconscious and the ways that cognitive structures shape society. While metaphor is often dismissed as mere linguistic playfulness, Lakoff has argued that most complex, subjective, and abstract concepts are defined according to a metaphorical structure. To use one of Lakoff and Johnson's examples, Western cultures talk about "arguing" using the metaphor "argument is war":

> Your claims are indefensible, He attacked every weak point in my argument, His criticisms were right on target, I demolished his argument, I've never won an argument with him, You disagree? Okay, shoot!, If you use that strategy, he'll wipe you out, he shot down all my arguments. (2003, 4–5)

More than merely shaping the way people talk, this metaphorical frame informs behavior and makes arguing a competitive and combative activity. A culture in which arguing was conceived as a dance might have a very different set of argumentative practices (Lakoff and Johnson 2003, 5). Lakoff and Johnson identify countless metaphorical frames, such as "life is a journey" (1999, 64), "time is money" (2008, 7), and "affection is warmth" (1999, 46). These prevalent metaphors, they claim, "go beyond the conceptual; they have consequences for material culture" (1999, 63). In cultures that do not have a "life is a journey" metaphor, for instance, "people just live their lives, and the very idea of being without direction, or missing the boat, of being held back of getting bogged down in life, would make no sense" (1999, 63). In each instance, speech and thought in these areas are organized according to metaphors, and, in that sense, the dominant conceptual metaphor can be considered the frame.

It should be noted, however, that the cognitive linguistics that informs Lakoff's work has a specific conception of frame and its relation to metaphor, which is quite different from the treatment of these concepts in media scholarship and sociology. For instance, Lakoff and Johnson's theory differs significantly from Gamson and Modigliani's (1989) treatment of metaphors, catchphrase, and idioms as "framing devices." In their analysis of interpretive packages, Gamson and Modigliani found that metaphors can be deployed as shorthand for broader interpretive frames or packages. This relationship is reversed in Lakoff's conception (2008, 2014) with metaphors forming the overarching interpretive structure and frames forming its basic subunits. For Lakoff, every given word has an associated frame, made up of semantic roles and normative relationships between these roles. Thus, the word fork is inseparable from the concepts of spoon, knife, food, plate, eating, and table, which form the frame's semantic roles. These are rigid, embedded inferences that are triggered in the brain upon hearing the word fork and can be supplemented with more specific data: restaurant, steak, waiter, and date. Accordingly, the title of Lakoff's popular manual for the re-framing policy debates is, "Don't think of an Elephant" (2008, 3), which also serves as the book's first lesson:

> I've never found a student who is able to do this. Every word, like elephant, evokes a frame, which can be an image or other kinds of knowledge: Elephants are large, have floppy ears and a trunk, are associated with circuses, and so on. The word is defined relative to that frame. When we negate a frame, we evoke the frame.

Such frames are often normative, what Lakoff termed ideal cognitive models (ICMs) (1987, 9). These normative frames suggest a logical order and relationship between each semantic role. For instance: one uses a knife and fork to eat the food on the plate. Our knowledge of specific scenarios associated with words, that Lakoff terms "source domains" (2008, 256), provides a rich resource for metaphorical reasoning about the nature and normative structure of a range of subjective and abstract phenomena, termed "target domains." Thus, metaphorical reasoning takes the guise of common sense by implying the logical, proper, and moral order of something else.

THE MORAL POLITICS OF LEADERSHIP

The most relevant discussions of metaphorical framing, for the purposes of this research, involves Lakoff's later work on political morality and the evaluation of leadership and policy through metaphor. He found that common areas of political discourse—such as the environment (2010), immigration (Lakoff and Ferguson 2016), and taxation (1996, 179)—are mostly reasoned about according to certain dominant metaphors. He identified discursive struggles over the application of preferred metaphors and the imposition of "metaphorical common sense" on key policy areas (2016, 5). For example, Lakoff noted the emergence of the term "tax relief" after George W. Bush won the presidency. The word "relief" triggers a frame that imposes a certain moral interpretation on tax policy:

> For there to be relief there must be an affliction, an afflicted party, and a reliever who removes the affliction and is therefore a hero. And if people try to stop the hero, those people are villains for trying to prevent relief. When the word tax is added to relief, the result is a metaphor: Taxation is an affliction. And the person who takes it away is a hero, and anyone who tries to stop him is a bad guy. This is a frame. (2016, 3–4)

Thus, partly because of the president's symbolic power and partly because of the innocuous formulation "tax relief," the term was readily taken up by news outlets, "and soon the New York Times is using tax relief. And it is not only on Fox; it is on CNN, it is on NBC, it is on every station because it is 'the president's tax-relief plan' " (Lakoff 2008, 4). Like Trojan horses, frames enter the public consciousness through innocuous idioms. In Lakoff's view, such frames are "a trap: The words draw you into their worldview" (2008, 4). Accordingly, while metaphorical framing is an unavoidable part of cognitive life these metaphors can be weaponized in ways that, over time, structure the cognitive subconscious.

The idea of leadership is also reasoned about using metaphor. In his most famous work, *Moral Politics*, Lakoff (2016) argued that opposing conservative and liberal worldviews were reflected in family morality and, specifically, "two opposing models of the family" (2016, 33). "At the centre of the conservative worldview is a Strict Father model," where children learn discipline through punishment and through the example of a strong father figure, eventually internalizing self-discipline and individual responsibility (Lakoff 2016, 33). "The liberal worldview centres on a very different ideal family life, the Nurturant Parent model," where children become responsible, self-disciplined, and caring members of society by experiencing care themselves in a loving empathetic and equal family environment (Lakoff 2016, 33–34). Lakoff found that discourses surrounding contentious political issues, such as taxation, the environment, abortion, capital punishment, and healthcare, were structured according to either of these metaphorical conceptions of family morality. Centrally, these metaphorical schemas suggest the kind of leader that is best placed to govern society: a strong disciplinarian in the conservative worldview, and a kind and caring leader in the progressive worldview. Lakoff found that "the metaphor that is central to Strict Father morality is the metaphor of Moral Strength . . . beginning with: Being Good is Being Upright [and] Being Bad Is Being Low" (2016, 71). On the other hand, metaphors for empathy, such as putting oneself in another's shoes are central in progressive thoughts about leadership legitimacy.

While Lakoff's work was deeply embedded in progressive activism and his books on moral politics are often written as practical guides for community groups as much as for academics, the core of his approach is built upon sophisticated cognitive linguistic research. Conceptual metaphor is especially appropriate for analyzing solutions journalism because, for Lakoff, they guide public reasoning about political morality, policy propositions, and leadership legitimacy. Metaphor analysis is also a useful bridging methodology between field and framing approaches because it considers framing as linguistic and cognitive habits (habitus) where certain words trigger neural circuits, which become stronger the more often one encounters a given framing. Accordingly, the prevalence of certain words can indicate their symbolic value within fields (Sonnett 2010) but also their relative habituation as ways of reasoning about leadership legitimacy.

Interestingly, the method for discerning cognitive structures is not dissimilar to Bourdieu's text analysis in *The State Nobility* (1998) that sought to uncover the evaluative schemas of teachers' academic judgments in the French education system. Bourdieu's text analysis of evaluative schema in teachers' comments brought specific attention to the adjectives used, which were frequently metaphorical. For example, in committee reports from an entrance examination to a prestigious school, Bourdieu (1998, 18) highlighted examples of figurative speech, which were recorded and organized in a system of binaries. Frequently the words that Bourdieu highlighted were metaphorical: brilliant, dull, elegant, heavy, morose, labored, light, dense, methodical, ease, gifted, and earnest (1998, 25). This "constellation of epithets" (Bourdieu 1998, 22) euphemized the inherited cultural capital of "gifted" students, and the cultural deficits of working-class students and served to construct a common sense and neutral model of the ideal student as a student from a cultured family.

Like education, journalism relies on a rhetoric of impartiality, fairness, and objectivity and, therefore, presents an interesting model for uncovering schemas of symbolic valorization in the governmental field. In the same way that students from poor backgrounds are routinely denied education's highest awards (Bourdieu 1998, 2), it is similarly verifiable that journalism's sources, particularly in consequential news about propositions, usually originate from a relatively privileged and restricted range of professions, backgrounds, and genders—a prediction that is confirmed in the following chapter. Leadership, this research predicts, is one such area of abstract and subjective phenomena that is evaluated using metaphorical schemas or frames. As such, the data sample will include metaphorical language that relates to the discussion of the future. At the outset, such metaphorical constructions seem common but perplexing. Why do journalists refer to an idea for the future as a "push," or a "bid" or a "call"? What has "vision" got to do with the future? What is a "bold" plan? This research will examine these expressions in order to determine whether there is a broader metaphorical system within which these terms are coherent. If Lakoff's theory is correct, we should expect that a level of coherence will become apparent. Thus, it should be possible to categorize related metaphorical idioms. Following Lakoff's suggestion that metaphors can have powerful societal effects, this thesis will question whether metaphoric systems related to the future help circumscribe who has a legitimate voice in the debate and euphemize natural and ideal leaders in the governmental field.

CONCLUSION

Solutions do not just appear in journalism and enter the public imagination on the basis of their merits. Rather, articulating a solution and having that idea taken seriously by journalists is characteristically an act of leadership, or rather, as this chapter has argued, an act that corresponds with journalists' variable concepts of valuable leadership. As this chapter found, such conceptions of leadership vary dramatically in solutions journalism. In its standardized and autonomous form, solutions journalism posits an extended governmental field of global changemakers, whose grassroots projects and innovations serve as exemplars for similarly ambitious social entrepreneurs elsewhere. In contrast, the reporting of the future more generally, in heteronomous practice, may reflect existing power structures and commonsense valorizations of entrepreneurial and political leadership. The difference between the two approaches, however, can be studied empirically using a combination of field analysis and frame analysis techniques, forming the theoretical basis for the subsequent case study chapters regarding "New Tasmania" (for a detailed explanation of the methods conducted, see appendices).

In part II, the book will examine the ways in which hope and leadership, two core normative concepts of solutions journalism, were mediated by journalists operating, relatively speaking, in splendid isolation—both geographically and in relation to the orthodoxies of solutions journalism. This will provide a counterpoint to studies of solutions journalism that have, to date, primarily sought to refine and define solutions journalism as a genre and delineate an ideal practice (McIntyre and Lough 2019). In recognition of the dynamic structures underlying solutions journalism practices, part II will examine solutions reporting as a common but variable practice operating at the unstable and interdisciplinary intersection of heteronomous and autonomous forces.

Part II

Chapter 3

"New Tasmania"

Tasmania, the heart-shaped island to the south of mainland Australia, is home to a relatively small and mostly rural population. With its three daily newspapers, four broadcasters (three commercial and one public), and emerging online media platforms, Tasmania provides a tidy delimitation within which to examine the theoretical terrain traversed thus far. How do journalists report ideas for the future and distribute social hope? Who is given voice and who is excluded? And how is news access shaped by the routine use of metaphors to evaluate leadership? Due to its remote location, Tasmanian journalists are relatively unfamiliar with the orthodoxies of solutions journalism that have been refined in the northern hemisphere. This remote and rugged island, therefore, provides an opportunity to test this book's hypothesis: that solutions reporting is, in fact, a relatively common journalistic practice, yet one that is shaped primarily by elite sources belonging to a restricted "governmental field." If this is the case, it will provide support for my argument that, normatively, solutions journalism should be characterized not merely by its reporting of solutions, but by its sources and its method for identifying and evaluating newsworthy leadership.

While Tasmania is a usefully remote subject, it faces challenges that are, nonetheless, familiar. Like many communities that have historically relied upon primary industry and manufacturing, Tasmania is facing rapid transformations in its economy and workforce, mirroring disruptions and their associated inequalities worldwide (Department of Economic and Social Affairs 2020, 58). In Tasmania as elsewhere, the deepening divides between the beneficiaries and victims of economic globalization have provoked fiercely contested visions of the state's future. Often symbolized by certain controversial development proposals, these contested visions have been routinely mediated by Tasmania's news media.

Controversial propositions have long been a staple of Tasmania's political discourse and represent key flashpoints in debates over conservation and development. In 1972, the rose quartz beaches of Lake Pedder in Tasmania's South West Wilderness were submerged after the controversial damming of the Serpentine and Huon Rivers (Beresford 2015, 19). In their disappointment, activists formed the world's first environmental political party, the United Tasmania Group, later known as the Tasmanian Greens (Stephens et al. 2006, 77). The conservation movement has since opposed many propositions in Tasmania and provided a counterpoint to the development of extractive industries. The subsequent dam proposal for the nearby Franklin River was famously prevented as a result of strong local and national protests (Doyle 2005, 100). Likewise, in 1989, the Wesley Vale pulp mill was halted (Beresford 2015, 64). Most recently, Tasmania's former forestry monopoly, Gunns Limited, proposed a pulp and paper mill at Bell Bay in the State's north, a project that became the object of "the environmental equivalent of 'total war' " (Beresford 2015, 283). From 2007 to 2011, a coalition of local, national, and international activist organizations cooperated and ultimately frustrated construction of the mill after a long and bitter campaign. Shortly afterward, in September 2012, Gunns Limited went into receivership (Beresford 2015, 364), precipitating a cascade of job losses and an economic recession (Andrews 2012).

These historical disputes have etched themselves into the political discourse in Tasmania, leading to the common characterization of the state as polarized between conservationists and developers. The positions taken by conservationists—across issues as diverse as forestry, fish farms, trawlers, cable cars, mines, road construction, Aboriginal heritage, tourism development and agriculture—are frequently derided as obstructionist and anti-development (West 2013). Conservationists are seen as impervious to the poverty and unemployment suffered by Tasmanians who might benefit from these propositions and the jobs and investment that they bring, just as developers are perceived as blind to the ecological, spiritual, and tourism value of Tasmania's famously pristine environment. Jonathan West characterized this dichotomy as a stalemate where, "if any interest group regards itself as disadvantaged by a development proposal—whether materially or in terms its values—there is insufficient weight on the pro-development side to push through resistance to change" (2013, 55). As has been argued in the preceding chapters, this research seeks to unpick unconstructive binaries between corporate solutions, on the one hand, and community alternatives, on the other. Indeed, by examining more closely whose voices are included and excluded, it may become apparent that such binaries disguise more fundamental asymmetries in the distribution of power: between those whose voices are routinely privileged in articulating development proposals, and those whose ideas are reported sporadically, routinely ignored, or derided.

According to the historian, James Boyce (1996), even prior to 1856, when Tasmania was known as Van Diemen's Land, the island was governed by a restricted field of British colonialists. According to Boyce, "We have allowed our history to be defined by the authors of this small group of very powerful men whose direct experience of living here was buffered by capital and privilege" (1996, 40). While historians rightly drew attention to this historical accumulation of influence and capital, in doing so, Boyce argued, alternative experiences and connections between people and place have been hidden, experiences that demonstrate alternative pathways for Tasmania. In a passage that brings his critique into contact with contemporary studies of news media and communication, Boyce identified a continuing suppression and denigration of Tasmanian alternatives to the dominant narratives of progress:

> There is a lot of money and power dependent on the lie that there is no other way than the present "practical path" of "growth" and "development." An important part of this ideology is the historical claim, or assumption, that there has never been a realistic alternative. Early sustainable farming practices, for example, despite easily meeting the needs of the people involved, have become defined as "misguided," "irrelevant to . . . real needs" and blamed for having "produced stagnation in Van Diemen's Land," in language that is reminiscent of the clearfellers' condemnation of small-scale selective logging operations or agribusinesses' dismissal of the benefits of self-sufficiency today. As long as the past is presented in this way, those who profit from the present exile can misrepresent alternative economic and social structures, which might reconnect us with the earth and each other, as the impractical, untested dreamland of a crazy few. [Such ideas present] a challenge to an ideology which, by defining what is "normal" and "realistic," protects powerful economic interests today. (1996, 57–58)

From a media and communications perspective, Boyce's reference to ideas and proponents "becoming defined" as variously misguided, normal or realistic due to the way they are represented, invites the type of news frame analysis outlined in the previous chapter. The binary between realistic thinking about the future with idealistic or utopian propositions is also consonant with Ghassan Hage's assessment of the marginalization of alternative futures in neoconservative rhetoric:

> You only have to listen to neo-conservatives speaking today. Whether they are politicians or journalists, there is one theme that unites them: they always like

to project themselves as "realists." They are always proclaiming the importance of "thinking hard and realistically." They are always attacking others "for not seeing reality as it is" telling us to "stop dreaming." They act as if "reality is on their side." In fact, far from being realists, such people are "actualists." They reduce reality to actuality and empty it from all forms of potentiality. They have a vested interest in people seeing actuality as the only reality there is. This is because actuality is on their side, and the domain of the potentiality and the struggle over it is where their rule over actuality can be brought to an end. This is why "hoping" and "dreaming" and "not being realistic" are all dangerous to them. Not because they are intrinsically capable of changing things but because they all point to the domain where practical change is possible. (Hage and Papadopoulos 2004, 121)

In the context of ongoing conflicts regarding the future, and the historical consolidation of leadership in an exclusive governmental field, it is interesting to note that Tasmania recently embarked on an explicitly future-oriented project under the banner of the local neologism, "New Tasmania." As we shall see, the term "New Tasmania" represented an attempt by the governmental field to build consensus, draw a line under historical feuds, and drive public optimism though a newly future-oriented discourse, much in the same way that solutions journalism had sought to do in the northern hemisphere. As such, the 2014 case study represented a collective effort to re-engage the public through a diversification of leadership and the distribution of hope. While operating outside the orthodoxies of solutions journalism or constructive journalism, this discursive effort provides an interesting counterpoint for solutions journalism as an autonomous alternative to traditional practice.

LAGGING TASMANIA

Tasmania is Australia's smallest and most isolated state, located 230 kilometers south of the mainland's east coast. Despite occupying roughly the same land mass as the Republic of Ireland, Tasmania's 68,401 km² of largely mountainous terrain remains sparsely populated with only 519,000 residents living in Tasmania at the time of writing ("June Key Figures" 2016). The state's population is also uniquely rural compared to other Australian states. According to the Australian Bureau of Statistics' (ABS) 2014–2015 report, "Of all states and territories, Tasmania had the highest proportion of its population residing outside the Greater Capital City at June 2015 (57%)" ("Regional Population Growth, Australia, 2014–15" 2015).

Despite its isolation, Tasmania was one of the first parts of Australia to be "discovered" and colonized by European settlers. Van Diemen's Land, as it was then known, was sighted by the explorer Abel Tasman in 1642 and subsequently colonized by the English in 1803 for use as a penal colony for English and Irish convicts (Boyce 2008; Shipway 2005). The island's early history under colonial rule was marked by violence, both in the brutal treatment of its convicts but also in the massacring of Aboriginal land owners culminating with "The Black War" of 1824–1831 (Clements 2013; Reynolds 2013; Shipway 2005). This was the first and only war fought on Australian soil, which, according to historian Nick Clements (2013, xiii), "all but wiped out" the formerly extensive Aboriginal population.

Tasmania is sometimes seen through this lens as a backward community and, perhaps, not a likely choice for the study of solutions-oriented discourses. According to the historian Jesse Shipway, there is an uncomfortable juxtaposition between Tasmania as a site of genocide and imprisonment and Tasmania as a site of modernity epitomized by the construction of enormous and impressively engineered hydroelectric dams (Shipway 2005, 190–195). While there is a need to contemporize this stereotype, in some respects, Tasmania does appear to have been more resilient to the waves of social progress and modernization that swept through the rest of Australia in the twentieth century. Tasmania was the last state to decriminalize homosexuality in 1997 (Croome 2013, 31) and remains the least multicultural state in Australia ("Trends in Net Overseas Migration: Tasmania" 2011). However, this cultural inertia is coupled with more material discrepancies between Tasmania and the mainland states relating to consistently poor outcomes in employment, health, and education (West 2013).

ECONOMIC RECESSION

Tasmania has, for geographic and demographic reasons, always carried a competitive disadvantage economically compared to its mainland counterparts. It is further away from national and international markets and reliant on expensive shipping of its export goods, which cuts profits and dampens investor enthusiasm. In addition, Tasmania's small and aging population (Jackson and Kippen 2001) means that there are fewer taxpayers (Denny and Polkan 2015), a limited local market for goods, and a shortage of skilled labor in some areas (McInerney 2013, 160). Citing these inherent disadvantages, Tasmania, as part of the Federation of Australia, appeals to the federation's foundational commitment to "provide the same standard of services to its population" regardless of where they live in Australia (Searle 2002, 1). Accordingly, the Commonwealth Grants Commission returns tax revenues to the states in order to equalize state revenues where some states, such as Tasmania and the Northern Territory, have less capacity to raise revenues themselves (Stratford 2007, 578). In 2014, Tasmania received $1.63 back for every $1 dollar of goods and services tax (GST) revenue raised, whereas Western Australia (in the midst of a lucrative mining boom) received only 0.38 cents per dollar raised. Tasmania is also the recipient of a freight subsidy called, the Tasmanian Freight Equalisation Scheme, which seeks to provide a level playing field for Tasmania's export market by subsidizing the cost of shipping (Truss 2015). This effective subsidization of the poorer states of Australia has been the source of some friction within the Australian Federation with Western Australia's premier describing Tasmania as a "mendicant state" and overly reliant on welfare payments (Denny and Polkan 2015).

These policies have, until recently, been effective in supporting Tasmanian industries in areas, such as mining, metallurgy, hydroelectricity, forestry, tourism, aquaculture, and agriculture. However, in recent decades, Tasmania's stagnant unemployment figures and growth have left the state vulnerable to economic recession and rising unemployment. In 2012, global and national trends coincided with local events to produce a sharp drop in employment and state government revenues. The Global Financial Crisis (GFC) of 2008 continued to hamper consumer confidence and reduced GST revenues. In April 2012, a prominent Tasmanian economist, Saul Eslake, declared the state in recession after recording two consecutive quarters of negative growth (in Andrews 2012). This led the state government to make cuts to health, education expenditure, and public service jobs (Alessandrini 2012, 660).

The economic problem in Tasmania was examined in a widely read edition of the Griffith Review titled *Tasmania: The Tipping Point* (Schultz 2013) that sought to reposition Tasmania in the context of the economic challenges and emerging opportunities of the twenty-first century. The crux of the economic problem was established by Julianne Schultz (2013) in an introductory essay titled, "Oscillating Wildly: Learning from the Past to Create the Future": "The warning signs are clear—about a third of Tasmania's population depends on benefits, a third is employed by the public sector, a fifth in the services sector and only a tenth in the private wealth creation sector" (2013, 8). This perceived imbalance in Tasmania's economy, with its higher proportion of welfare recipients and much lower levels of employment in the private sector, singled Tasmania out from northern states and territories. Business and innovation Professor Jonathan West attracted controversy with his forlorn explanation of the state's problems, arguing that Tasmania's reliance on subsidization had fostered a culture of obstructionism, and a "social coalition that blocks most proposals to improve . . . problems and challenges are debated endlessly, with no resolution" (2013, 51). For West, the uncomfortable truth is simply that "Tasmania doesn't change because its people don't really want to. They don't *need* to" [original emphasis] (2013, 51). The hard truths that West aired in this essay did not go unchallenged. Demographer Lisa Denny

(2013) took issue with West's "less than flattering description of Tasmania and its people," noting that "both South Australia and the Northern Territory (and until recently, Western Australia) receive a greater proportion of GST receipts than they contribute" (Denny 2013). Tasmania, Denny argued, was not alone in its dependence on government subsidization and was leading other states in innovation and education. Other respondents, such as Fred Gale (2013), challenged the classical economics model on which West's critique relied, pointing to surveys that revealed Tasmanians' high level of happiness and satisfaction, a scale that is excluded in GDP and employment figures.

Foreshadowing the newly optimistic spirit of "New Tasmania," the caricature of a lagging Tasmania was moderated significantly in this volume. This was reflected in the redemptive tone most of the essays with authors employing metaphors alluding to the exciting potential of the state: "The cracks are where the light gets in" (Cica 2013, 9); "churning the mud [from which] something truly remarkable again springs forth" (Croome 2013, 38); or "a dry forest [where] a spark could set off all kinds of things" (Bibby 2013, 73). Historically, economic downturns and recoveries are not unprecedented in Tasmania, and casting a look back at recent slumps and recoveries, there was cause to expect another revival in the state's prospects. A previous bout of pessimism regarding Tasmania's economy occurred in the late 1990s when the Booker Prize winner Tasmanian Richard Flanagan, in characteristic fashion, wrote that "it's as though the war's ended and we're left standing in the rubble and nobody knows where we are to go now, nobody's got any maps for the future" (in Croome 1997, 136). Yet Tasmania duly emerged from the downturn in the early 2000s, leading Natasha Cica (2005) to characterize the local economy as "Turbo Tassie." It would seem that the bumpy road of development, much like Tasmania's landscape, is characterized by steep and unexpected change.

FORESTRY COLLAPSE

Concern surrounding Tasmania's stagnant economy was intensified by the liquidation of forestry company Gunns Limited on September 26, 2012 (Beresford 2015, 365), resulting in the loss of more than 300 Tasmanian jobs (Bibby 2013, 66). This episode is worth unpacking in detail because it illustrated the fragility of Tasmanian democracy, and how the public are variously invited or refused entry into discussions regarding the future, and how the question of leadership is valorized by journalists and editors.

Depending who was asked, Gunns Limited was alternately a rare, home-grown success story, a family business that made good or, according to its detractors, a rogue corporation that ultimately fell victim to its own hubris. Since the 1980s, the company had been the face of Tasmania's timber and woodchip industry, accounting for nearly 85 percent of all forestry operations (Krien 2012, 158). After buying out several competitors in 2001, the company came to boast a gigantic portfolio of businesses and properties including five sawmills, three timber veneer factories, four woodchip export ports, six hardware stores, a building construction arm, a nursery capable of handling 13 million tree seedlings a year, and huge swathes of private land; 100,000 hectares of which were hardwood plantation (Beresford 2015, 24). As a proportion of the Tasmanian workforce, forestry workers accounted for 1 percent of total employment; however, these workers tended to be concentrated in rural areas with few alternative industries, making the job losses all the more conspicuous (West 2013, 53). Outside of forestry towns, the demise of Gunns was more symbolic than material, "emblematic" (West 2013, 51) of the economic conditions facing primary industry industries nationally: the high Australian dollar, tightened environmental restrictions and fierce international competition.

For conservationists who had fought for the wood chipping and clear-felling industry for decades, the event was cause for celebration. Senator Bob Brown, the former leader of the Australian Greens party, declared that "a great millstone had been lifted off Tasmania's neck" (in Beresford 2015, 368). The "millstone" presumably related to both the ecological burden of forestry practices in Tasmania but also the company's political gravity. In making its case for a Pulp Mill, Gunns had been ruthless in its condemnation of critics and activists. In 2004, Brown and nineteen other critics of the company were targeted with a defamation suit worth $6.3 million, days before the company announced a feasibility study into the controversial Tamar Valley Pulp Mill (Beresford 2015, 207). While these legal challenges—often termed "SLAPP suits" (Strategic Lawsuit Against Public Participation)—were ultimately overturned, the company's "relentless pursuit and near limitless resources did intimidate its defendants and other potential critics in the wider community" (Krien 2012, 172).

While supporters of Gunns and its pulp mill condemned activists for "dancing on the grave" of the company (*ABC Tasmania* 2012), it was apparent that, even outside of activist circles, mainstream opinion had turned against Gunns' heavy-handed approach to consultation and development under the leadership of CEO John Gay. According to novelist, Richard Flanagan, "Opposition to Gunns long ago outgrew any conservation group and Gunns was in the end undone by the many, many people who refused to give in to its threats, lies and intimidation" (2012). In addition to the infamous SLAPP suits, Gay had controversially leveraged great influence with Tasmanian politicians, most notably the then-premier, Paul Lennon, but also the former Liberal premier,

Robin Gray, who became a Gunns board member (Denholm 2013). Forestry had long been a cooperative effort between government and business with the state-owned Forestry Tasmania responsible, by law, for supplying the industry with no less than 300,000 cubic meters of resource each year, which, according to West (2012, 2), was an inherently unsustainable volume. In 2007, the close association between forestry and government became controversial when, in attempting to push the company's controversial pulp mill through environmental assessment, Gay was able to secure an exception from the standard process with the introduction of the "Pulp Mill Assessment Bill," to fast-track approval of the project (Beresford 2015, 275–276). According to the Tasmanian correspondent for *The Australian* newspaper, Matthew Denholm (2013), this special treatment "further undermined mainstream public support for the project" with the charge of corruption and cronyism impacting the company's efforts to secure financial investment and public support for the project. Forestry contractors, investors, and owners of plantation forests also felt betrayed by the mismanagement of the company under the leadership of CEO John Gay (Beresford 2015, 367), leading Flanagan (2012) to summarize the case against Gunns as "a parable of corporate hubris":

> You can, as they did, corrupt the polity, cow the media, poison public life and seek to persecute those who disagree with you. You can rape the land, exterminate protected species, exploit your workers and you can even poison your neighbours. But the naked pursuit of greed at all costs will in the end destroy your public legitimacy and thus ensure your doom. Gunns was a rogue corporation and its death was a chronicle long ago foretold. The sadness is in the legacy they leave to Tasmania—the immense damage to its people, its wildlands, and its economy. (Flanagan 2012)

One benefit of Gunns' capitulation, however, was that it provided an opportunity for Tasmania to have a more thorough discussion about the state's economic future outside the myopic focus on the company's proposed pulp mill. For Eslake, this future involved a shift away from extractive industries toward "the production of highly differentiated goods and services, embodying higher intellectual content which can be sold at higher prices" (in Beresford 2015, 368). Formerly Tasmania's most successful business and the southern hemisphere's largest woodchip exporter, the company's spectacular demise intensified pessimism regarding the state's economy and left a hole in Tasmania's understanding of its purpose and destiny. It was, according to Will Bibby, "as much a psychological shock to Tasmanians as it was economic" (2013, 66). However, besides the recriminations that accompanied Gunns' demise and the downturn in forestry generally, the question began to be asked, what now?

"NEW TASMANIA"

The local neologism, "New Tasmania," refers to a deliberate reformation of Tasmania's image, economy, and social policy: away from the state's historic association with social conservatism and heavy industry, and toward the burgeoning tourism, hospitality, gastronomy, real estate, and arts industries (Stratford 2006, 2007; Altman 2003, 2003b). The discourse was spearheaded by the Australian Labor Party (ALP) premier Jim Bacon and followed a series of speeches and articles in 2003 (Altman 2003). In his first term as premier, Bacon had succeeded in securing a number of key infrastructure projects that, in his view, would encourage a diversification of economic development. These included the installation of an undersea gas pipeline and a "Basslink cable" to connect Tasmania to the national energy grid, and two new ferries to transport goods and tourists. The delivery of these projects along with the increased uptake of internet technologies promised to transform Tasmania's isolation from a disability to a resource (Stratford 2007): diminishing the costs of distance (communication, energy, and export access) while marketing the benefits (clean air, wilderness, fresh produce, ocean views, and artistic excellence). In *The Australian's* special report, "The New Tasmania," the premier celebrated these changes and the possibility that "Tasmania really is, at long last, starting to benefit from where we are geographically, where for so long that was seen as a disadvantage" (in Altman 2003).

In addition, Bacon's tenure was also marked by advances in social policy, most prominently, the introduction of legislation to recognize and give legal entitlement to lesbian and gay couples (Baird 2006, 965). Having been one of the last Australian states to remove sodomy laws and decriminalize homosexuality, this world-leading policy complimented the infrastructure developments of "New Tasmania" with social progress (Baird 2006, 965; Croome 2013, 31). According to Eslake, this reform would encourage artists and creatives to move to Tasmania and participate in new cultural industries (in Altman 2003). While it would be cynical to explain this legislation as purely instrumental and motivated by the pursuit of "creative migration," progressive social policy does fit within current trends in urban planning and economics that place a high value on tolerance and liveability (Verdich 2010). This school of thought is associated with Richard Florida's concept of "the creative class" (2006) and Charles Landry's "creative city" (Landry 2008). Here, creativity is not intended in its usual artistic sense but refers broadly to energetic communities of innovators and technology professionals who, in their view, constitute the engine room of "new economies." According to Florida, the contemporary world is "shifting from an economy based on physical inputs—land, capital, and labour—to an economy based on intellectual inputs, or human creativity" (2006, 22).

This creates a global demand for innovative people and a global competition to attract these desirable migrants (Hage 2003). As Florida suggested, a prerequisite for attracting talented and creative people is "tolerance": "The regions that are most open to different lifestyles and to people who think differently or who express their creativity differently have the kind of ecosystem that attracts talented and entrepreneurial people across the board" (2006). Accordingly, the imperative of local governments is to market their region (its liveability, lifestyle, and tolerance) to this international group of changemakers. For "New Tasmania," as Stratford (2006) suggested, this involved an increasing emphasis on Tasmania's cosmopolitan credentials as opposed to its isolation that had formerly been used to attract government subsidies. Thus, in a globalized world, Tasmania's isolation became a valuable commodity in the eyes of tourists, professionals, and property developers; "an open and accessible island imaginary of global international desire" (Stratford 2006, 577).

The retention of educated, young people has long posed a problem for Tasmania with governments developing strategies to attract and retain skilled young people (Easthope and Gabriel 2008, 175). However, critics of the "New Tasmania" discourse argue that, rather than attempting to retain talented students on the island, the newly cosmopolitan and professional Tasmania aimed to attract professionals from abroad seeking a tree-change from mainland cities. This preference for outsiders' ideas over those of locals, according to some, was alienating and discouraging. Flanagan complained of a cultural cringe associated with new Tasmanian ideas and innovations:

> There is also a new economy forming in Tasmania. It is an economy in which distance is no longer a tyranny. [However] one of the great problems for Tasmania is the belief of those in power that if something is Tasmanian it is mediocre. You come across this belief again and again: if Tasmanians have done it, it's no good. But if someone comes in from outside with a proposal or a business there's an implicit faith that it must be good. (in Croome 1997, 138)

Rejection of Tasmanian originality was, according to other writers (Cica 2005), making Tasmania the same as everywhere else and unwittingly discouraging people from visiting and living there. As Cica argued, "I don't like a lot of the look, smell and taste of New Tasmania because it's making Tasmania look, smell and taste more like everywhere else" (2005, 14). This globalizing effect, according to Stratford, is "simultaneously homogenizing and destabilizing" (2007, 577). There is a self-defeating contradiction in the terms of "New Tasmania" that both celebrated the island's uniqueness while instrumentalizing this uniqueness to pursue development in ways that homogenize and devalue Tasmanian originality.

There is, likewise, a tendency to dismiss the concept of "New Tasmania" as masking processes of gentrification and disguising the state's ongoing reliance on destructive forestry practices (Cica 2005; Flanagan 2012). As the previous chapter alluded, in the early 2000s, Premier Bacon's vision of Tasmania had forestry and mining industries as assumed and non-negotiable parts of the economy. Outside pro-forestry circles, however, the discourse of "New Tasmania" often corresponded with a disparaging attitude toward the state's traditional industries in favor of the burgeoning tourism, niche agriculture, and knowledge-based industries. Human rights lawyer, Greg Barns, identified as a myth the notion "that we are moving or "transitioning" from an "old" industrial economy into a "new" clean, green and clever economic nirvana" (Barns 2013). The term "New Tasmania" conceals a view that "Tasmania should be hip and cool and it is embarrassing to have a zinc processing plant in Hobart" (Barns 2013). Indeed, the juxtaposition between creative and heavy industries in "New Tasmania" is geographical as well as cultural. The Nyrstar Zinc Works, alluded to by Barns, is located on the Derwent River, only a few kilometers upstream from MONA. Their proximity, and the absence of mutual embarrassment, would appear to support Barns's assertion that these industries can work in concert. In fact, rather than representing a new exclusive high culture, MONA purports to be an amalgam of high culture, anti-elitist hedonism, and working-class sensibilities. In 2011, the professional gambler, millionaire, and art collector, David Walsh opened his outlandish art museum in the outer suburb of Berriedale, not far from the street where he grew up. Hewn into the river's sandstone cliff embankments and perhaps borrowing a brutalist aesthetic from its industrial neighbours, MONA has planted itself at the forefront of Tasmania's new tourism and arts economy. "The MONA effect," like the Bilbao Effect, brought international renown to Hobart when, in 2015, the institution was listed as one of the Seven Wonders of the World by *Lonely Planet* (Franklin 2014). While it is located in one of the state's most disadvantaged suburbs and adjacent to heavy industrial plants, the extent to which MONA does incorporate these cultural influences and invite patronage and support from working-class Tasmanians has been questioned (Booth et al. 2017). As Booth and colleagues suggested, the discourse of transformation surrounding MONA elides existing cultural and artistic communities in Hobart's northern suburbs that, in comparison, are dismissed as a "cultural desert" (2017, 27). At the heart of this cultural transformation, then, is a negotiation between "the creative class," which Florida and Landry considered as a migratory class of workers in the new economy, and more local sensibilities regarding the cultural transformation of Hobart. This tension highlights the importance of an examination of how cultural and economic propositions are framed in local media and who the sources are that "frame the shape of the new" (Beers 2006, 121).

REFUGEES OF THE INTERIOR

For Tasmanians who celebrated the end of the forestry wars and the dismantling of the bullish forestry company Gunns Limited, the subsequent period of optimism and cultural revival in "New Tasmania" represented a welcome development and a source of hope. However, hope for one group can be predicated on its extraction from others (Hage 2016). In particular, according to Hage, the cultural competition for transnational investment and workers, typical of "New Tasmania," offers hope primarily to "mobile managers and workers associated with these global firms, so that they will desire to come and live among us," while simultaneously denying hope and homely belonging to locals, the poor, and marginalized who, "like pimples," are constructed as an "aesthetic nuisance" (Hage 2003, 19–20). Thus, "New Tasmania" "involves an architectural and touristic aesthetics" (Hage 2003, 19–20) designed to instill confidence in new residents and investors.

In particular, many rural areas of Tasmania continued to struggle economically, uncomforted by new cultural institutions in the capital cities, and suspicious of popular conservation movements and their promises of tourism jobs (McGaurr and Lester 2017). Thus, "New Tasmania" produced "refugees of the interior" whose solutions and propositions are devalued as a result of Tasmania's newfound cosmopolitanism (Hage 2003, 21). Adopting this metaphor, Boyce described a uniquely Tasmanian and rural feeling of living in exile at home (1996). While activities such as hunting, fishing, and felling have long been "integral to a whole way of life here," these foundational experiences of subsisting with the Tasmanian landscape tend to be denigrated or ignored by environmentalists in their advocacy for wilderness conservation, free from human interaction (1996, 56). This, for Boyce (1996), helps to explain why ferocious conflicts over conservation proposals "are understood as 'locking it up' [and therefore] produce deep fear and a corresponding anger today" (1996, 56). While Boyce suggested that such fears have been effectively manipulated by corporations who are, themselves, intent on locking up and privatizing public land for profit, he encouraged conservationists to consider "the fullness of the human story" regarding Tasmania's environmental history and to reject the convenient myth "that 'Love of this island came late' " (1996, 57).

Rural voices have, historically, not occupied a central place in Australian or Tasmanian political discourse. In recent decades, however, this has changed. In an essay titled, "Fair Share," Judith Brett charted the relationship between country and city interests within Australia, noting the sudden reappearance of country voices within mainstream politics. "Since at least the 1970s in Australia, the city has had the upper hand and the country has been pushed aside" (Brett 2011, 3). However, she continued, recent elections have delivered rural representatives' strategic power, a platform for reorientating public debate toward the economic injustices facing rural communities (2011, 3). In Tasmania, this trend was reflected in the election of Jacqui Lambie from Tasmania's north-western region to the Australian Senate. Lambie, formerly of the Palmer United Party, has since started her own party, the Jacqui Lambie Network, that commentators have likened to right wing, populist political movements globally (Kefford and McDonnell 2015). What was perhaps most surprising was the especially furious tenor of these new rural voices. Compared to the previous generation of country representatives, who gave voice to a calm and considered conservatism, the new anti-politician politicians, such as Jacqui Lambie, Pauline Hanson, and Bob Katter, give voice to a sentiment of furious dispossession, often framed in explicitly racial terms. This wave of populist outsider politicians arguably owed its visibility to growing exclusion from the culturally dominant modes of hoping. According to Katherine Murphy, the new wave of support for racist populism was "because governments have failed to give them hope for the future, and we need to acknowledge that perhaps part of the reason politicians have been insufficiently attentive to the losers is because journalists—under pressure, battling shrinking newsrooms, unable to get out into the field—haven't done enough to tell their stories" (Murphy 2016, 47). Thus, according to Murphy, journalists and politicians are jointly responsible for distributing hope in the form of stories and, consequently, policies. However, arguably, the partnership between journalists and political elites also needs to be reconsidered. Dominant cultural frames for evaluating leadership may structurally privilege elite sources and exclude different forms of community leadership. Populist political movements are consequently energized by this discursive exclusion, forming their own insurgent values of leadership and their own insurgent truths constructed in opposition to journalistic truths and evaluations of leadership.

NEW TASMANIA UNDER NEW MANAGEMENT

The year 2014 was chosen for the case study sample period as an especially eventful year in the recovery of Tasmania following the economic slump of 2012. Two newly elected conservative governments, at state and federal level, handed down their inaugural budgets. The president of China, Xi Jinping, visited Tasmania for the first time, purportedly at the behest of Launceston primary school students (Vowles 2014), sparking a week of trade bargaining and investment pitching between the world's largest economy and Australia's smallest province. There were numerous articles on the potential of Tasmanian industries, including dairy, agriculture, aquaculture, and tourism. Debate swirled around controversial developments and infrastructure upgrades. The tentative truce between loggers and environmentalists was dissolved with the incoming Liberal government rescinding the Tasmanian Forests Agreement (TFA). Reporting of these events, which were frequently proposed as solutions, success stories, and opportunities for Tasmania, were delivered primarily by a restricted sphere of government and business sources.

SOLUTIONS

The six-month sample, taken from April–May, August–September, and November–December 2014, produced 1,172 solution-centered stories and 342 prospective solutions. Most propositions in these articles received fleeting attention in news reports, appearing in only one or two stories. However, the most-discussed proposition in the sample, Tasmania's blossoming trade relationship with China, was reported in thirty-five articles. The relative prevalence of propositions varied according to outlet location with Hobart-specific propositions such as the Royal Hobart Hospital (RHH) rebuild and the Mount Wellington Cable Car proposal appearing less often in Launceston's daily newspaper, the *Examiner*, compared to the Tasmania-wide ABC and Hobart's the *Mercury*. However, many propositions were common across the whole state. Foremost among these was the historic first visit of a Chinese head of state to Tasmania.

Trade with China

The historic first visit of the President of the Peoples' Republic of China to Tasmania took place one afternoon, on November 18, 2014. However, eager anticipation of the event and subsequent coverage of the trade negotiations generated seventy-one articles state-wide, including numerous editorials and op-eds, making this the most reported solution in the sample. The *Mercury* celebrated the arrival with an additional wrap-around front and back page, colored red and spangled with yellow stars, welcoming the powerful leader and his wife.

China had long been an object of political and business opportunity in Tasmania. As an importer of Tasmanian forest products, politicians from both sides of politics have traveled to China to secure markets and liaise with investors (Richards 2014a, 11). Recently, trade missions also sought to counter the lobbying of environmentalists who had successfully warned importers of the controversial nature of Tasmanian wood products (Richards 2014a, 11). However, with forestry exports shrinking after 2012, emerging industries have clamored for Chinese attention. For example, the University of Tasmania has sought to capitalize on Chinese demand for higher education (Hope 2014); Chinese importers, catering for a swelling middle class, had discovered Tasmanian alcohol, milk powder, minerals, and beef, while Chinese tourism in Tasmania has also increased markedly. In this context, the visit by the president represented a range of new opportunities that were symbolic of "New Tasmania."

Besides exports, efforts were also made to invite the purchase of Tasmanian assets by Chinese investors. An investment forum, TasInvest, was orchestrated to coincide with the visit and encourage an entourage of Chinese investors to tour the state's attractions. A lavish dinner was organized for the premier and participants, attended by Australian business and political leaders (Smith 2014b). Simultaneously, the federal government signed a preferential free trade agreement with China—lowering tariffs for many products, some of which (notably apples) proved beneficial for Tasmania (Clark 2014b).

As a solution, the idea of fostering stronger economic ties with China was relatively uncontroversial in Tasmanian news outlets, the groundwork for the visit having been laid by both sides of politics over many years (*The Mercury* 2014r). However, some sources did seek to qualify the bipartisan enthusiasm. Greens party MP, Nick McKim, highlighted the poor human rights record of China, especially in Tibet, and encouraged leaders to use trade negotiations to leverage some influence over the premier on that issue (McKim 2014). Human rights lawyer Greg Barns (2014b) took issue with free trade agreements generally on the eve of the signing of the agreement with the Chinese government while the historian, Randall Doyle, warned that Tasmania could become another Chinese "agri-natural resource colony" (2014). However, editorials sought to sooth popular anxieties around Chinese investment, and reassure readers that Tasmania was not "selling the farm" (*The Mercury* 2014t).

The Royal Hobart Hospital

The second-most discussed solution concerned RHH. The future of the hospital has been a perennial issue in state-wide debates about healthcare. Successive Tasmanian governments had attempted to secure a timely renovation of the ostensibly inadequate facility. In 2011, Hobart's independent Federal Member of Parliament, Andrew Wilkie, negotiated a $340 million investment from the Labor federal government for the much-needed renovations. However, the awkwardness of renovating the asbestos-laden structure while housing delicate long-term patients proved costly and time consuming. While the proposed renovation faced financial and deadline blowouts, in 2014, the story took a sudden turn when developer Dean Coleman proposed an entirely new "greenfields" hospital design for the Hobart waterfront (Smiley 2014). News outlets were instrumental in circulating images of the modern design and mobilizing political and expert support for the project. In total, there were fifty-three articles addressing these proposals from across the dataset. Yet, ultimately, the proposal was deemed unaffordable by Health Minister Michael Ferguson: the state needed to protect its credit rating and would not be borrowing the necessary sum to complete the ambitious waterfront design. This was a controversial decision with many stakeholders taking contrary positions on the issue in local media.

The Mount Wellington Cable Car

Mount Wellington is a 1,271 meter, cliff-faced mountain that dominates the Hobart skyline from every angle of the city. While it is an important tourist attraction, some operators and developers have argued that leaving the mountain in its mostly natural state squanders its potential as a tourism asset (Smith 2014a, 4–5). With seasonal snowfall preventing access to the summit, the proposed improvements have centered on a cable car that would ferry passengers above the forest canopy and cliff face to the summit. While the proponent, Adrian Bold, made the case that there would be minimal visual interference, the issue aroused great passion among Hobart locals.

The debate over this proposal was reflected in thirty-nine articles across the *Mercury* and the ABC. In terms of jobs and dollars, the project was of limited consequence compared to the propositions mentioned earlier. Its prominence in the sample was likely due to the conflict between conservationists and developers, making this a symbolic controversy in the context of Tasmanian environmental politics. Since 1994, when conservationists opposed building a tourism road through the Tarkine wilderness in the remote North-West of the state (Mcgaurr et al. 2015, 274), tourism developments have increasingly drawn the attention of conservationists rather than traditional conflicts over forestry and mining development. In 2014, Premier Will Hodgman also became the first leader to take the Tourism and Hospitality policy portfolio, signaling the importance of this economic sector.

Budget Cuts

The sense of change in Tasmania in 2014 was also a product of a new, conservative political landscape at state and federal levels. On 15 March 2014, Tasmania elected its first Liberal state government of the new millennium, overthrowing sixteen years of ALP rule. Six months earlier, the Liberal Party had won the 2013 Australia Federal Election, installing Tony Abbott as prime minister after six years of Labor Party government. These new conservative governments brought with them a raft of propositions, both Tasmania-specific and Australia-wide, which were highly prominent in local news reporting in the sample.

Many of these propositions were bundled into two inaugural state and federal budgets. Federal budgets are of particular interest to Tasmanians. With its small workforce and inherent trade disadvantages owing to its geographical isolation, Tasmania is reliant on support from the Commonwealth to provide basic services and infrastructure (Stratford 2006). With poor health, education and employment statistics, Tasmania usually makes a strong case for support from the Federal Budget. On May 13, 2014, the Liberal federal government handed down its first national budget that featured dramatic cuts to health, education, and welfare programs. Considering the state's precarious economic position, these were highly controversial. The most contentious policy in these new budget measures became known as the "Earn or Learn" precondition for unemployment benefits (Clark 2014a). The government proposed that school leavers face a six-month waiting period before applying for unemployment benefits to encourage them to enroll in higher education rather than apply for welfare support, thus providing a solution for youth employment and overreliance on welfare. However, with Tasmania's high rate of youth unemployment and a shortage of available local jobs, critics warned that the policy could leave many young people without sufficient support or the option of study or work. Controversially, Prime Minister Abbott suggested that if jobs were not available locally, then unemployed Tasmanians should leave the state to find work elsewhere (Clark 2014a). In response, the *Mercury* initiated the campaign "Our Kids, Our Future," which sought to give visibility to the stark choices facing young unemployed Tasmanians (Kempton 2014b).

In the wake of this controversial Federal Budget, the Liberal state government aimed to reassure Tasmanians that its own August 2014 State Budget would be a "nip and tuck budget" (Wells 2014). However, the state treasurer, Peter Gutwein, indicated that spending patterns would ultimately have to change in the face of a "$1.1 billion budget black hole," which was blamed on the excesses of the previous Labor government (Richards 2014b). Gutwein provided funding for $400 million of pre-election promises and sought to balance the spend with a public service "pay freeze," the shedding of 700 public service positions and an increase in the size of dividends taken from state- owned businesses (Bolger 2014).

Forestry

Lastly, a great number of propositions in the sample were concerned with the ongoing forestry dispute. Liberal state and federal politicians promised to "rebuild forestry" and undo the conservation gains of the previous minority Labor-Greens government. At federal level, Prime Minister Abbott sought to recapture the newly minted World Heritage Area extension in the West of Tasmania for logging (Clark 2014). A delegation was sent to lobby the World Heritage Committee to reconsider its decision proved to be an ultimately fruitless trip with committee maintaining its position (Clark 2014).

The state government, immediately after gaining office, claimed a mandate to dismantle the TFA. This deal, brokered between environmentalists and forestry representatives under the previous government, had exchanged 504,000 hectares of new forest reserves for the support of environmental groups in the industry's bid for Forest Stewardship Certification, and an industry compensation package. The compensation was retained by the logging industry in order to rebuild, despite the protected forests being reopened (albeit with a six-year logging moratorium) (Ikin and Nightingale 2014).

The year also featured a scandal around the dismantling of Tasmania's main woodchip port and mill in Triabunna, a renowned logging town on Tasmania's east coast. The mill was sold to environmentalist entrepreneurs, Graeme Wood and Jan Cameron, who intended to create a large tourism and arts hub in the struggling region. However, when it emerged, the new owners had allowed the machinery to be destroyed, preventing any forced-acquisition of the property as part of the "forestry rebuild," an inquiry was called by the new Liberal government (Richards 2014a).

THE TASMANIAN GOVERNMENTAL FIELD

Considering these relatively diverse solutions, one might imagine that the stories involved a similarly diverse range of sources: trade with China might require economists, political scientists, farmers, and diplomats; RHH—doctors, nurses, patients, and architects; forestry policy—loggers, environmentalists, biologists, and economists; budget policy—economists, unions, teachers, public servants, and welfare charities; Mount Wellington cable car—tourism operators, engineers, conservationists, and locals. Indeed, all of these professions made some appearance in the sample; yet, business and political professions were by far the most quoted. Across the news outlet, politicians were the most quoted profession in solution-focused articles, with 40 percent of all quotes. Business spokespeople and industry representatives, together, comprised 31 percent of quotes. Politicians and business interests together represented 71 percent of all sources. In comparison, civil society sources—that included unions, non-government organization (NGOs), activists, nursing and teacher associations, welfare advocates, community groups, and interest groups—made up 10 percent of sources. Experts such as

Chapter 3

Table 3.1   Distribution of Professions

Fields	The Mercury	The ABC	The Examiner	Total	Percentage of total
Business	210	155	73	438	19%
Civil Society	113	86	37	236	10%
Culture	48	31	25	104	5%
Expert	97	35	16	148	7%
Public	40	14	10	64	3%
Industry Representative	130	78	53	261	11%
Health & Education	12	19	4	35	2%
Public Servant	40	18	24	82	4%
Politician	387	323	193	903	40%
Business and Industry	340	233	126	699	31%
Business, Industry and Politicians	727	556	319	1602	71%
TOTAL	1077	759	435	2271	

scientists, researchers, analysts, and academics made up to 7 percent of all sources (table 3.1).

The relative dominance of political and business sources was even more pronounced when considering the twenty most-quoted sources. These individuals represented the most familiar voices; the "state nobility" (Bourdieu 1996b) of the Tasmanian governmental field, whose leadership credentials were the most recognized and recognizable. Politicians represented the majority of these top sources, with slightly fewer industry representatives and entrepreneurs and only one public servant and one cultural source. The *Mercury* appeared to offer a more even balance of business and political sources. However, even in the *Mercury*, there were no nonpolitical or non-business professions in the top 20 most-cited news sources. Across the three news outlets, the only nonpolitical and nonbusiness sources were found in the *Examiner*. While the *Examiner* gave the impression of having a diversity in its top twenty sources, this is likely due to the smaller sample size taken from the newspaper, which had consequently fewer sources overall. The list of the twenty most quoted sources provides a good indication of the main leaders in the governmental field and indicates some of the attributes that are valued in leaders.

Besides the professional makeup of these leaders, the top twenty sources were also conspicuous in terms of the prevailing gender, ethnicity, and age of these leaders. Overwhelmingly, the top sources were men and predominantly of European heritage. By gender, only six women appeared in this list compared to thirty men. The gender imbalance was even more pronounced when comparing the number of articles these top male and female sources were quoted in. The six women sources were quoted in a total of 70 articles while the top thirty male sources were quoted in 636 articles, a ratio of nearly 1:10. Using information from Wikipedia, LinkedIn, and other publicly available webpages, it was estimated that the average age of the people on this list was fifty-one with only three of the thirty-six individuals on the list being in their thirties. In addition, using the same online sources, there did not appear to be any people in this source list from non-European backgrounds.

CONCLUSION

Politicians and businesspeople were the most prominent voices in the construction of the prospective future, but also, implicitly, in the legitimation of leadership capital within the governmental field. Their prominence was at the expense of a range of other professions, such as public servants, experts, scientists, doctors, teachers, civil society, welfare organizations, the public, and artists, people who, in another time, might well have been called on to imagine the future of their locality and, implicitly, defend their right to do so. While politicians are elected to make future-altering decisions, and businesses have a responsibility to their shareholders and employees to make the most of opportunities, there is also a risk of overreliance on these two professions for solutions and propositions, and a corresponding risk that the wider community's expertise and imaginative resources could be underutilized. From this perspective, the great benefit of solutions journalism as it is practiced in the United States and Canada is that it provides a discursive space that is largely quarantined from the usual political and business voices, making room and providing a platform for a diversity of expertise and, consequently, a diversity of solutions to common problems. As such, this research denaturalizes the dominance of political and business sources, except to argue that it is only the natural outcome of historical efforts of cultural and economic legitimation by politicians and businesspeople over time.

Chapter 4

"An Entrepreneurial Spirit"

In many respects, New Tasmania was a mediated cultural phenomenon. Part of the construction of a newly optimistic future for Tasmania was journalists' routine identification of who was leading this economic and social revival, and whose voices would be featured in articulating its goals, pathways, and success stories. The concept of New Tasmania was popularized through the press and most notably by a special report in the *Australian* titled 'The New Tasmania' (Altman 2003). Across eighteen stories in the *Australian*, Australia's only national daily newspaper canvassed a range of Tasmanian industries and leaders that were suddenly prospering in splendid isolation: wilderness tourism, real estate, gay rights, dairy, agriculture, and the cultural industries. In 2014, Tasmania was again emerging from a ferocious conflict over the pulp mill and an economic recession and was on the verge of a new wave of economic success. As such, newspapers and editors canvassed the state's advantages and future prospects by sourcing ideas and proposals from a range of Tasmanian leaders.

As chapter 2 argued, leadership evaluation is an important corollary of solution reporting, with news access often depending on journalistic perceptions of effective, legitimate, and consequential leadership. This chapter seeks to test this hypothesis and understand how and why leadership featured in the construction of Tasmanian optimism. In this regard, news editors are central leadership figures within news organizations who also provide regular commentary regarding leadership quality. An important insight regarding journalistic evaluations of leadership, therefore, was a pair of interviews with the editors of Tasmania's two local newspapers: Simon Tennant of the *Examiner* (based in the northern city of Launceston) and Mathew Deighton of the *Mercury* (based in Tasmania's capital city of Hobart). These semi-structured conversations sought to traverse the editors' perceptions of the new cultural climate and asked who they considered as effective and newsworthy leaders. I sought to understand how editors approached reporting of solutions, how they identified news sources and how they evaluated leadership. I then triangulated their responses with an analysis of their editorials to examine how their ideas were born out, often implicitly, through the use of metaphor.

Editors have a decisive role in news organizations and in the journalistic field. They are responsible for maintaining standards of accuracy and ethics (the autonomous laws of journalism) while also negotiating the demands of readers, advertisers, important sources, and shareholders (the heteronomous laws of journalism) (Benson 2006; Champagne 2005, 60). While some have argued that editorial power has been eroded with current digital media transformations (Ihlebk and Krumsvik 2015), this was not apparent from direct observation conducted at the *Mercury*'s and the *Examiner*'s newsrooms. Matt Deighton and Simon Tennant, both relatively new in their positions, appeared to occupy central roles in facilitating these news meetings, and guiding the priorities of their organizations. At the *Mercury*, where news meetings involved a considerably larger number of reporters and staff than at the *Examiner*, participants congregated in a circle at the center of which sat Matt Deighton and head of news, Sarah Fitzpatrick-Gray. The meeting began in democratic fashion with each reporter taking around thirty seconds to outline their intended focus and anticipated stories for the day and were generally offered encouragement or advice on a possible point of interest, but were never contradicted or censured. While there was certainly ample time for other reporters to contribute to these routine discussions, editorial authority was exercised in the final selection of the front page and the positioning of stories in the newspaper. By comparison, the *Examiner*'s editorial meeting was smaller and less structured than at the *Mercury*, despite maintaining a similarly democratic dynamic between editor and reporters.

TASMANIA'S JOURNALISTIC FIELD

While there was a perception of editorial authority in news meetings, interviews with editors revealed that their influence was tempered by less visible constraints. As field theorist Patrick Champagne argued, journalists are "structurally condemned to produce—variably, depending on the period and outlet—under political and/or economic constraints" (2005, 50). One economic constraint that editors mentioned frequently in interviews for this study was the need to tailor reporting to the community that the newspaper sought to represent, including the range of political and policy perspectives therein. According to Deighton, the diversity of the Hobart audience is an important structural difference compared to mainland metropolitan newspapers, where their audiences are segmented. When asked to compare his recent experience working at Australian metropolitan newspapers in Sydney and Melbourne, Deighton recalled a very different audience and set of reporting considerations:

> Sydney is a blood sport. So you've got *The Sydney Morning Herald* which looks after one part of the population, and *The Daily Telegraph* which looks after another. Both know their readers really well and, sort of, never the two shall meet. So it is very much, up there, two different media speaking to different segments of people. Whereas here [in Tasmania], you've got a Labor state, which had 16 years of Labor rule, now with a Liberal Government, and also here with Denison, one of the biggest Green electorates in the country. So, as a local paper, you can't afford to be particularly partisan . . . . It's impossible to be all things to everyone but you've got to try. Because there are so many sort of demographics to traverse. (Deighton 2015)

For Deighton, writing for a one-paper city such as Hobart involved a heightened sensitivity to its diverse political audience. While Simon Tennant, editor of the *Examiner*, did not highlight political considerations to the same extent he did state that his newspaper's allegiance was firstly to the community as a whole. In his estimation, other rival news organizations, despite supposed ideological differences, were really just doing "the same job" of representing their plural communities (Tennant 2015). The *Examiner*, he stated, was highly driven by audience analytics in deciding the type and quantity of coverage a particular story would receive:

> From my perspective, it's important to understand your audience, and things like Google analytics have given us an insight into what people want to read. I know from our perspective, we will try to tailor how much a story will run depending on what we know, digitally, people are reading about. (Tennant 2015)

For both editors, balance was central in their production context. In particular, Deighton celebrated the breadth of views in the *Mercury*'s opinion pages. However, he stated that, when it came to the newspaper as a whole, the default position was to be more circumspect. While the newspaper can outsource a wide range of opinions through sources and opinion columns, the daily editorial column would presumably represent an area of heightened sensitivity by constituting, as it does, a statement from the news outlet as a whole. In these routine but delicate opinion pieces, the question of leadership became an especially convenient focus for editors.

"AN ENTREPRENEURIAL SPIRIT"

In the context of the politically diverse readership in single-paper towns such as Launceston and Hobart, opining on leadership quality rather than on ideology or policy detail was a sensible strategy for editors. While proposition-centered stories have been divisive flashpoints in Tasmania's recent history, there is relative consensus about desirable leadership attributes. Virtues such as honesty, decisiveness, and thoroughness, for instance, are widely accepted as virtues in any leader, whereas particular development proposals and policy initiatives have, especially in Tasmania, sparked fierce partisan conflict.

For Deighton, as he stated several times in the course of the interview, an "entrepreneurial spirit" was a leadership virtue that, in his view, Tasmania sorely needed. One such leader, according to Deighton, was the founder of the controversial Museum of Old and News Art (MONA), David Walsh. Despite being credited with turning around Tasmania's tourism fortunes, the provocative contents of Walsh's gallery—with its subversive themes of sex and death—were initially met with alarm by conservative and religious sections of the community. However, as Deighton stated, these controversies are effectively nulled by the undeniable success of the project and the benefits it has brought to Tasmania. "Whether you like what he does or you don't is irrelevant. The fact is that he has achieved it," said Deighton (2015). By focusing on the sheer success of the project under the leadership of Walsh, the controversial elements of MONA were eclipsed. This demonstrates how a leadership focus can defuse divisive propositions, which explain the prevalence of leadership evaluation as a theme in editorials.

This outcome-focused evaluation of leadership was regularly celebrated in both the *Mercury*'s and the *Examiner*'s editorializing on propositions. Walsh's success was symbolic of a new entrepreneurial optimism, exemplifying a virtue that Tasmania ought to cultivate locally or, indeed, import from elsewhere. According to Deighton, "David Walsh has shown what an entrepreneurial spirit can achieve [and] for me, an entrepreneurial spirit is really really important. You see it all the time in places like Sydney, you don't see it as much down here." Because Tasmania was less endowed with this specific leadership quality, Deighton recommended importing entrepreneurial skills and energy from elsewhere:

A lot of the successful people here are people that have worked elsewhere; like your guys at Tassal, your Liz Jacks and Mike Grangers, and some of the big business people around town who have national or international exposure. Bring that back to Tassie. So, I think to harness that you need to bring people in from outside. (September 28, 2014)

Simon Tennant expressed a similar sentiment, favoring the independence and effectiveness of entrepreneurs, against businesses that are reliant on government subsidization in order to operate:

> I've always been suspicious of businesses that rely on [government] funding to do anything. Probably not start-ups. I think start-ups are wonderful. It's fairly new that we have start-ups. I was at a Chamber of Commerce awards on Saturday night and one of things I found really refreshing and exciting was the number of niche businesses and start-ups that are coming up. (Tennant 2015)

Thus, while both editors gave only general statements about the types of propositions that might help Tasmania, they were specifically in favor of the innovation and energy of entrepreneurialism to reshape the future of Tasmania. Common to both these editors' statements favoring entrepreneurialism was a celebration of the independence and proactivity of businesspeople. For Deighton, entrepreneurs like David Walsh have achieved incredible things, "without a cent of government money," while Simon Tennant appreciated the independence of businesses that get things done without government support. This is an especially salient point in Tasmania where forestry and energy businesses continue to benefit from government subsidization, and where there have been accusations of corruption between business and government leaders.

Entrepreneurial leadership, evidenced through a record of independence and achievement, can be considered a type of symbolic capital within the governmental field. Having a record of "getting-things-done," being a "doer," being proactive rather than just talking about doing something, these are recognized as evidence of an entrepreneurial spirit. The pragmatism of the entrepreneur has been specifically commended by solutions journalists in their reporting of social entrepreneurialism (Bornstein 1998). Entrepreneurs, according to Drayton, "know from the time they are little that they are in this world to change it in a fundamental way" (in Bornstein 1998, 37). The entrepreneurial spirit, the determination to act and make change, inheres in certain rare leaders but not others. Whereas the social entrepreneur draws upon social capital to get things done (deep reserves of community trust, cooperation, and networks of likeminded people), the private entrepreneur draws primarily on economic capital to materialize propositions. Indeed, the entrepreneurial spirit might be considered the symbolic legitimation of sheer economic power. In places such as Tasmania, with strong egalitarian and democratic norms, having money does not automatically equate to legitimacy in the governmental sphere. In fact, business interests can be used to delegitimize politicians or business voices, especially when their pronouncements are seen as self-serving. Accordingly, sources that are perceived to be wealthy usually make an effort to appear as responsible benefactors and conscious of the wider effects of their action. Euphemizing their economic clout as pragmatic rigor usefully transforms wealth into a culturally sanctioned virtue of leadership that is valuable within the governmental field.

According to Ron Kerr (2008, 204) key concepts relating to leadership are "homologous" (logically similar) across the fields of politics and business: crisis-driven leadership, competition with an enemy and the charisma of the leader are common themes in public and private fields (Kerr 2008, 204). The "new spirit of capitalism," according to Boltanski and Chiapello (2005), is apparent in the widespread acceptance of management and leadership theory across a range of fields. Likewise, political scientists have shown that politics, political movements, and parties have also adopted strategies and structures from the world of businesses and marketing (Lock and Harris 1996). Branding, logos, focus groups, and merchandising are now ubiquitous political practices, just as privatization and market solutions are increasingly preferred in the policy sphere. Bourdieu noted that the authority of any politician is vitally dependent on maintaining a perception of entrepreneurial effectiveness. Thus, "in politics, 'to say is to do,' that is, it is to get people to believe that you can do what you say" (Bourdieu 1991a, 190). Following Rodney Benson's term, we might also suggest that there is a "habitus affinity" between successful business and political leaders (2013, 88). Typically educated in the fields of law and economics and rising through hierarchical institutions, politicians and entrepreneurs arguably develop a recognizable leadership habitus. This leadership habitus may also be linguistic (Dodd 2020) producing habitual ways of evaluating leadership that implicitly legitimize the symbolic capital of business and political sources. The relative consensus regarding leadership virtues makes this a safe (hence common) moral question for editors to elaborate upon daily editorial columns; however, as the following chapter will explore, the specific metaphorical constructions of leadership varied.

TESTS OF LEADERSHIP

Leadership quality was a prevalent focus in editorials in the sample and presented a "sphere of legitimate controversy" (Hallin 1994, 54) for editors. While commenting on leadership quality is an inherently subjective and moral question, editorials adopted an empirical tone that suggested their evaluations of leadership were factual observations. A common formulation was to describe important decisions facing politicians regarding new ideas and solutions as constituting "tests of leadership." A proposed solution would be described as "a test for Hobart [that] the city cannot afford to fail" (*The*

Mercury 2014m). Solutions and propositions typically require leaders to offer a response: whether to support the idea, dismiss it, or refer to a proper process of formal assessment. For example, a proposed new hospital required the health minister to consider the idea and make a judgment, making this story a test that could undermine or demonstrate leadership credentials. For example, Greg Barnes warned the new Liberal government that if they failed to privatize public assets, as had been proposed, they would "have failed the first test of political courage and caved into their well-honed populist instincts" (Barns 2014a) Similarly, the proponents of an idea were also scrutinized through this frame, with editors questioning whether they possessed the right mettle to successfully prosecute the idea and see it implemented. Such editorial tests of leadership constructed the editor as an objective examiner that could adjudicate whether the criterion of success has been met, a role that sits comfortably with journalistic norms of independence and impartiality. As objective scorekeepers, journalists, and editors could state that pressure is mounting on a particular leader or that someone has "a poor record" with apparent objectivity. However, by testing leaders on established criterion of good leadership, journalists and editors arguably become involved in the policing of the governmental field as a whole.

REFLECTIONS AND BALANCE

While there was enthusiasm for the catalyzing effect of entrepreneurial leadership in Tasmania, Deighton and Tennant were also concerned with community well-being, pride, and self-belief. Indeed, there was a nurturing ethic of community self-care that seemed to inform editors' approach to reporting Tasmanian solutions and success stories. I asked Deighton whether he thought the *Mercury* occupied a unique position within Tasmanian journalism. In his answer, he alluded to a reaction against what might be considered a strict, authoritarian style of editorial leadership—in favor of a more nurturing and inclusive role:

> I'm really trying to make *The Mercury* a mirror looking onto its community. So this is a reflection of what people are talking about, this is a reflection of what people are saying, that does stand up for things when they're wrong, that does stand up for people, but is optimistic, and does think we live in a pretty special place, that does care about its people, that is a big community paper. (Deighton 2015)

As an explanation of journalistic practice, mirror metaphors have been criticized for overplaying journalists' passivity, underplaying the level of social mediation involved in constructing news, and ignoring the contested nature of the knowledge that is being "reflected" (Lester 2010, 63). However, as Lakoff and Johnson (2003) argued, metaphors are cognitive tools that appear in complex and abstract reasoning about moral questions and can provide nuanced answers. Accordingly, one might consider the place of mirrors in a wider network of signifiers and semantic roles (Lakoff 1987), especially in the many human situations where mirrors occur in daily lives. Two important yet overlooked components of mirror situations (source domains) are vanity and recognition, both of which figured heavily in Deighton's remarks. Rather than just reflecting events occurring in the community, Deighton was concerned with whether the community recognized itself in what was being reported, and whether that reflection appealed to the community's positive self-image. This, it could be said, goes beyond mere replication of physical events and objective knowledge to include a mutual recognition and convergence of values. Accordingly, Deighton notes that the reflection also includes a reflection of the community's moral expectations: "a reflection of what people are talking about, this is a reflection of what people are saying, that does stand up for things when they're wrong, that does stand up for people" (2015).

Mirrors are central objects in what might be termed everyday self-care. A similarly bathroom-situated metaphor for news can be found at the beginning of Tom Wolfe's book, *The Painted Word*: "People don't read the morning newspaper, Marshall McLuhan once said, they slip into it like a warm bath" (1975, 3). Indeed, reading a newspaper is a solitary, almost antisocial activity. However, using a mirror metaphor, reading the newspaper becomes an expression of care for oneself and provides a valuable self-care service at a community level. In a subsequent conversation with Deighton, he noted that the *Mercury* had a role in conveying the beauty of Tasmania: "I never want readers to pick up the paper and feel anxious. I want people to have a sense of optimism and a sense that, 'it was a great idea to decide to live in Tasmania' " (2015). Rather than a professional ethic of objectivity, Deighton expressed concern about readers' subjective, emotional experience upon picking up the newspaper. Likewise, the routine examination of oneself in the mirror can help to instill recognition, familiarity, and confidence. Indeed, showing the community an image of itself involves some sensitivity about how the reader might respond. Often these considerations are literal. During observation of news meetings at both the *Mercury* and the *Examiner*, a large proportion of time was routinely spent examining the day's photographs, which were projected onto a large screen in the center of the open-plan office. Editors would comment on the facial expressions, the lighting and the composition. Finally, the perceived quality of the photographs (normally portraits) would often determine where the story would appear in the paper. Showing the community in its best light is an important consideration that appeared to be articulated through the concept of a mirror as a reflexive tool in community self-care, an interpretation that helps make sense of Deighton's description of MONA having "changed the whole face of Hobart" (2015).

A contrast can be made here between prevailing attitudes to source selection at the *Examiner* and the *Mercury*. Whereas Deighton appeared to use mirror metaphors exclusively, Tennant spoke stridently about the fundamental importance of balance and his insistence that this rule be adhered to by his newsroom:

> One of the things we're really strict on with a news story is that, as I mentioned earlier, if it's a story about forestry, you get the forestry side and you get the conservation side. Absolutely must. And any time I personally get a story the next day, and I see it in print, and I see you've only got the one side of it, I'll but a big red ring around it and email it off to the reporter and say, "why isn't this story balanced"? And to me that's the most, I mean, that's the fundamentals of journalism, being fair and balanced. And that's one of my very strong ethics. (Tennant 2015)

Research and criticism of the journalistic balance norm has brought attention to this metaphor and how it shapes, and potentially skews (Boykoff and Boykoff 2004), source selection. According to Wahl-Jorgensen and colleagues, the concept of impartiality in the British Broadcasting Corporation operationalized two metaphors relating to balance: a see-saw and a wagon wheel metaphor (Wahl-Jorgensen et al. 2017). The Bridcut Review of the public broadcaster (2007) recommended a wagon wheel metaphor that would, in their view, better encourage the inclusion of multiple perspectives. The prevailing see-saw metaphor was found to reduce stories to binary perspectives, whereas a wagon wheel metaphor valorizes a plurality of viewpoints as the necessary spokes that prevent the wheel from collapsing (Wahl-Jorgensen et al. 2017, 4–5). Similarly, the mirror ideal of journalism might also be considered as informing practices of source selection, encouraging editors to represent the diversity of people and perspectives in the community. Sources should be relatable and recognizable while also, as Simon Tennant alluded, reflecting the best parts of the community by "promoting people in our own community that are doing good things" (Tennant 2015). But, importantly, the range of voices and political perspectives in newspapers should realistically reflect the spectrum of voices in the community. In this vein, Deighton was critical of restricting the debate to two opposing sides of a given debate and highlighted the importance of finding the people in the middle by "trying to get a wider spectrum of what people are saying" (Deighton 2015).

CONCLUSION

These interviews highlight an interesting contradiction. Whereas editors were outspoken about the importance of representing a diversity and balance of news sources in their coverage of solutions, the 2014 content analysis revealed that 71 percent of all quoted material was from political, business, and industry leaders who were the dominant voices in "New Tasmania." Thus, the interviews revealed something of a contrast between editors' commitment to the ideals of impartiality (a necessity in one-paper towns) and their enthusiasm for entrepreneurialism as an emerging necessity in post-recession Tasmania. The diversified economic base of "New Tasmania"—building on emerging markets in higher education, tourism, real estate, art and agriculture—idealized entrepreneurs as central protagonists. Start-up businesses and entrepreneurial success stories arguably constituted a more vibrant and diverse range of economic actors compared to previous government-owned and subsidized forestry and hydroelectricity that have historically dominated Tasmania's destiny. However, by profession and gender, these dominant sources were relatively homogenous: 40 percent politicians, 30 percent business leaders, and overwhelmingly male. To understand this contradiction—between the ideal of pluralism and reality of news access patterns—the following chapter will explore how leadership was evaluated, framed, and legitimized through conceptual metaphor.

Chapter 5

Governmental Metaphors

Solutions reporting in New Tasmania was a richly metaphorical discourse, with metaphors adding color and drama to these, at times, dry governmental pronouncements. While metaphors have tended to be discounted as mere rhetorical flourish, this chapter will consider these metaphorical devices as figurative frames (Burgers et al. 2016) and conceptual metaphors (Lakoff and Johnson 1999, 2003) that give insight into how leadership was evaluated and hope distributed in Tasmanian reporting. Indeed, metaphorical justification for leadership is arguably more important when solutions are reported without the characteristic rigor of autonomous solutions journalism. Instead of empirical support for the selection of sources, journalists often relied on metaphorical legitimation, often using metaph supplied by the sources themselves.

This research has hypothesized that metaphors in solutions journalism would correspond with the symbolic capital of dominant sources in the governmental field, which, as the previous chapter suggested, were typically celebrated as entrepreneurial. Pressures and professional considerations in the journalistic field compelled editors to evaluate associated entrepreneurial leadership qualities rather than speculate on the future benefits or risks associated with controversial propositions. While journalists avoided taking strong positions in relation to specific solutions, journalists and editors were more willing to articulate a typology of desirable and undesirable leadership virtues that were applicable across a wide range of propositions. This evaluation and description of valuable leadership—as an inherently subjective, political and moral area of discourse—was often conducted implicitly through a range of metaphorical devices.

A close reading of 1,172 articles in the sample revealed that metaphorical language was pervasive with 3,671 instances of metaphorical language at an average of 3.13 metaphorical figures of speech per news article. These metaphors were categorized into three conceptually related "source domains" navigation, nurturance (child and health care), and construction. Describing and evaluating leadership, hope, and expertise in solutions journalism, journalists regularly drew upon these source domains to form myriad idiomatic and figurative expressions across editorials, opinion pieces, and news reports.

Overwhelmingly, navigational metaphors were the most common metaphor occurring at a rate of 1.77 per article and reflecting (61 percent of all metaphorical expressions in the sample). By comparison, the second most prevalent metaphorical expressions were nurturance metaphors (parental and health care), which appeared much less commonly (19 percent of metaphors) while construction (9 percent of metaphors) was the third most common. The analysis also revealed two minor metaphors relating to gambling (7 percent) and theater (5 percent). While these latter metaphors were revealing, this chapter will primarily explore the three most common conceptual metaphors: navigation, nurturance, and construction. A full illustration of the distribution of these metaphors and the expressions that comprised them is listed in the appendices. Overall, these governmental metaphors[1] often appeared to legitimize the leadership of an exclusive field of elite news sources in proposing and commenting upon solutions.

NAVIGATION

Navigation was the most common metaphor for evaluating, describing, and prescribing leadership. Language relating to maps, journeys, visions, pathways, steps in the right direction, charting a course, a firm hand on the tiller, launch, drive, turn around, and landmarks form part of a semantic network relating to navigation. The application of this language to leadership formed a metaphor: leader as navigator. Navigators of planes, boats, or walking parties are invested with significant responsibility and their skills of navigation are determined, very simply, by whether they lead their fellow travelers safely to a given destination. The frame involves several semantic roles: A navigator, passengers, a map, movement, obstacles, stops, a final destination, and an expected time of arrival. The navigational metaphor is spatial and constructs time, the past and the future as positions in space, therefore, providing a very simple, hence common, rhetorical tool for editorializing on leadership quality while holding responsible leaders to account. For example, in the following passage from an editorial in the *Mercury*, framing devices related to location, direction, and ultimately navigation were salient: "How the Government *handles* the state's health-care problems will be *pivotal* to its fortunes, and ultimately the fortunes of our people . . . . If things *turn around*, it will be one of this Government's greatest legacies" (*The Mercury* 2014v). According to this metaphor, the leader is responsible for setting the direction and charting a course between the past (behind) and the future (ahead). In the context of this navigational frame, "handles" suggests steering rather than manually handling or touching. Metaphorically, the navigator is the leader, the passengers are Tasmanian citizens, the map is a plan, movement is progress, stops are goals, and the destination is the realization of the proponent's objective or promise.

Besides the strictly spatial aspects of the metaphor, a number of related navigational leadership virtues were typically implied. This could be seen in relation to the proposed rebuilding or renovation of RHH. Long considered an urgent priority, the hospital's redevelopment became an issue suddenly in late 2014 when a radical new proposition emerged in conflict with the planned renovation of the hospital at its original location. The development stalled while Health Minister Michael Ferguson considered his options. Large artist's renderings of Dean Coleman's new design appeared in the *Mercury* while opposition parties lent conditional support to the project. Amid this debate, editorials reflected on Mr. Ferguson's record in office and assessed his leadership credential and suitability to make the crucial decision: "Mr. Ferguson has been one of the Government's *strongest* performers since taking power. Calm and collected, he has *taken the proverbial bull by the horns* and *set the health system on a course of* meaningful restructure and reform" (*The Mercury* 2014v). This passage, that likened good leadership to a captain's firm grip on the wheel in stormy seas was invoked even more explicitly in another favorable assessment of the Liberal Party's time in office:

> THE State Government has provided a largely *steady hand* since taking office in March. [however] Of course it has not all been *smooth sailing* . . . but all up, we would argue it's been a *solid* first six months. . . . But while facing such *hurdles*, the Government must also be careful not to overlook its grassroots responsibilities in the process. (*The Mercury* 2013)

Legitimacy is often euphemized in descriptions of body, a tendency that Bourdieu termed "bodily hexis" (1996b, 35–36). The importance of physical strength as a leadership virtue was highlighted, to an absurd degree, in the celebration of the toreador-like ability to take "the proverbial *bull by the horns* and *set the health system on a course* of meaningful restructure and reform" (*The Mercury* 2014v). In particular, strength of hand appeared to be an important signifier within a navigational metaphor. The exaggerated, vice-like handshake of powerful business and political men, for instance, could be interpreted as a symbolic reference to this metaphorical virtue of navigational leadership. The supposedly innate suitability of men for leadership roles, and especially those men whose voices dominated the governmental field, was thus euphemized in bodily form. Good navigational leadership appeared to involve a level of physicality and athleticism in other domains. This could be seen, especially, in two common variants of the navigational metaphor that adapted the spatial language of sport and war.

Sport

Sport and war share similar leadership virtues of courage, determination, and physical prowess. As Bourdieu once observed, by providing an alternative criteria of social achievement to purely intellectual and scholastic endeavors sport is considered, in elite circles, "the training-ground of character" (1991b, 361). As seen in the following editorial titles—"Hodgman on the ball," "Keep eyes on the ball," and "Time to play ball"—the *Mercury* regularly used ball sports to conceptualize key moments of opportunity and excitement, while euphemizing desirable leadership virtues. This idea was captured in an end of year editorial titled "Our Chance to Shine" (*The Mercury* 2014x): "The Government needs to make sure 2015 is a time when it *grasps* the opportunities and *forges ahead* with projects that have been delayed too long." A missed opportunity, on the other hand, was often characterized as having "dropped the ball" (*The Mercury* 2014l), highlighting the importance of reaction time, teamwork, and focus in good navigational leadership. This construction implied that leaders should make sure to grasp fleeting opportunities as though they were rugby balls and forge ahead against adversity.

Military

Determination, courage, ruthlessness, decisiveness, and discipline were suggested in the heavy use of military language used to celebrate good leadership in the *Mercury*. One editorial in particular, titled "Hodgman on the Ball" (*The Mercury* 2014h), constructed his leadership style using military language within a navigational metaphor:

> The state desperately needs a leader *to chart a course* out of its economic malaise. . . . . But in recent days Mr. Hodgman has *raised his head above the trenches* to *lead the state's charge against* the Federal Government's $80 billion cuts to health and education. It is *a battle well worth fighting* . . . . It is good to see Mr. Hodgman *showing some ticker* and *fighting* for Tasmania's fair share of resources. It shows people are at the *forefront* of the Premier's concerns—right where they should be. (2014a)

In this dramatization, what was essentially a press conference by Premier Hodgman became an act of heroism and a sign of leadership. The military virtues of patriotism and the ability to inspire bipartisanship among one's compatriots were frequently highlighted as important for navigational success. An editorial titled "Fists Fly but still No Jobs" (*The Mercury* 2014k) noted that "Tasmanians desperately want to unite and look forward." Meanwhile, other editorials recommended "eschewing parochialism and nepotism [and] placing the needs of the state front and centre" (*The Mercury* 2013). When Chinese Premier Xi Jinping visited the state in 2014, an editorial credited leaders from both sides of politics, noting that the event "represents *a journey* almost 40 years in the making . . . *a victory* for cross-party politics" (*The Mercury* 2014r). Thus, while military language dramatized the physicality and courage of leaders, this was constrained by the need for regimented and cooperative fighting in the interests of the Tasmanian public. As we will see, internecine conflict was routinely condemned as one of several leadership vices.

Lost Causes and Rescue Missions

As well as providing an account of successful leadership, the navigator metaphor was also used to construct instances of navigational failure and reason about leadership vices. A good example of this frustration with a flawed navigator was during the rollout of new optical fiber internet for Tasmania. "The National Broadband Network was going to enable our island state to once and for all *break through the barrier* created by Bass Strait," opined one editorial (*The Mercury* 2014a). In describing the subsequent failures and frustrations rolling-out the technology, editorials continued to use the navigation theme: "*Somewhere along the line we dropped the ball*. The advantages of the early rollout of the NBN appear *all but lost* amid a political, logistic and engineering debacle. The state is not as far advanced *along the IT road* as many imagined it would be" (*The Mercury* 2014l). Indeed, the editorial concluded, "Far from *pioneering* the NBN or using Tasmania's early rollout to *steal a march* on the rest of the country and *forge a technology-driven future* for the state, these businesses have been *left languishing*" (2014e). In the final editorial on the issue, aptly titled "The Long and Winding Road," the *Mercury* labeled the rollout a "convoluted saga" that had become "mired in controversy" that has "lurched" from problem to problem (*The Mercury* 2014o). However, it ended optimistically by noting that the CEO of the operation would personally visit the state, which was finally "*a step in the right direction*" (2014g).

Becoming lost is an especially discrediting error within a navigational conception of leadership. This metaphor featured extensively with a health "Rescue Taskforce" initiated by the incoming state government. The Liberal state government came to power at the beginning of the sample, in March

2014. At this early stage, many of the state's problems, including health and RHH, were attributed to the mismanagement of the previous Labor government. Accordingly, the Liberal Party established a "rescue taskforce" to manage the redevelopment of RHH (*The Mercury* 2014v). By announcing a *"rescue* taskforce" the government brought to mind a responsible new navigator taking control of a stricken and lost ship with a mandate to *"set the health system on a course* of meaningful restructure and reform" (*The Mercury* 2014v). While this appellation served to underline the poor navigational skills of the previous Labor administration, editorials in the *Mercury* sought to remind the new government that it was now the navigating leader: "it is no longer in opposition and needs *to firmly grasp the reins and lead the way*" (*The Mercury* 2014f). Navigation thus provided narrative options for politicians and editors to construct and evaluate flawed navigational leadership. Within the scope of this metaphorical device, as the following section will elaborate, are the many descriptions of being lost, directionless, purposeless, wavering, cowardly, blind, or turning around. Even the policy "back-flip," frequently used to deride a policy change, is only an absurdly dramatized version of "turnaround" within this navigational metaphor. Within this navigational frame, however, failures in securing health and infrastructure outcomes were attributed to metaphorical distractions and character flaws that make good navigation difficult or impossible. In particular, dreams, drunkenness, and distractions were frequently tied to instances of poor navigational leadership.

Dreams

One consequence of the editors' use of a navigation metaphor was the frequent warning that leaders should not be seduced by dreams and delusions that might lead the state on the wrong path. The request for governments to be more realistic in their goals and promises often took the form of an anti-utopian discourse, which played upon the contrast between clear vision (indispensable for navigation), and delusions, dreams, short-sightedness, or blindness (which make navigation near-impossible). An editorial in the *Mercury* titled "Dream the Achievable" (*The Mercury* 2014j) listed a range of failed projects in Tasmania that had promised a way out of Tasmania's economic mire but had proven unrealistic. Their mirage-like quality, the editorial suggested, was a product of public relations pyrotechnics, so visually appealing that they distracted the state's leaders, taking them off-course. These included: "grand designs," "big projects announced in a blaze of publicity that often failed to materialize," or "big-ticket developments," "proudly spruiked as a saviour" (2014e). In the editorials, such projects were ultimately unsubstantial, delusional, or absurd—"bread and circuses built on hot air" (*The Mercury* 2014d), or "like a movie without a script" (*The Mercury* 2014q). Elsewhere, the *Mercury* described a controversial cable car proposal for Mount Wellington as "a mirage—a wonderful vision that disappears the closer you look" (*The Mercury* 2014c). Leaders should guard against these tempting visions, sirens of the governmental field. The soundest way to avoid waking dreams is to proceed methodically and step by step, which, as this passage suggests, can ultimately bring the state to a grand utopian future:

> The new Liberal Government would do well to instead concentrate on creating a development climate for projects that are achievable and sustainable. A number of successful, smaller developments can easily add up to create a vibrant economy, jobs, and a future for coming generations—a big dream come true. (*The Mercury* 2014j)

This prescribed style of navigation could be interpreted ideologically. Hage has argued that neoconservatives "always like to project themselves as 'realists' . . . telling us to 'stop dreaming' " (Hage and Papadopoulos 2004, 121). The preference for small steps can be considered as opposed to large government-funded interventions in the market and in favor of a market-based approach where projects emerge organically without subsidy.

Inebriation

Part of the distraction of dreams and delusions within this metaphor is a dangerous proclivity for drunkenness, which is constructed in opposition to sober rational judgment. While journalists have been known to euphemize parliamentary drunkenness by describing politicians as "tired and emotional" (Paterson 1993), conversely, this sample found that emotional states such as anger and passion were metaphorically euphemized as drunkenness. In the *Mercury*, good leadership often required "sober heads and a calm approach" (*The Mercury* 2014d) and encouraged leaders to proceed with "a due sense of prudence and sobriety" (*The Mercury* 2014s), or "a calm sense of urgency and a clear head" (*The Mercury* 2014u). Metaphorically, sobriety and intoxication are commonly used to reflect on emotional states of mind with the implication that strong emotion is inimical with sound rational judgment. As Lakoff and Johnson in this metaphorical frame, "The vices of drunkenness and gluttony make us unfit for rational deliberation and thereby diminish, or even discard temporarily, our autonomy as rational beings" (1999, 434). According to a "strict father" worldview, drunkenness is especially dangerous, because the highest moral good is considered "moral strength" and "strength of will," which are weakened under the effects of intoxication leading to moral failure (Lakoff 2016). In a navigational metaphor, heady emotions were constructed as dangerous distractions. Often these emotions expressed themselves in, what editors perceived as, hasty and thoughtless decision making: "Too often projects and ideas are met with a sudden and often harsh 'no,' which is based on emotion and historical differences" (*The Mercury* 2014n). This critique of poor leadership played upon the deafness and insensitivity of the drunk who does not respond to the needs of others. On controversial issues, editorials called for open and calm discussion, implying that sober community engagement is overlooked when leaders act with "malice, or with a fool's haste" (*The Mercury* 2014t) ("Tasmania ready to go," November 18, 2014). As we shall see, the discrediting of emotion as drunkenness was frequently deployed in regard to civil society.

Politics

A perennial distraction for political leaders is politics. Successful navigation and the "hard work" of leadership was frequently constructed in opposition to the rancor, spin, and talk of politics. This critique of political leadership took several shapes in the sample; however, a common construction in the sample contrasted political "talk" with constructive and timely "action." Political talk was characterized as negative and unconcerned with reaching concrete outcomes. For instance, one editorial in the *Mercury* noted that "The Tasmanian Government has been extremely keen to talk about the size of the Budget black hole this week," and that, generally, "there has been constant talk in recent times about flagship projects to send a message that Tasmania is open for business" ("Fix hole in city's heart," May 3, 2014). However, rather than talk, the editorial continued, action was required: "This is *the point where* a can-do government *steps in* to ensure the project *goes ahead. This* is where a can-do government *joins the table* to negotiate a successful outcome for all. This is where the Hodgman Government can *show its mettle*" (*The Mercury* 2014g). This passage suggested that not all political talk was unconstructive, and that negotiation and consensus-seeking would be considered valuable. By comparison, editorials identified the most distracting and unconstructive type of political talk as political point-scoring and bickering. A particularly vociferous editorial in the *Examiner*, titled "Focus on State's Potential" (Prismall 2014c), chastised leaders of all persuasions for their political preoccupations:

> The major parties should be made to invest equally in policy development as much as they invest in opposition to each other. We are not interested in manufactured abuse and parliamentary antics. We understand that they oppose aspects of each other's policies but we also know there's a lot they agree on. We expect them to propose solutions, rather than some deceitful teaser on more detail being revealed closer to the next election. (Prismall 2014c)

This passage, in combination with the title's emphasis on "focus," high-lighted the difference between distracting political talk and constructive action. A similarly strident editorial in the *Examiner* asked, "Where are our federal MHRs [Members of the House of Representatives] and Senators on this? Collecting their pay in return for playing endless politics is the usual answer" (*The Examiner* 2014). A related critique of politics was also aired in this construction: that politicians are insiders with no knowledge of the real world of hard work and struggle. While this was not stated explicitly, it was arguably implied in the common directive, "roll up their sleeves and get to work" (*The Mercury* 2014f). This phrase appeared four times in the *Mercury* over the sample and was often used in contrast with political inaction and negativity: "It is at times like these when the courageous roll up their sleeves and get to work . . . as long as we remain stubbornly locked into negativ-ity, we will get nowhere" (*The Mercury* 2014f). Negative political talk was framed here as a distraction from the *real* work of navigation, an unconstruc-tive attitude that can take the state off-track.

One reason that political partisanship and negativity is so discouraged within the navigational metaphor is because it causes leaders to look the wrong way. Navigators should always be looking forward in order to pre-empt obstacles and make the most of opportunities; however, political debates make politicians look backward in bitterness at historical differences, rumi-nating over old wounds rather than focusing on the path ahead. This structure can be detected in the frequent directive to put political differences "aside or 'behind us' " so that we can "move on." An important cause of political fighting in Tasmania has been forestry, an issue that became newly divisive in 2014 when the Triabunna woodchip mill that was controversially purchased and secretly dismantled by environmentalist entrepreneurs, to repurpose the site for tourism and the arts. As details of the dismembering of the machinery emerged in the *Monthly* magazine (Van Tigglen 2014), Tasmania's history of violent ecological conflict became newsworthy once again. The Liberal Party, whose efforts to reboot the forestry industry were sabotaged by the sale of the mill, formed an inquiry to determine what had occurred. However, the *Mercury* editorialized against this move labeling it a distraction:

> The scab is being torn from the wounds of this sordid issue, and the lives and livelihoods of Tasmanians continue to be secondary to this *no-holds-barred, winner-takes-all stoush* that has *waged* over four decades. We must *move on* . . . . Learning from the past is critically important but, when it becomes purely raking over the coals, *looking backwards* can have a debilitating effect. If the truth be known, most Tasmanians desperately want to unite and *look forward*. It was this "*let's move on* and get the job done" attitude that *swept* Will Hodgman and the Liberals into power. (*The Mercury* 2014k)

The editorial, titled "Fists Fly, but still No Jobs" (August 14, 2014), paints the combatants as selfishly absorbed in their fight while the tired public waits for their leaders to refocus on their needs and move forward.

Democratic Implications of Navigation

The quality of navigational leadership is tested, first and foremost, according to whether obstacles are avoided and destinations are reached in a timely fashion. Accordingly, the navigation metaphor corresponded with certain government priorities where other norms of governance such as consultation are contingent or secondary to overriding navigational imperatives. In the sample, politicians would invoke navigational language at the same time as justifying unilateral and unshakable leadership decisions, thereby placing limits on dissent, transparency, and legitimizing the concentration of power in the hands of a few responsible navigators rather than a plurality of voices.

The state budget of 2014–2015, for instance, was notable for using navigational imperatives to counter dissent. In the lead up to the budget, Treasurer Peter Gutwein unveiled a "$1.1 billion Budget Black Hole" in the state's finances (*The Mercury* 2014e). While the navigation metaphor included many obstacles and dangers such as hurdles and red tape, a "black hole" is a particularly potent navigational obstacle for the (intergalactic) traveler. Not only are black holes best avoided, but due to their famous suction, they present a danger to stationary objects as well. Something of this traction was implied by the treasurer when he warned that "a $1.1 billion black hole . . . will have consequences for Tasmania because interest payments will rob Tasmanians of basic services they need" (Gutwein in Richards 2014b). Thus, according to Gutwein, the compound interest on the state's existing debt could leave the state spiraling toward bankruptcy and financial oblivion. This navigational device was readily taken up in leads and headlines in the sample and often accompanied defiant statements. For example, it was reported that "Mr. Gutwein would not rule out increasing cuts to the public service beyond the 500 fulltime equivalent jobs the Liberals said would be cut under natural attrition and vacancy control. 'I'm not going to deal with hypotheticals,' he said" (Richards 2014b). The construction of government debt as a navigational danger appeared to valorize these opaque official statements about government policy as an expression of the steely resolve and determination required of a skilled navigational leader. The claims of unions and public sector workers were subordinated to the overriding need to get the budget "back on track" and "out of deficit" (Richards 2014b).

Navigational metaphors, which were the most prevalent and homologous way of evaluating leadership across the sample, appeared to valorize a relatively narrow range of relevant leadership styles. This frame corresponded with a celebration of the physicality of good leadership as involving strength, a firm hand, quick reflexes, and an unbending determination. Considering the overwhelmingly masculine voices in the governmental field, this metaphor arguably served to naturalize this gender imbalance by equating good leadership with archetypally masculine characteristics. This finding affirms feminist scholarship and cultural criticism regarding the exclusion of female voices from the public sphere (Fraser 1990) and masculine leadership styles in the workplace (Eagly et al. 1992). In particular, the gender-role-congruency hypothesis posited by Eagly et al. (1992, 16)—"that women are negatively evaluated when they exhibit masculine leadership styles"—may partially explain the correspondence between the low levels of women included in solutions journalism in the sample. Navigational imperatives were also, arguably, deployed to rationalize a unilateral and undemocratic approach to public consultation in government. When combined with militaristic language, this metaphor marginalized alternative voices in favor of a highly regimented and disciplined governmental field that is idealized as marching together into a better future.

The myopic focus demanded of navigators as leaders, according to this frame, can lead to the claims of activists and protesters falling into the category of navigational distractions. In the navigational metaphor, it makes sense for the navigator to stay in touch with the metaphorical passengers (citizens) to make sure everyone is "on-board" with the leader's "direction" for the state and "moving forward together." However, there is a risk that this duty of communication with passengers is broken by the loud, distracting, or misleading speech of protesters and activists. Protesters' claims were often described with accompanying reference to the volume of their speech. Thus, there were "noisy objectors" (*The Mercury* 2014g) or "grumblings from some quarters" (*The Mercury* 2014s) and "too often projects and ideas are met with a sudden and often harsh 'no' " (*The Mercury* 2014n). In the *Examiner*, this point was made explicitly where an editorial warned against taking the words of "leftist lentil lovers" as representative of the broader community (Baker 2014). Tasmanian politics risks, it continued, "heading towards the same old situation where a handful of people with differing vested interests tell us their view is representative of the majority" (Baker 2014). Implicit in these references to the volume of protesters and their unrepresentative status is the fear that they drown out the sensible political center and prevent the type of sober, calm, rational community consultation that is part of a navigator's duty of care to its passengers.

It is also worth noting the prevalence of the military word "quarters" in describing the location of these protestations. The word was used three times in the *Mercury*'s editorials where it was attached to a group that had a marginal or minority standing in the debate and that the editorial ultimately disagreed with. Tasmanian Premier Will Hodgman was "criticized in some quarters . . . but in recent days Mr. Hodgman has raised his head above the trenches to lead the state's charge" (*The Mercury* 2014h); "The general perception of the state in certain poorly informed offshore quarters is that the island is a complete economic failure" (*The Mercury* 2014p); and "there have been grumblings from some quarters within the Aboriginal community for some time that the term wilderness discounts the ancient culture that helped create the Tasmanian landscape over the past 40,000 years" (*The Mercury* 2014s). The term "quarters" frames their perspective as a minority segment of overall opinion. Within a navigational metaphor, the polysemy of the word includes inferences that are explicitly military and maritime. "Quarters" usually refers to sleeping areas in army barracks or ships, which are typically divided according to rank with the low-level crew members separated from the officers and captain. This regimented and discipline expected in army barracks contrasts with the outbursts of protesters breaking rank. Indeed, used metaphorically, grumblings and criticisms from the quarters is an ominous sign of possible mutiny from below decks that the crew must ignore or act quickly to silence. The likelihood that this inference is still resonant is also suggested by the fact that other similar class-based maritime references were present. Notably, the word "flagship" was used five times in the *Mercury*'s editorials to highlight certain symbolic projects of considerable importance for the state. Flagship refers to the leading ship in a fleet where the highest-ranking official has his flag visibly raised. The term was used metaphorically to describe a project with official government support and has, for instance, "become a flagship of Premier Will Hodgman's leadership" (*The Mercury* 2014c). Occasionally flagship and reference to loud and illegitimate protestations occurred together. One editorial (*The Mercury* 2014g) noted that "this critical project has no noisy objectors, unlike so many other developments jousting for flagship status." This passage brings together the idea that, metaphorically, each project in Tasmania is a semi-autonomous navigating vessel with its own captain, occasionally bearing the official insignia of the Premier when he symbolically or materially supports it. Often, however, each project contains a rag-tag crew of illegitimate protesters dwelling in the bowels of the ship, so to speak. As navigators, the responsibility of leaders in the governmental field is to put the views of the community front and center and exercise courage by disregarding the ill-disciplined protesters in their minority quarters.

However, ideologically, free-market idealism entails a more circumscribed role for political leadership in directing economic activity. Governments, in this view, provide the requisite security, confidence, and monetary policy for businesses to invest and expand—with businesses providing employment and revenues in return (Harvey 2007, 2). Implicit in this idea is a revaluation of government and business leadership experience. People with business experience are considered qualified to drive progress in society, whereas centralized government or public service leadership is devalued. This can be seen in the devaluation of "navigational" political leadership in some neoliberal writing. For instance, Friedrich von Hayek, the father of neoliberal philosophy, titled his most famous critique of centralized government, *The Road to Serfdom* (Hayek 1976). Beginning with the opening chapter, "The Abandoned Road," Hayek characterized the intervention in the free market as a step in the direction of the "authoritarian horror" and made regular use of navigational metaphors to furnish the critique. However, with its unpalatable policy prescriptions of welfare reduction, flexible pay, work hours, and heightened competition, neoliberalism required cultural legitimation and a moral argument. This "cultural work," turning now to construction metaphors, took place in the sample metaphorically through a romanticization of its most important protagonists: businessmen, investors, and marketing professionals.

CONSTRUCTION

A familiar historical example of the construction metaphor is the phrase "nation-building" that has typically been used to legitimize Keynesian government infrastructure developments. The vast Tasmanian hydroelectric infrastructure investments were, for instance, archetypal nation-building projects. However, government projects of this magnitude were treated more skeptically in the new economic rationalism of the post–Cold War period with financial risk and profit outsourced to private companies that are equipped to interpret consumer demand and incentivized to increase efficiency through a profit motive. However, rather than dispensing with this metaphor altogether, proponents of market rationality and small government have altered the internal logic of construction implied by a nation-building metaphor.

In the wake of the Global Financial Crisis, the former prime minister of Australia, Kevin Rudd, initiated the "Nation-Building Program" as a form of financial stimulus. This program funded ambitious education, health, and technology infrastructure upgrades—as enormous government investment designed to prevent job-losses (Grube 2011). However, with the change of government federally in 2013 and at a Tasmanian state level in 2014, this discourse received a radical revaluation. Interestingly, the term "nation-building" was conspicuously absent in the sample. Where it did appear, it took on a pejorative meaning, tied to government irresponsibility and bureaucratic inefficiency. In the ABC, it did not appear at all, and in the *Examiner*, it was only used in reference to the television program *Utopia*, which parodied the bureaucratic incompetence of the public service of the fictional

"Nation-building Authority" (Stevenson 2014). In the *Mercury*, however, it appeared twice: once in an opinion piece by Labor Federal Minister Anthony Albanese (2014), noting that the new Liberal government seemed determined to "expunge the term 'Nation-building' from government programs and avoid any accountability in infrastructure investment decisions by the Abbott Government." It also appeared in quotation marks in a critical editorial of the new internet infrastructure upgrade, the National Broadband Network (NBN), that was progressing far slower and at greater cost than predicted: "What a far cry from the lavish promises of four years and two federal elections ago, when Tasmania was chosen to be the pioneer in this great 'nation-building' enterprise" (*The Mercury* 2014b).

However, while nation-building vanished from the political lexicon in 2014, construction metaphors persisted. Indeed, there appeared to be a deliberate reformation of this metaphor, conforming with a shift toward a more market-centric political landscape and toward limited government and business-led development. A reconstructed construction metaphor formed the basis of state treasurer, Peter Gutwein's, first budget speech, titled "Keeping our promises, Laying a foundation for the future" (Gutwein 2014). Rather than "nation-building" the government would be, instead, "laying the foundations" on which businesses can be built with confidence. The logic of this new formulation can be seen in this selection of quotes from Gutwein's budget speech:

This budget *lays the foundation* for a brighter future for all Tasmanians . . . by making Tasmania the most competitive place in Australia. Our energy sector *underpins* that. The *foundation stone* of our energy sector is Hydro Tasmania, which is why the Liberal Government is committed not to sell this Tasmanian icon . . . . The Government and the Board of Forestry Tasmania are currently working together to consider options to place Forestry Tasmania back onto a *financially sustainable footing* . . . . The budget was left in an unsustainable position. This wasn't caused by a *collapse* in revenues. Rather, it was caused by the previous Government's unsustainable spending. During the past four years, revenues have been more than *stable* . . . . Every household in Tasmania knows that you cannot *build* a prosperous future if you continue to spend more than you earn and keep living off credit . . . . We also believe that we can't tax ourselves to prosperity and while there are signs that the economy is starting to grow again, increasing the impost on Tasmanian businesses could *damage that fragile recovery* . . . we have a plan for Tasmania's future. A plan to deliver *strong, stable* majority government to get things done . . . . And a plan to *rebuild* essential services . . . . Madam Speaker, this is a Budget that keeps our promises; begins *fixing* the budget *mess*; and most importantly, *lays a foundation for the future*. (Gutwein 2014, 1–13)

Coming to power after more than a decade in opposition, Gutwein sought to frame the party's platform as beginning the work of "rebuilding" the state economically after the "collapse" that occurred under the previous government. By stressing the government's role in "securing the foundations," Gutwein effectively placed limits on the government's role and reframed the division of labor in policy making. In this metaphor, businesses will do the building and decide what is to be built and the government will restrict itself to providing the necessary preconditions and foundations.

In this construction metaphor, which was pervasive throughout the sample, buildings are businesses and entrepreneurs, vital structures that must be built for the good of society. However, they are also fragile, prone to collapse and vulnerable to (economic) shocks, shakes, and instability. People rely on these buildings and can be harmed if they collapse. For this reason, it is vital that a responsible engineer (the government) secures the foundations that will safeguard the structure into the future. It follows that, once a building is constructed, tampering with the foundations can risk bringing down the entire building. This idea captures businesses' frequently stated need for confidence, stability, and certainty.

The function of the metaphor is apparent in the most commonly used phrase within this metaphor: "base." "Base," which was used metaphorically 69 times in the sample, usually appeared as "based on," but also appeared in constructions such as "evidence-based." This common usage served to highlight assumptions that were central to action. For instance, Industry Minister Paul Harriss's new forest strategy would be "based on science" (Edwards 2014). Or, in relation to the possible legalization of medicinal cannabis, the Labor Party would defer to experts who are "making informed decisions based on research" (Billings 2014). Usefully for leaders and businesspeople who are bound by norms of accountability, this metaphorical device has an implicit qualification: that the decisions are only as good as the foundational information on which they are built. This rationalist, technocratic style of accountability is an important part of business operations and investment decisions. It is also a concept that lies at the heart of journalism historically. The earliest examples of "news letters" that passed between the market-cities of Europe (Conboy 2004, 11) were primarily concerned with informing important business decisions by providing reliable information about conditions in other parts of the world. Loading a ship with stock and crew, ready for a perilous journey to a distant port, was a hugely risky and expensive investment. It was, therefore, imperative to know whether the port city was at war or peace, in famine or flood. In this sense, news has always had a role in providing the factual foundations upon which rational, enlightenment self-interest could operate.

Accordingly, a shrewd business mind looks at these foundational assumptions prior to an investment in the same way that an engineer might examine a blueprint. Under transnational capitalism, the equations are much more fluid and the assumptions more contingent. The engineer's leadership habitus is even more vital in these unsteady times. A central virtue implied by a construction metaphor is, therefore, "responsibility." An editorial in the *Mercury* suggested that financial responsibility was the primary virtue of the current Liberal Party government: "But the bottom line is the people of Tasmania elected Will Hodgman and his Liberal team to bring a new financial prudence to the job. They were elected on the premise that they would be more responsible" (*The Mercury* 2014w). Construction metaphors appear when issues of trust and responsibility arise and, as this quote shows, this included the trust and expectations of voters. Accordingly, politicians are elected on a policy "platform" or "on" the basis of the promises they make. However, this metaphor's application to economic leadership implies that politicians have responsibilities beyond the promises they make to the electorate. They are also responsible for the economic integrity of businesses, which have to make important decisions based on existing policy settings. Accordingly, politicians will seek to appear as the most qualified, predictable, and responsible economic engineers while casting their opponents as reckless and dangerous. For instance, Peter Gutwein stressed that his budget was not a "slash and burn" budget but a "disciplined and responsible" budget (Richards 2014b). Labor Party, however, sought to make the budget decisions appear reckless and even violent with references to "slashed jobs," "deep cuts," a "brutal budget" that will "hurt" Tasmanians and destabilize the economy. The legitimization of the Liberal Party's budget used construction metaphors to differentiate itself from economic irresponsibility of the previous Labor government.

A Business Is an Edifice

It is no accident that a city's most powerful businesses are represented by the tallest office blocks and skyscrapers. They are symbols of the work taken to build them, of stability, ambition, and, importantly, independence. They do not lean against anything. They stand straight and tall, exuding moral strength, will power, and independence. The reason that global business culture traditionally prefers tall straight buildings over, say, buildings that take up a lot of horizontal space is partly metaphorical. According to Lakoff, the founding metaphor of a conservative "strict father" morality is the idea that "Being good is being upright" and "Being bad is being low" (Lakoff 2016, 71), and that uprightness must be enforced, through punishment and privation if need be: "Thus, to remain upright, one must be strong enough to "stand up to evil." Hence, morality is conceptualized as strength, as having the moral fiber or backbone to resist evil. "Morality Is Strength" (Lakoff 2016,

71). Thus, in this worldview, wealthy individuals and businesses are virtuous and moral because they are strong and have achieved independence and self-reliance. Powerful businesses tend to make a virtue of their success by signaling their uprightness and strength architecturally. This could be seen in the sample, where poor economic performance was described as a childlike failure to stand strong and tall. As the editor of the *Mercury* noted, "With so much going for it, it's difficult to imagine why the state is still struggling to *stand on its own feet* economically" (*The Mercury* 2014x). However, while virtuous independence and strength can also be symbolized by posture and other personal characteristics, being slumped and weak can symbolize dependence, poverty, laziness, and stupidity. In his analysis of teachers' comments about good or bad school students, Bourdieu observed how the social class of students in the classroom corresponded to descriptions of the student's manner, posture, pronunciation, and facial expression—projection of class distinction through learned bodily dispositions that Bourdieu termed a "bodily hexis" (Bourdieu 1996b, 35). Particularly in oral presentation assessments, he found that teachers often noted idiosyncrasies, which were used euphemistically to judge personality, erudition, and, ultimately, award marks, favoring the wealthy urbanite students over the poor rural students. Like bodies, buildings too—their straightness, tallness, grandness—can project characteristics of their occupants including their governmental legitimacy.

Failed Urbanism and Economic Leadership

In the sample, descriptions of dilapidated buildings were used to symbolize leadership dysfunction and neglect in Tasmania. In particular, the C. H. Smith building in Launceston, a famously dilapidated "eyesore," was marked as "a symbol of stalled development and halted progress" by Launceston's Mayor, Albert van Zetten (van Zetten in Maloney 2014b). The building's presence in the city belied what other commentators considered to be a pervasive economic and business incompetence in the leadership culture of the state.

Several opinion pieces in the *Examiner* alluded to its broader significance in the context of critiques of leadership and economic management. These appeared to draw on a metaphorical schema relating to buildings, architects, and leadership. Barry Prismall, deputy editor of the *Examiner*, was a consistent critic of Tasmanian leadership failure, writing five forceful editorials against weak leadership and economic inaction across the sample period. In the context of these critiques, his description of the dilapidated building took an accusatory tone. His editorial titled "Time to Act on Future of Eyesore" (Prismall 2014a) described the famously dilapidated C. H. Smith Building as "an eyesore on Launceston's landscape and its future should be determined one way or the other." The symbolic quality of the building was inferred by continuous reference to its visibility: the reference to "eyesore" in the head-line and lead, that it "sits there in all its neglected glory for all tourists to see," and that "it is an embarrassment, occupying a prime city cite with potential for both tourism and commercial usage but going nowhere. A crumbling wreck" (Prismall 2014a). By highlighting its prominence, Prismall suggested locals and tourists would be familiar with the building and what it stands for: neglect and idleness. By way of contrast, it was described as being "opposite a major retailer" (Prismall 2014a) and as hampering potential tourism and business development of the area. In comparison to these promising and pro-ductive uses, the building represented economic failure and unemployment.

Importantly, the editorial tied the building's condition to what Prismall considered to be a pervasive attitude in Tasmania: a preference for care over responsibility, for easy populism rather than necessary decisiveness. This weak attitude was considered an anathema to good economic leadership:

> A decade ago critics described it as a product of the usual heritage farce—a building subjected to all care and no responsibility. Nothing has changed. Once again those concerned enough to save buildings never have to look after them. A set-and-forget culture, while ratepayers or taxpayers are left to pick up the tab. (Prismall 2014a)

Interestingly, there is a conflation of language used between parenting (in a Lakoffian sense), governance, and urban decay in these critiques of failed urbanism. The reference to "all care and no responsibility" in the first paragraph, and having to "look after them" is a metaphorical critique of a nurturant parent mentality: if you spoil your children they will not become strong, upright, independent adults—they will be weak and will have to be looked after by other people such as the welfare state when they grow up (Lakoff 2016). Economically, it is a leadership style that leads to derelict buildings and unemployment. By being overly sentimental about the heritage value of the C. H. Smith Building leaders squander the business potential of the site. What was needed, Prismall implied, was a stricter parenting style of governance that is capable of making a hard decision. He begins the article by complaining that "we seem incapable of dealing with it" (Prismall 2014a). According to Prismall, "Its future should be determined one way or the other . . . . Let's have a hard look at it and make a tough decision" (Prismall 2014a). Again, responsibility emerged as a key leadership virtue in this construction metaphor, albeit responsibility within a "strict father" moral framework.

Unemployment and idleness were common themes in Prismall's other editorials (2014b, 2014c) and were present, obliquely, in this description of the abandoned warehouse (2014a). The theme of unemployment was invoked symbolically through his description of the defunct C. H. Smith construction site: "Even the heavy machinery deployed long ago to expedite development at the rear of the building's facade is developing rust and cobwebs" (Prismall 2014a). The description of the defunct construction site and abandoned machinery symbolized the unemployed workers who should be operating the machinery but are, like the machinery, redundant and idle. The description of the construction yard was also taken up by another Launceston journalist, Matt Maloney, in his article titled "Long Struggle to Redevelop City Eyesore": "Today, a lonely piece of earthmoving machinery remains in the same slumped position it had 12 months ago, with weeds growing around it. Blue and black spray paint decorates the backside of a heritage-listed crumbling facade and an unsecured, semi-derelict warehouse" (Maloney 2014b). Describing the machinery as in a slumped position seems to anthropomorphize the object. In relation to Lakoff's moral politics, this posture may imply moral failure or laziness within a "strict father" moral frame work in contrast to moral "upright-ness" (Lakoff 2016, 65). In addition, Maloney noted the blue and black graf-fiti on the building—evidence of dangerously unoccupied and unemployed youths—with the colors reminiscent of bruising or, perhaps, depression.

This conflation of failed urbanism with youth unemployment was espe-cially salient because of the political context of the sample. In 2014, youth unemployment was a central theme in reporting with the federal govern-ment's controversial "Earn or Learn" policy attracting considerable atten-tion. The policy, which sought to quarantine young people from applying for welfare for six months, was interpreted by some as imputing a moral failure on young unemployed Tasmanians when, in fact, there were simply not enough jobs (Webb 2014). The application of a construction metaphor did not directly blame youth unemployment on young people. Rather, the moral failing was directed at the leadership of Tasmania, reasoned about in terms of parenting. It implied that young people's idleness and lack of inde-pendence was due to a weak, overly nurturant leadership style. This implicit accusation appeared in the common conflation of failed urbanism with failed parenting in, for instance, Matt Maloney's critique of Launceston's Brisbane Street Mall:

> The Brisbane Street Mall is a depressing place to be, for any length of time. It's grey, it's drab, and those creepy hard-plastic cushions make me jump out of my skin every time they utter inaudible words at me in a creepy child-like voice reminiscent of a horror movie. Add to this the screaming, swearing, narcissistic youths that slump themselves over the mall's dull furniture, and you have cre-ated one of the circles of my personal hell. (Maloney 2014a)

Where Maloney noted the graffiti on the C. H. Smith Building, in this case, he described the youths in physical form, occupying another example of failed urban planning. They are slumped rather than upright and are distinctly threatening with their screaming and yelling. "The council has some massive work ahead to make the centre a place where people want to be," he continued (Maloney 2014a), overlooking the fact that apparently the youths already want to be there (and are people). Brisbane Street is described as almost Soviet in its grayness and drabness, with furniture that are "creepy" inhuman automaton. Again, this site is contrasted with other uses that are characterized by vibrant businesses, and more productive and legitimate members of society:

> Imagine cars and asphalt replaced by beautiful paving, architecturally designed wooden furniture, garden beds, food carts, shady trees, grassed embankments, and the hum of quality buskers and warm chatter. This could be a place to encourage weekend markets, a hub for cafes, restaurants, bars and alfresco dining, concerts, and hopefully the odd flash mob . . . . It would provide a stage for market trade and events that will bring people together and promote an image of a thriving community. More activity in the centre would support existing businesses, and new businesses would have confidence to open in some of the small and narrow tenancies around the centre. A town square historically has been the heart of a town or a city. (Maloney 2014a)

Between this imagined free-market utopia and the current urban dystopia, there lies the specter of obstructionism and an overly nurturant leadership mentality:

> Of course, such a dramatic overhaul of the city's centre will cause some initial pain, frustration, and confusion, and it is unlikely to be cheap if the job is done correctly. People will complain about the inconveniences of two small sections of road closed to traffic. Others will fear a "bogan" influx, and some will simply hate the idea because it is something different. (Maloney 2014a)

These statements anticipate the same weak, obstructionist mentality to which Prismall alluded. A culture that does not tolerate short-term pain in the interest of making a necessary tough decision. A contrast was also made between different performances of youthfulness—a different "bodily hexis," to use Bourdieu's (1996, 35) term—that might be expected from a refurbished town square: buskers and warm chatter instead of screaming and swearing, and "hopefully" a flash mob (a caricature of youthful aerobic activity) rather than slumped bodies on ugly furniture.

The *Mercury* also had a preoccupation with the built environment, noting a number of projects that were symbolic of the economic circumstances facing the state. However, Hobart and Launceston represented two very different economic realities during the period, a point that Tennant emphasized in his interview by noting a "two speed economy in Tasmania" (Tennant 2015). This economic discrepancy appeared to inform the tone in the editorializing between the two newspapers. While articles in the *Examiner*, such as those by Maloney and Prismall, seemed pessimistic about the prospects of an economic revival and despairing about in the city's urban wastelands, there was a pervasive sense of optimism in the *Mercury*. Several articles praised the development of the Brook Street Pier building, a floating retail and hospitality building on Hobart's waterfront. It was a symbol of innovation and new optimism in Hobart's economy. In an editorial titled "Wonderful Waterfront," the editor celebrated the new floating building: a miracle of innovation and symbolic of "New Tasmania" (*The Mercury* 2014i).

NURTURANCE

In the discussion thus far, leadership was legitimized by metaphors that were, in a Lakoffian sense, consistent with a "strict father" moral politics (Lakoff 2016, 65). Navigational, military, and construction metaphors legitimized symbolic capital relating to responsibility and discipline over care or empathetic imperatives. Construction metaphors celebrated uprightness and the morality of independence and stability while navigation and military metaphors identified sobriety, rationality, and focus as necessary qualities for perceiving and avoiding the obstacles facing the state. In comparison, as Lakoff suggested, a nurturant moral politics centralizes care, empathy, and mutual respect as key leadership virtues. In a nurturant morality, "children become responsible, self- disciplined, and self-reliant through being cared for and respected, and through caring for others" (Lakoff 2016, 108). While we tend to think of nurturance as naturally endowed—that someone has a kind heart or a sensitive soul—there is also a sense in which nurturance is form of expertise and can be considered as a form of symbolic leadership capital in the governmental field that leaders may allude to in their public pronouncements.

Nurturant language occupied an important place in the discussion of the future, with metaphors relating to health and child-care accounted for 19 percent of all metaphorical language in the sample. In particular, nurturant language was typically borrowed from two specializations: health care and child-care. Idioms and metaphors relating to the education, support and protection of children were common devices that legitimized a caring leadership habitus. Likewise, the technical skill of caring for someone was highlighted by references to health and medicine. A *sick, ailing, stunted* economy, for instance, required a caring leader who could find the appropriate cure and *inject* money into the economy or *resuscitate* a *near-dead* industry. These statements about one's character can be considered as legitimize nurturing virtues of leadership, rather than more disciplinarian navigational or construction values. Indeed, audiences often expect nurturing virtues from their leaders. Public outrages at breaches of trust, preventable accidents, or abuses of power are typically regarded breaches of nurturant care. However, in the sample, this frame was often applied strategically in public relations campaigns for private interests—stretching credulity, perhaps, regarding the authenticity of these nurturing pronouncements.

Children Are the Future

Solutions too are frequently reasoned about in reference to nurturance because children symbolize the future, and often our moral obligation to future generations. Distinctions between young and old, child and adult, are apt metaphorical devices for reasoning about the future. Aging mirrors the passing of time. Representations of old or young people can symbolize, variably, the past or the future. They are also basic concepts in everyday life. Differences in stature, power, and age are some of the first distinctions that one encounters in life. The first "other" for children is usually "the adults." Children, likewise, present a powerful symbol of hope, creativity, care, and opportunity to the older generation. As such, related language has come to furnish many political discourses. Australia famously celebrates youth in the national anthem. Omitting the fact that indigenous Australians are some of the world's oldest living cultures, the first stanza begins with "Australians let us all rejoice, for we are young and free." The figurative youthfulness represents a perceived national characteristic belonging to a range of old and young people. Australians are metaphorically young at heart: optimistic, innocent, and trusting.

During the sample period, both the *Mercury* and the *Examiner* took steps to provide a platform for young voices. During National Youth Week, for example, the *Examiner* invited five young people from Northern Tasmania to share their vision for the state's future in opinion columns. Sarah Wright (2014) contributed a piece titled "Don't Stifle Our Voices" that drew attention to young people's disparagement within the Tasmanian governmental field. "An individual's view should not be judged or swept away due to the year they are born. Age is not a justifiable excuse to dismiss an idea," she wrote. Interestingly, the *Mercury* initiated a similar campaign "Our kids, our future" that also sought to amplify the voices and opinions of young Tasmanians:

> THEY are the faces of Tasmania's future. A group of typical 18 to 24-year-olds who are passionate about their futures but struggling to find their feet

amid a worsening unemployment crisis. Today, the Sunday Tasmanian and the Mercury launch a landmark campaign: Our kids, our future. The aim is simple: we want to tell the issue of youth unemployment through the eyes of those it most affects—our young people. (Smith 2014)

The *Examiner*'s Youth Week initiative offered a statesman-like space for young people to outline their vision for the future and a temporary position in the governmental field. By comparison, the *Mercury*'s initiative aimed to convey the everyday reality of young Tasmanians, "typical 18-24-year olds," struggling in a tough economic climate. While inviting greater understanding and empathy with young people was important in the context of the Earn of Learn policies of the 2014 federal Liberal government, it did not confer leadership capital on young people as did the *Examiner*. In the *Examiner,* the young visionaries were anything but ordinary. As the biographies on each of their contributions showed, these were the state's future leaders (scientists, artists, activists) sharing their hopes and aspirations for the community as a whole.

The special effort to profile young voices was also a metaphorical reference to Tasmania's future. In the sample, metaphorical references to children and child-care were used in a number of different contexts. One common usage could be termed "Ideas are Children," and mapped as follows (prevalence indicted in brackets):

I *conceive* (5) of an idea. I want to bring my idea *to life* (35). I may want others to *adopt* (24) the idea. However, if the idea is not working I may have to *abandon* (26) it.

We have *inherited* (13) a *legacy* (9) of bad ideas, debt, and *aging* (6) infrastructure from previous governments that must *be renewed* (4).

This first construction captures the love, care, and investment of time that proponents have for their projects and their commitment to seeing them implemented in the future. Used negatively, however, this metaphor relates to a lack of care for the future, and hence, the future generations who have to live with their parents' mistakes.

This negative usage was deployed frequently in the sample with newly elected state and federal governments seeking to attribute current economic and policy problems to the previous administration. The new Liberal government made frequent references to *the legacy* of debt and deficit that the previous Labor administration left to Tasmania (Gutwein in *The Mercury* 2014e). The previous government, according to Gutwein, having over-spent during its tenure, had breached its responsibility of care for its constituents and jeopardized the future of welfare programs and other "basic services."

Considering Lakoff's schema of moral politics, it may be surprising that Gutwein, a conservative politician advocating fiscal restraint, would choose to frame his argument using nurturant metaphors. However, both progressive and conservative moral perspectives make appeals for intergenerational equity. This constitutes a rare area of agreement, and hence competition, between these political world views. An example of a progressive articulation of this idea is the appeal to safeguard the environment for "future generations" that has become a central feature in environmentalist politics and sustainability (World Commission on Environment and Development 1987). In this view, future generations, often symbolized by children themselves, must be protected and cared for in an uncertain and dangerous future. This argument has arguably attracted widespread support compared to eco-centric and precautionary ecological principles due to its applicability within a conservative "inheritance" frame. However, its relative applicability to conservatives and progressives has also led to a discursive struggle, which could be detected in the sample. In the previous term of government, the ALP had controversially enacted strong environmental policy by introduced carbon pricing legislation to mitigate climate change. This move was accompanied by the now familiar appeals to consider the welfare of the next generation. After passing the legislation, Prime Minister Julia Gillard addressed the National Press Club stating that it was time "to do what is best for Australian families, what is best for future generations, what is best for this country" (Gillard in *Australian Associated Press* 2011). However, upon losing the election in 2013, the legislation was repealed by the incoming Liberal government, who also sought to reclaim this floating signifier within conservative economic ideology. Possibly seeking to redirect care for future generations from ecological to economic considerations, the then Australian Treasurer Joe Hockey began his 2014 budget speech with a call for intergenerational prosperity:

> Our future depends on what we as a nation do today. For our children, for our seniors, for individuals, for families, for our disabled and for our frail, for all of us, the government's solemn duty is to *build a stronger Australia*. . . . Every generation before us has contributed to the quality of life that we enjoy today. (Hockey 2014)

This framing of conservative fiscal restraint using child-care concepts, along with the similarly innovated construction metaphor, could be seen as a way of re-owning this political concept, which had been in danger of becoming embedded in ecological considerations.

Xi Jinping as a Nurturant Parent

While nurturant language appeared frequently throughout the sample, nurturance was frequently performed—often by leaders seeking to convey their kindly nature. Central to credible nurturant leadership is a healthy love of children, and all the potential and opportunity for the future that they represent. A clear example of this strategy of legitimation was during the tightly choreographed visit of the Chinese President Xi Jinping. The visit coincided with a campaign to familiarize Tasmanians with China and Chinese culture in anticipation of the nation becoming an increasingly important trading partner for the state. Daniel Chan from the Chinese Community Association offered to "work with the State Government's new China Investment and Trade Unit to come up with a week of business and cultural activities to tie in with the visit" (Shannon 2014). This cultural celebration was likely intended to assuage xenophobia regarding Chinese foreign investment and land sales and reframe the public image of China.

A central feature of this highly anticipated visit and associated promotion was a vast array of metaphorical references to President Xi Jinping's nurturance and respect of children. This began with long before the visit with media reports explaining why the president chose to visit Tasmania in the first place. Despite elsewhere reporting the long-standing, bipartisan effort of politicians and diplomats to secure the visit, journalists readily took up the remarkable story that the Chinese couple had been summoned to Tasmania at the behest of Launceston primary school students. An article in the *Mercury* titled "Letters to Melt a President's Heart" read like a fairy tale:

> IN May, 23 pupils from Scotch Oakburn College each wrote a letter to Chinese President Xi Jinping inviting him to visit Tasmania and offering suggestions about what he could see and do. Those letters, written in Mandarin, were responsible for securing last week's state visit by President Jinping and his wife Madame Peng Liyuan. The Grade 5 students, and their teacher Katie Marson, had never expected the letters to even reach the President, but on November 12 they were visited by Chinese Ambassador Ma Zhaoxu and Consul-General Song Yumin, who had a very special message for the children. "The ambassador told the children their letters were the reason Mr. Xi had decided to visit Tasmania," Mrs. Marson said . . . . "Then we were told the President had received the letters and had sat down with his wife to read each letter, making corrections as they went" . . . . "Next, we received an invitation to meet the president at Government House and found out the ambassador and consul-general were going to visit the school to personally deliver a letter from the President" . . . . The President's letter complimented the children on their beautifully written Chinese characters and told them language was *the bridge to connect hearts and minds among people. "Children are the future and hope of a country or a nation,"* he wrote.

> "*They are also the hope of state-to-state relations.* Your letters have given us great confidence in future China-Australia relations." Mrs. Marson said she thought the letters had struck such a chord with the President because they were written in Mandarin and were very child-centred. (Vowles 2014)

In this richly metaphysical construction, the president and his wife take on the authority of parents or teachers, correcting the students' homework, gently encouraging and complimenting them. While the president's letter states that "children are the future and hope of a country or a nation [and] also the hope of state-to-state relations," it is clear that this is a shared-future that, metaphysically, the Chinese president is claiming some authority over as a caring, responsible, nurturant parent figure. As the *Examiner* reported, this association with Tasmanian children was reinforced throughout the opening day at almost every stop on the couple's crowded itinerary:

> A number of Tasmania's high profile leaders will be at the airport to greet them, along with Bobbie the Bear . . . . Two lucky Tasmanian primary school pupils will present Mr. Xi and Madam Peng with the lavender-filled bear, along with a vibrant bunch of locally grown, deep red peonies. From there it's straight to Government House, where the couple will meet a class of grade five pupils from Launceston's Scotch Oakburn College. Mr. Xi specifically requested to meet the 21 pupils after receiving their letters urging him to visit the state. The President will plant an ancient Chinese native tree at the vice-regal residence to commemorate his visit, before being introduced to three baby Tasmanian devils. (McCulloch 2014)

Needless to say, the tree planting ceremony (the sapling itself is a symbol of nurturance and care) was accompanied by "a choir of 5-10-year-old girls from St Michael's Collegiate" (*ABC Tasmania* 2014). The juvenile Tasmanian Devils were also suitably chosen to reinforce the leader's empathetic credentials: a vulnerable species at a vulnerably young age being cuddled by one of the world's most powerful men.

There were only a handful of articles that brought some scrutiny to this important repositioning of Tasmania and Australia with China. While this saturation level of nurturance was arguably marketed at a Chinese audience as much as it was at a local audience, it would presumably have softened Tasmanian perceptions of China's (apparently benevolent) interest and intentions regarding the state and its natural resources. In an opinion piece in the *Mercury*, Professor of East Asian and US history Randall Doyle (2014) cautioned against naiveté regarding the visit:

> China's unending addiction and thirst for the world's natural resources must be recognised by Tasmanian state officials and handled with great caution.

Tasmania has the kind of natural resources that China desires with great intensity. I believe there is a great danger that Tasmanians could find themselves embroiled in another internal firestorm over its extractive policies concerning its natural resources and the demands of the Chinese market. There is the real danger that Tasmania could be an agri-natural resource colony of China's. . . . Therefore, it is imperative Tasmanians understand President Xi is not travelling to Hobart as a sightseer or tourist. In reality, he is a head of state whose country is now seen as the second most powerful nation-state in the world. And, perhaps, the most powerful in Asia. Hence, the Chinese president is coming to Hobart as part of a calculated public relations strategy to present China as a positive factor in Tasmania and Australian society in general. (Doyle 2014)

This sobering assessment of the trip, while providing a welcome counterpoint, did not appear to inspire much caution in the otherwise celebratory reporting. A separate opinion piece in the *Mercury* by the Tasmanian Greens' leader, Nick McKim (2014), encouraged diplomats to use the visit to pressure China on its occupation of Tibet and environmental record. The *Mercury* noted: "A small group, including Greens MP Nick McKim, protested about Tibet" (Killick et al. 2014). The *Examiner*, however, representing Tasmania's investment-starved north, offered no criticisms.

The strategic placement of children in political rhetoric is a familiar public relations technique for most Australians. Politicians make a point of appearing at public schools, kissing babies and playing with school students in the playground during election campaigns. There is also a common tradition of children being deployed in celebrations of multiculturalism such as that which accompanied the Chinese president's visit. Children are innocent of many of the enculturated suspicions and prejudices of adults. Official citizenship ceremonies, where new migrants pledge their allegiance to the nation, are almost always accompanied by a choir of children and, often, the offering of a native plant to each migrant family to grow and nurture. To adults, children represent a caring bond and agreement, as well as the future generally.

Emerging Industries and Child-Care

While political sources frequently appeal to different ideals of parenting, emerging industries and businesses are, correspondingly, constructed as akin to children. Central to the distinction between child and adult is a difference in stature. Children are small and will often struggle to overcome obstacles such as chairs, steps, or fences, requiring a responsible adult to lift them up. Accordingly, there were many phrases that alluded to this specific type of parental care. Solutions were often predicted as likely to "boost" or "lift" a particular section of the community. "Boost" was the most common metaphorical expression of the 385 nurturance metaphors recorded, appearing 131 times in the sample. Boost indicates some upward force such as a leg-up or a lift. While it can be used as shorthand for "more" within the common metaphor "More Is Up" (Lakoff and Johnson 2008, 15), there is an implicit suggestion of stature in the word boost that is reminiscent of an adult's relation to a child. By examining the context of its use in the sample, the primary usage appears to be nurturant rather than relating purely to quantity. Boost appeared when a solution was predicted to assist a community, especially a community that appeared to be struggling or emerging economically. For instance, dairy farmers were offered "increased financial incentives to help boost a North-West dairy company's milk production" (Kempton 2014a). The frequent coincidence of "help" with "boost" highlighted nurturant inference within a child-care metaphor, implying that these industries were metaphysically in their infancy, having great potential but requiring support or a "helping hand" so they can "find their feet."

In comparison, established and successful businesses within existing industries appeared to take on the mantle of an older family member in comparison to fledgling businesses and industries. For example, the founder of Lark Distillery, Bill Lark, was one of the first Tasmanian whisky makers to gain international recognition. The headline of one feature article described Lark as the "Godfather of the Tasmanian whisky industry" (Abey 2014b). In relation to forestry, Tasmanian boat-builder, John Young, was likewise introduced as "the grandfather figure of Tasmania's acclaimed wooden-boat industry" (Bevilaqua 2014). Unsurprisingly, perhaps, given the low profile of female leaders in the sample, there were no reference to industry grandmothers or mothers. These father figures made frequent appearances in the sample as voices of wisdom, mentors to the newer players, and proof that new industries can achieve success. Interestingly, Lark offered his own nurturant metaphor in advising how the governmental field should seek to nurture the burgeoning Tasmanian whisky industry: "Mr. Lark cautioned against rushing into large-scale production to satisfy a thirsty world market, saying it could risk killing the big, oily and malty golden goose that had won the state so many plaudits so far" (Abey 2014c). Thus, as this reference to animal husbandry might suggest, a nurturing ethic is not necessarily a selfless endeavor. Rather, the governmental field should properly nurture budding industries with an eye to their future success from which we might benefit.

CONCLUSION

Metaphors pervaded "New Tasmania." Through a kind of linguistic dramatization and staging, new solutions—which were perhaps mundane pseudo-events, press releases, or photo opportunities (Boorstin 1992)—were transformed into daring navigational dilemmas, precarious construction project or family dramas. These metaphors, however, did more than merely add color, drama, or rhetorical flourish. They were also schematic, providing a structure, logic, and seemingly objective grounds for identifying and evaluating leadership and hence governing the governmental field. The most prevalent metaphors corresponded, in many instances, with fundamental asymmetries in news access. Hypermasculine navigational metaphors of sport and war, which fixated on the physicality of leadership, the firm grasp and steely resolve of a natural leader, arguably corresponded with the high profile of men and the low profile of women. As Lakoff and Johnson stress, conceptual metaphors "structure what we perceive, how we get around in the world, and how we relate to other people" (2003, 4). Accordingly, the cultural habituation of certain metaphors shapes who we perceive as a leader and who we think might legitimately and usefully propose a solution and frame the future. These metaphors provided a schema of virtues and vices against which leaders could be evaluated, and against which their actions could be tested.

Often metaphors were pioneered by leaders themselves to legitimize themselves and delegitimize their rivals. In particular, the new Liberal government pioneered a range of metaphorical constructions to narrativize themselves as protagonists and the previous Labor government as antagonists. Metaphorically, the Labor government was construed as lost and requiring rescuing; reckless and leaving a trail of disrepair; profligate and leaving Tasmania legacy of debt and deficit. Their metaphorical appellations and slogans—*laying the foundations, rescue taskforce, budget black hole*—were readily taken up by journalists and editors, embedding these frames in their reporting of important policy areas. This is not an uncommon journalistic practice, and a new government has, perhaps, a discursive mandate to reframe the debate: the symbolic spoils of an election victory. However, journalists (and the broader governmental field) were arguably naïve and remiss in their near-total cooperation with the Chinese government in reproducing and staging what was frankly propaganda.

Outside of discursive battles between political sources, metaphors also corresponded with the marginalization of all professions besides businesses and politicians. Disciplinarian, navigational or construction metaphors often coincided with moments when leaders sought to bracket deliberation and dissent. In the face of tough decisions and crucial solutions, metaphors were often deployed to enforce a spirit of bipartisanship, to bring warring parties together, marginalize protesters and, in a more regimented fashion, move forward together and get to work. Indeed, these metaphors all related to domains of work: navigators, engineers, architects, parents, doctors and nurses. As the following chapter will explore, this figurative interdisciplinarity was especially curious considering the limited diversity of professions in the sample, and most notably the near invisibility of expert sources.

NOTE

1. In this chapter metaphorical language will be italicised within quoted material for emphasis.

Chapter 6

Expertise

While solutions journalism has been refined and formalized as a reporting practice in the Northern Hemisphere, journalists and news organizations in other parts of the world, such as those examined in Tasmania, nonetheless report solutions. In Tasmania, ideas were proposed and reported, success stories were celebrated, alternative ideas debated, and the future mediated, variably, through the professional practices of journalists. What distinguishes solutions journalism then, I have argued, is not its reporting of solutions so much as *who* is routinely given space to propose solutions. Heteronomous reporting of solutions tends to reflect and legitimize the governmental field without autonomously stipulating or proposing an alternative journalistic criterion for valuable leadership and news access. On the other hand, a characteristic feature of autonomous solutions journalism—yet one that tends to be executed implicitly—is that journalists report the responses and solutions of an alternative governmental field, a networked field of social entrepreneurs, changemakers, community leaders, project managers, and innovators whose ideas provide a counterpoint to existing practices, and whose leadership operates in a different mode to the prevailing governmental voices. Whereas Tasmanian solutions journalism tended to be concerned (reactively) with power and consequence, autonomous solutions journalism—and I believe this is its distinguishing feature—is proactive and rigorous in its assessment of expertise.

Compared to business and political sources, who provided 70 percent of the quotations, experts provided 7 percent of the quoted material in the Tasmanian sample of solutions reporting. Experts and scientists are commonly imagined at the helm of social progress, according to a familiar meta-narrative of progress (Gamson and Modigliani 1989), making experts and their institutions a seemingly obvious place for journalists to seek comment regarding solutions. Additionally, there was little in the pervasive use of navigational, construction or nurturant metaphors that could easily account for this discrepancy. Indeed, the three primary forms of metaphor corresponded with different forms of expert knowledge. Navigation metaphors might be deployed to legitimize expertly produced maps, good directions and clear vision; construction metaphors might highlight the solidity of information on which decisions and businesses could be based or necessitate a skilled engineer to design the foundations; nurturant metaphors might celebrate the skills of a health practitioner, pharmacist, or surgeon. Thus, each of these common formulations could easily be adapted to legitimize expertise in the governmental field, yet no correspondence between metaphors of expertise and actual experts was apparent.

"INDUSTRY EXPERTS"

A key reason for the low number of experts in the sample could be divergent definitions of expertise. For the purposes of coding, I defined experts as knowledge-based subject authorities. Included, therefore, were historians, demographers, economists, biologists, engineers, architects, climate scientists, data analysts, indigenous scholars, and maritime researchers, among others. It was not taken to include public servants, such as teachers and doctors, or cultural professionals such as artists or musicians. This seemed an uncontroversial definition of expertise, and corresponded with Schudson's definition of an expert as "someone in possession of specialized knowledge that is accepted by the wider society as legitimate" (2006, 499). However, the sources that journalists explicitly nominated as experts in the sample did not correspond with the types of people I was including as experts. Indeed, there was a somewhat postmodern slippage in the definition and standing of the expert evident in the sample. This is worthy of further exploration, not least because the definition and value of expert is contested by solutions journalists, who occasionally argue for a broadening of expertise to include knowledge derived from practical firsthand experience in implementing change (Bansal and Martin 2015, 7).

In the sample, articles did refer to "experts" with the word "expert" appearing 119 times at a rate of 0.1 per article. The *Mercury* had the highest proportion of expert quotes compared to other Tasmania outlets, with 9 percent of the quoted material coming from sources I coded as experts. In fact, this figure arguably underplayed the salience of expert voices in the *Mercury*, since experts would regularly author opinion columns in the paper, which I counted as a single lengthy quotation. This multi-genre delivery in the *Mercury*, with a greater mix of opinion and straight news reporting, appeared to correspond with a more multi-perspectival range of sources, a finding in line with Benson's analysis of the debate ensemble format of the French press (2009). However, there did appear to be some slippage in the concept of expertise in this reporting, as in the reporting across the Tasmanian sample.

For example, a story titled "Acres of Options on Jobs Horizon" stated, "Experts predict tourism, agriculture and aged care will be the drivers of a vibrant Tasmanian economy as the state emerges from recession towards a diversified industry base" (Abey 2014a). However, the experts referred to in the lead were, in order of appearance, the chief executive of the Tasmanian Farmers and Graziers Association, Jan Davis; the chief executive of the Tasmanian Chamber of Commerce and Industry, Michael Bailey; Bank of America Merrill Lynch chief economist, Saul Eslake and; quoted last, University of Tasmania demographer Dr. Lisa Denny. Of these sources, I identified only Eslake and Denny as experts (who were the least salient in the article). Eslake had been appointed as the University of Tasmania's vice-chancellor's fellow, based on his research expertise in economics, while Denny is a well-recognized demographer at the same university. On the other hand, I categorized Davis and Bailey as "industry representatives": Davis as representing the interests of farmers, and Baily as representing Tasmanian businesses. Likewise, a commentary on Chinese investment titled "Are We Ready for the Great Leap Forward?" began by stating "Chinamania itself won't get the job done, experts are warning," before quoting, Michael Baily of the Chamber of Commerce and Industry, two politicians, the CEO of Reid Fruits, Jan Davis of the Farmers and Graziers Association, and, quoted last, Chinese Business expert Dr. Fan. The conflation of industry interests with expertise was most apparent in the dual term "industry expert" that appeared several times in the sample. For example, an article in the *Examiner* began by stating that "the aged care industry requires rebranding and government investment before Tasmania can capitalize on the sector, *industry experts* say" (Baker 2014). The article went on to quote a company employee in aged care and then a demographer, thus eliding their differences and including both voices under the dual category.

Across several examples, the conflation of expertise with stakeholders overlooked the fact that, in their relationship to democracy, these categories should be mutually exclusive. According to Schudson (2006), the value of expert voices in democracy is premised on their ability to prioritise their professional reputation, as judged by legitimate peers, over their own interests or the interests of their employers: "they desire to please their professional peers more than their clients" (2006, 500). Thus, while news sources such as Baily and Davis do possess considerable expertise in marketing and agribusiness respectively, their status as experts should be forfeited by the fact that they are speaking on behalf of clients and members. As such, their intervention in the press was to convey the policy or message of the organization, when, according to Lippman, the last thing a decision maker should "tolerate in [their] experts is the suspicion that they have a 'policy' " (1922, 382). For Lippman, the best governance occurs when "the divorce between the assembling of knowledge and control of policy is most perfect" (1922, 382–383).

METAPHOR AS MASQUERADE

These observations cast new light on the expertise metaphors in Tasmanian solutions reporting, which were incongruously prevalent considering the low profile of actual expertise in the sample. Arguably, expertise metaphors may have effectively simulated or supplanted independent expertise in the governmental sphere. Entrepreneurs, industry representatives, and politicians were granted, metaphorically, a range of expert competencies that could be tested, not by expert peers in an autonomous fashion, but by the public and journalists. As Lippman argued, public opinion can only realistically be expected to say "yes" or "no" (1922, 230), but the questions posed to it can be metaphorical: "Does the doctor's injection cure the ailment"? "Are the expertly designed footings supporting the structure?" "Has the cartographer lead us astray?" These questions pose tangible and testable hypotheses about the effectiveness of leadership and provide seemingly objective grounds on which their effectiveness can be adjudicated. Expertise metaphors are, to use Alasdair MacIntyre's term, "moral fictions": "they purport to provide us with an objective and impersonal criterion, but they do not" (MacIntyre 2007, 70). These metaphors allow editors, journalists, and the public to evaluate, in particular, *the effectiveness* of leadership, a function that was specifically identified by MacIntyre in his provocative book *After Virtue*. He identified the corporate manager as an archetypically modern character, whose authority rests on "the claim to possess systematic effectiveness in controlling certain aspects of social reality" (MacIntyre 2007, 74). However, due to the hazy causal link between long-term goals and the manager's actions in securing them, and the absence of any verifiable body of knowledge that might inform their expertise, the claim to managerial effectiveness that underwrites their authority is ultimately, in his view, a masquerade, a moral fiction:

> Consider the following possibility: that what we are oppressed by is not power, but impotence; that one key reason why the presidents of large corporations do not, as some radical critics believe, control the United States is that they do not even succeed in controlling their own corporations; that all too often, when imputed organizational skill and power are deployed and the desired effect follows, all that we have witnessed is the same kind of sequence as that to be

observed when a clergyman is fortunate enough to pray for rain just before the unpredicted end of a drought; that the levers of power—one of managerial expertise's own key metaphors—produce effects unsystematically and too often only coincidentally related to the effects of which their users boast. Were all this to be the case, it would of course be socially and politically important to disguise the fact, and deploying the concept of managerial effectiveness as both managers and writers about management do deploy it would be an essential part of any such disguise. (MacIntyre 2007, 75)

Thus, to entertain this hypothetical scenario, metaphors of managerial effectiveness have a crucial legitimizing function. At best, such metaphors simplify complex causal mechanisms, enabling audiences and editors to impute success or failure; or, at worst, they paper over impotence and reassure the public of control, accountability, and expertise when outcomes, in many instances, are beyond their control. MacIntyre's rejection of any valid base of knowledge or expertise on the part of corporate managers is, perhaps, unfair. However, when such managers and corporate spokespeople appear in the news to speak on behalf of their clients rather than on behalf of a community of expert peers, they arguably need recourse to a range of expertise metaphors to simulate the expertise that they have forfeited. Politicians, as Bourdieu argued, are likewise dependent on maintaining the impression of effectiveness to legitimize their symbolic power (Bourdieu 1991a, 190). They are variously beneficiaries and victims of journalists' participation in this metaphorical masquerade of effectiveness. They are credited when their policy corresponds with success, and discredited when it does not—despite these outcomes often taking place in conditions of radical uncertainty, or even, as Brian McNair might suggest, chaos (2006). In a small economy such as Tasmania where economic fortunes depend on a range of external factors, the masquerade of effectiveness is especially necessary and prevalent. However, an autonomous journalism that is concerned with alleviating the "oppression of impotence" (MacIntyre 2007, 75) goes beyond the legitimizing myths of managerial effectiveness by positing its own schema of effective leadership.

In contrast, autonomous solutions journalism, while similarly concerned with the search and evaluation of effectiveness, is characteristically rigorous, proactive, and empirical. Indeed, solutions journalism is frequently defined as *rigorous* reporting of *effective* responses to social problems, where the effectiveness must be demonstrated empirically rather than rhetorically (The Solutions Journalism Network 2020). For example, according to prominent solutions journalist at the *Seattle Times*, Janet Horne Henderson, "there needs to be some way to measure the effectiveness of [a solution]. If it's just anecdotal, if we just have people saying, "Oh, this is great," that's really not enough. We need some way to measure it." Likewise, after interviewing a range of solutions journalists, McIntyre and Lough elaborated upon the concept of rigor, concluding that

> the rigor of a solutions journalism story can be operationalized by ensuring that the story thoroughly describes how a tangible response to a problem is being implemented, contains reliable numerical data that show the effectiveness of that response, and mentions limitations of the response. (McIntyre and Lough 2019, 10)

Through its stipulated rigor, solutions journalism is autonomous in the sense that it relatively impervious to the rules and evaluations of external fields (of business and politics) that grant a solution gravitas outside of empirical measurement. By identifying solutions and leaders through such practices as analyzing data for "positive deviants," solutions journalists are proactive in their search for effectiveness rather than retroactive. A solutions journalist seeks verification and empirical grounds before reporting the solution, whereas other journalists present the solution as a test of prevailing leadership virtues.

However, interestingly, solutions journalists have expressed skepticism about the value of disinterested expertise and academia in generating effective solutions. For example, the *Solutions Journalism Network* advocated for including "sources who have a ground-level understanding, not just 30,000 foot expertise"—listing this as one of ten distinguishing characteristics of solutions journalism (Bansal and Martin 2015, 7). Likewise, Bornstein defined a social entrepreneur—the news source par excellence for solutions journalism—as intolerant of academia. For Bornstein, "Unlike artists or scholars, entrepreneurs are not satisfied with merely expressing an idea. . . . To be effective, they must remain open to signals from the environment. They do not fare well in academia, because they have no interest in specializing" (Bornstein 1998, 37). Arguably, the anti-elitist spirit of solutions journalism can be traced to public journalism, which, in turn, was heavily informed by deliberative democracy and John Dewey's democratic idealism (Schudson 2006). Indeed, nothing surmises solutions journalism's mission as clearly as Dewey's pragmatic maxim that "to foresee future objective alternatives and to be able by deliberation to choose one of them and thereby weigh its chances in the struggle for future existence, measures our freedom" (1922, 311). Thus, rather than evaluating expertise and effectiveness on the basis of their academic and institutional consecration, solutions journalists seek to weigh the proposition in terms of its future viability and empirical proof of effectiveness.

UTILITARIAN RIGOR

Solutions journalism's characteristically rigorous assessment of effectiveness—evident in its preference for data-based evidence, analysis of positive deviants and investigation of the responses and their limitations (McIntyre and Lough 2019, 9–10)—can be understood as operating within a utilitarian moral framework. Here, journalists seek to calculate, in consequentialist fashion, whose response is most likely to maximize the aggregate utility of a community. Thus, measuring the effectiveness of a response, adhering with Smart's definition of the utilitarian method, "depends only on the total goodness or badness of its consequences, i.e. on the effect of the action on the welfare of all human beings (or perhaps all sentient beings)" (Smart and Williams 1973, 4).

A utilitarian evaluation of proposed solutions was specifically what Tasmanian editors and journalists appeared reluctant to engage in, falling back, instead, upon a virtue ethics of valuable leadership. Rather than asking which solution would maximize happiness and well-being, editorials preferred to evaluate whether the proposal or implementation corresponded with appropriate virtues of strength, decisiveness, rationality, and a constellation of other minor entrepreneurial virtues. This was informed by the need to distance the paper from controversial policy debates, which, in the context of one-newspaper towns such as Hobart and Launceston, was an important economic necessity. For Bourdieu, it is a fundamental law of journalism that "if a newspaper or other news vehicle wants to reach a broad public, it has to dispense with sharp edges and anything that might divide or exclude readers" (Bourdieu 1998, 44). Indeed, a utilitarian assessment of solutions, as Tasmanian journalists perhaps foresaw, does involve a controversial "sharp edge." The divisiveness of utilitarianism has also been identified as an important philosophical weakness of this moral framework (Dewey 1922; MacIntyre 2007; Nussbaum 2006). Where there are contested definitions of the good life, different individual preferences, and different pursuits of happiness, utilitarianism proves unable to adjudicate between them—or when it does, as Haas and Steiner surmised, it requires journalists "to take sides in political conflicts, and forces them to gloss over complex problems for which no simple solutions exist" (Haas and Steiner 2006, 248). Human happiness is arguably too ephemeral and varied a concept on which to build a rigorous calculation because, as MacIntyre surmised, "there are too many different kinds of enjoyable activity, too many different modes in which happiness is achieved" (MacIntyre 2007, 64). Therefore, the rigor of solutions journalism is unable to provide an entirely objective moral standpoint to adjudicate between rival solutions.

A good example of contested utility can be found in a *British Broadcasting Corporation* story, identified by the *Solutions Journalism Network* as acceptable practice. The story profiled the conversion of underground car parks in Paris into vast mushroom farms, suggesting this was an exemplary repurposing of these increasingly redundant spaces, spaces that had been cleared by a recent decrease in car ownership. However, the issue of transportation in Paris, and the campaign to disincentivize car ownership had been enormously controversial, inspiring the Yellow Vest (*gilets jaunes*) protest movement. For these protesters—workers who felt locked out of the gentrifying Parisian inner city and penalized by the fuel taxes and other disincentives—the conversion of their former car parks into mushroom farms would have represented gentrification and exclusion, rather than increased utility. The story also somewhat flippantly described the farms as clearing out resident drug dealers and sex workers, a euphemism for a range of undesirables including the homeless, the mentally ill and the unemployed. Hage observed a similar tendency for city managers to hide marginal members of society, in order to make cities more attractive to the transnational creative class:

> More so than any of its predecessor cities, the global city has no room for marginals. How are we to rid ourselves of the homeless sleeping on the city's benches? How are we to rid ourselves of those underclasses, with their high proportion of indigenous people, third world-looking (i.e. yucky-looking) migrants and descendants of migrants, who are still cramming the non-gentrified parts of the city? (Hage 2003, 20)

Inevitably the preferences of the least governmentally legitimate members of society are sidelined, much in the same way urban renewal discourses in Tasmania were accompanied with well-meaning concern regarding dangerously unemployed youths. Urban renewal stories may only suggest maximizing the utility of under-utilized spaces. However, the utility preferences in renewal stories are, to use Martha Nussbaum's phrase, "adaptive": "people adjust their preferences to what they think they can achieve [thus] women and other deprived people frequently exhibit such 'adaptive preferences,' formed under unjust background conditions" (Nussbaum 2006, 73). Thus, while renewing derelict buildings may seem a mutually beneficial proposition, often solutions are predicated on historic injustices and exclusions that generate the opportunity. Thus, in the context of radically different preferences and ideas of utility and in conditions of increasing inequality, it is nearly impossible for a journalist, even with rigorous calculations of effectiveness, to adjudicate between rival solutions and visions of the good life without implicitly endorsing these fundamentally unequal conditions.

Utilitarian journalistic rigor seems on firmer ground when focused on negative utility and the avoidance of suffering (Smart 1958). Examining which responses are most effective in preventing the spread of malaria, for example, would seem a less controversial journalistic investigation than weighing up solutions to improve society's aggregate fitness and aerobic health where solutions might cut across different ideological lines, preferences and understandings of the good life. Indeed, the alleviation of negative utility does appear to be the preference of solutions journalists. Horne Henderson, for instance, argued that for there to be solutions journalism, first of all, "there has to be an established problem or common agreement that there's a problem" (in Bansal and Martin 2015, 42). However, if effectiveness is measured by its capacity to reduce negative utility, this would seem to place reporting firmly in the "disease model of the world" (McIntyre and Gyldensted 2018). In the same way that post–World War II psychology sought only to cure pathologies and mental disorders by empirically testing a range of effective treatments (McIntyre and Gyldensted 2018, 663–664), so too solutions journalism's preference for negative utility might prioritise social pathology, differing from traditional reporting only by proceeding to report effective treatments. Solutions journalism should, like positive psychology, foreground human strengths, flourishing, and virtues by profiling solutions that promote positive utility rather than only alleviate negative utility.

Rather, extending the discussion of hope in chapter 1, journalists might evaluate solutions in terms of their capacity to distribute social hope rather than maximize utility. As Hage argued, societies are mechanisms for the distribution of hope (2003, 9) and journalism is part of that mechanism. This distribution, according to Hage, refers "not only a distribution of 'amounts' of hope but a 'distribution' of intensities" (2016, 465). A solutions journalist might consider whether the proposed solution gives intense hope to a highly restricted audience segment. Indeed, this type of calculation is already evident in the selection of solutions with, for example, Horne Henderson suggesting:

> If the response or solution came about because somebody just threw a ton of money at it, we're probably not interested in that because that precludes a lot of other places from being able to replicate it or try it out themselves. Which speaks to another thing we look for. Is the response or solution scalable? Could it be replicated? (in Bansal and Martin 2015, 42)

This statement speaks to a democratization of social hope in solutions journalism, where those without economic capital are included rather than excluded, thereby making the story available for the hope cognitions of a wider audience. Indeed, this seems to be an important focus of solutions journalism where, looking beyond the direct beneficiaries of a given solution, a journalist seeks to maximize a sense of agency in the audience and a feeling that they, too, might create change in their community using the proposed pathway. However, the distributional model of hope proposed by Hage does face similar challenges to a utilitarian approach to evaluating effectiveness. The reported alternative pathways that inspire hope in parts of the community will depend on audience's own goals—and pathways will likely cut across agonistic goals with journalists potentially unable to adjudicate between them. Indeed, Hage subjected his distribution approach to "self-critique" in a recent essay, arguing that a distribution focus can "blind us as to the process of production" (2016, 466). In reality, Hage argued, the production of hope for one group is often premised on the extraction of hope from another: "It is one thing to say: there is an inequality in the distribution of hope and that group A receives more hope than group B, and it is another to say: group A receives more hope than group B because group A exploits group B" (2016, 466). Such an analysis of the extractive production of hope is necessary, in his view, in order to properly understand hope in the context of colonialism and ecological crisis, where "hope for someone is built on the sucking of the very possibility of hope from someone else," whether human or nonhuman (2016, 466). Extractive hope complicates journalistic judgments regarding their evaluation of expertise and effectiveness. Stories that are highly applicable for a wide range of hope cognitions may be premised on the extraction of that hope from others, much in the same way that utility preferences may be adapted to background conditions of inequality and constrained options (Nussbaum 2006, 73). However, as the utilitarian philosopher, Peter Singer, argued, we should not turn our backs on the complexity of the consequences our actions, difficult though they are (1980, 328), and indeed these are important issues to dwell upon. However, in distinguishing between rival preferences and goals, whether in relation to hope or happiness, the issue is not complexity but undecidability, since the objective moral criteria and metric turns out to be contested and subjective, providing an unstable basis for journalist's proactive and rigorous assessment of effectiveness.

HOPE, VIRTUE, AND PRACTICAL WISDOM

I would like to use this section to advance a possible alternative method for identifying and evaluating effective solutions based, instead, on a virtue ethics tradition of moral evaluation. In contrast to a utilitarian approach, virtue ethics recommends actions according to whether they correspond with relevant virtues, such as honesty, benevolence, and justice (Nussbaum 2007; MacIntyre 2007; Borden 2008). Indeed, a leading definition of "positive deviance" by Spreitzer and Sonenshein (2004) recommends moving away from utility consequentialism, by defining positive deviance as "intentional behaviors that depart from the norms of a referent group in honorable ways" (2004, 832). As such, their definition "focuses on behaviors with honorable intentions, independent of outcomes" (2004, 833). However, profiling individuals with honorable intentions alone would be too general for solutions journalism, likely falling within a trope of reporting the *Solutions Journalism Network* terms "Hero Worship" (Bansal and Martin 2015). Instead, based on the ideas developed regarding hope and expertise, it is possible to advance a more specific range of relevant virtues that might form the basis of solutions journalism reporting.

Indeed, a specific type of pragmatic optimism, which Aristotle termed "practical reason," would seem to be an especially pertinent virtue might inform the evaluative criteria of solutions journalists. In this, I share Nancy Snow's argument for considering "hope as a civic virtue, especially well-suited to democracies, that is most valuable in times like the present, when democracy faces significant challenges" (Snow 2018, 408). Snow based her argument, as did I, on Hage's theory of hope with reference, too, to Snyder's hope theory. Hope, for these thinkers, is dispositional—a trait that is learned over time, that has benefits for the individual and for society more broadly: "a democratic civic virtue" (Snow 2018, 419).

Hope itself, however, could be further refined since as some forms of extreme hope are maladaptive and unrealistic (Schneider 2001). To tighten the focus, then, regarding the types of virtuous hope that might be most relevant for solutions journalism, it is necessary to consider hope in relation to expertise and effectiveness. According to Aristotle, virtues (*arete*) and practical wisdom (*phronesis*) are interdependent (Aristotle 1999, 97). In the same way that Snyder observed that hope cognitions rely on a combination of goals and pathways, the goals of action (*telos*) are properly determined by the virtues (*arete*), yet achieving those goals requires a certain intellectual competence in deliberating and identifying the best pathway. For Aristotle, this latter skill is constitutive of practical wisdom. For Aristotle, practical wisdom is acquired in relation to particular practices since "those who have experience, are more practical than others" (1999, 97). Hoping, then, brings together virtuous goal setting with practical wisdom derived from experience and expertise in assessing pathways and, on that basis, offering advice to others.

The relationship between virtue and expertise is discussed directly by MacIntyre, whose conception of virtue is specifically in relationship to practices. Practices—defined as "any coherent and complex form of socially established cooperative human activity" (2013, 187)—offer participants external and internal goods as rewards for achieving excellence in them. This division between internal and external goods is central to MacIntyre's account of the virtues. He illustrates this division through the analogy of a child being taught to play chess (2013, 188). In order to secure the child's cooperation and interest, a teacher offers a child 50c worth of candy if the child plays one game of chess with the teacher each week, and double if she is able to win. However, this "external good" alone does not provide a reason not to cheat and every reason to cheat, provided she can cheat effectively. However, cheating would prevent the child gaining the "internal goods" to the practice of chess: "a certain highly particular kind of analytic skill, strategic imagination and competitive intensity" (MacIntyre 2013, 188), a habitus of chess. These internal goods can only be gained by participating virtuously, that is to say, without cheating. Accordingly, there are two levels of excellence in any practice: the demonstrable skill within a given practice but also a kind of meta-excellence which allows one to achieve that skill. The latter excellence is what MacIntyre calls a virtue:

> A virtue is an acquired human quality the possession and exercise of which tends to enable us to achieve those goods which are internal to practices and the lack of which effectively prevents us from achieving any such goods . . . . For it is not difficult to show for a whole range of key virtues that without them the goods internal to practices are barred to us, but not just barred to us generally, barred in a very particular way. (2013, 191)

The most relevant virtues that allow one to develop practical intelligence, for MacIntyre, are justice, courage, and honesty. These virtues govern the behavior of participants within a practice, which enable the recognition of excellence and progress in the field. In a field that was riven by dishonesty, injustice, and cowardice, there could be no practical wisdom since its deliberations would be arbitrary, unreliable, and ineffective. Thus, virtues enable the pursuit, not only of internal goods, but ultimately aim at human happiness and flourishing (*eudaimonia*) (2013, 148) by producing shared goods that "extend human powers" (2013, 199). Accordingly, in the virtuous pursuit of internal goods, practitioners create the necessary preconditions for discoveries, innovations, and breakthroughs that improve the well-being of those outside of the practice. They are literally examples of "best practice" as acknowledged by a community of fellow practitioners and, on this basis, the proper subjects of a solutions journalism rigorously testing the effectiveness of solutions.

The distinction between internal and external goods provides an interesting basis for examining journalism's reporting of "best practice," and a normative guide for how journalism might evaluate expertise and effectiveness. Journalism, according to Bourdieu, tends to favor fast thinkers and talkers who can talk in easily accessible "received ideas" (1999, 28–29), and experts who make uncontroversial moral rather than political statements (1999, 45–46). Journalism, therefore, risks creating a class of heteronomous "media-experts" and undermining "the conditions necessary for the production and diffusion of the highest human creations" (1999, 65). Heteronomous virtues serve the practical requirements of journalism, which Gans called "source considerations" (1979, 128–131). These considerations included reliability, openness, trustworthiness, authoritativeness, articulateness, and interestingness, all of which "have one overriding aim: efficiency" (1979, 129). As Gans explained, "Reporters who have only a short time to gather information must therefore attempt to obtain the most suitable news from the fewest number of sources as quickly and easily as possible, and with the least strain on the organisation's budget" (1979, 129). However, considering the centrality of journalism in consecrating information, the structural preference for eager and powerful sources threatens the integrity of other fields of cultural production by bestowing entertainment value on their spokespeople rather than values according to their field-specific criteria. With the rise of the public relations industry (Davis 2000), sources are more regularly spokespeople for institutions who, from a journalist's point of view, can be relied upon to provide useful, succinct, and official comments (Gans 1979, 129). However, these sources cannot provide the requisite practical wisdom to articulate pathways to given goals, since they are not practitioners themselves but concerned with well-being of the institutionalized aspects of the practice. Practices rely on institutions to be sustained (MacIntyre 2013, 194) yet there needs to be a clear division of labor, with practitioners maintaining the integrity of the internal goods (cultural capital), while the institution manages the external goods (economic and social capital). Thus, while spokespeople tend to speak on behalf of the institutionalized aspects of the practice, practitioners can speak with practical wisdom regarding best practice pathways to specific goals.

CONCLUSION

Solutions journalism cannot do without the concept of expertise but can do without experts. Solutions are dependent on claims of effectiveness, and such claims are hollow without recourse to a form of expertise or experience that can attest to their effectiveness. However, in my analysis of solutions reporting in "New Tasmania," effectiveness and expertise were more often simulated via expert-centric metaphors or by conflating experts with interests, rather than interviewing independent experts. Likewise, established solutions journalists tend to balance expertise with on the ground experience implementing change. In light of this ambiguous category in reporting solutions, this chapter has sought to restore expertise as a normative ideal in evaluating the effectiveness of solutions and informing news access.

While the definition of expertise is perhaps uncontroversial (Schudson 2006), expertise is perhaps less straightforwardly mobilized in adjudicating between rival solutions. Solutions journalists have foregrounded a rigorous assessment of effectiveness as a characteristic and objective method, reflecting a utilitarian moral calculous. However, in the context of rival conceptions of utility—different worldviews, values, priorities, and unequal social locations—utilitarian rigor may mask a subjective or unreflexive evaluation of solutions. Instead, I argued that virtue ethics, based on the ideals of practical wisdom and realistic hope, represents a more useful model for evaluating news sources, solutions, and effectiveness. In the same way that solutions journalists themselves are virtuously involved in promoting best practice within journalism (with less regard for strictly external values or market pressures), so too should solutions journalists seek out correspondingly autonomous individuals within other fields, experts with the requisite practical wisdom to apply the insights of their field to contribute to human flourishing generally.

Chapter 7

Conclusion

Four years after the 2014 case study, Tasmania finds itself in a comparable position. The Liberal government is facing its first Tasmanian state election since winning office. Each day, journalists relate new political policies, propositions, initiatives, success stories, and opportunities to their audiences. And, through the local news media, editors and opinion leaders relentlessly evaluate leadership and imply the type of stewardship that Tasmania requires. Many of these challenges are the same: health remains a pressing concern for many Tasmanians, the Mount Wellington cable car hangs in limbo, enthusiasm about Chinese investment has turned to concern about foreign donations and influence, and the booming tourism industry is putting pressure on public roads and rental markets. There is a mood for action on these issues, and strong polling for the Tasmanian Labor Party under the new leadership of Rebecca White suggests it could be a mood for change.

Perhaps sensing this, Will Hodgman launched the election campaign with a different construction metaphor than Treasurer Gutwein (2014) deployed in his first state budget speech. Instead of "Laying the Foundations" the Liberal Party would now be "Building Your Future" and "Taking Tasmania to the Next Level." The warning implied in this construction metaphor was that changing the government would shake the economic foundations, risk economic collapse, and prevent Tasmania from reaching its true potential on the next level. Thus, the economic construction metaphor served to legitimize the government's economic stewardship while casting newcomers as recklessly endangering the structure. Indeed, as in 2014, a number of voices were marginalized who might have otherwise been offered the opportunity to contribute their vision for a different Tasmania.

Despite this optimistic tone, in terms of policy solutions, the election was uniquely myopic and negative. One solution dominated the debate and arguably decided the outcome: the proposed banning of poker machines from Tasmanian pubs and clubs. Gambling addiction and debate over the extent of poker machine distribution throughout Tasmania's poorest suburbs had been a perennial and deeply controversial issue. The history of how one interstate family, the Farrell family, came to possess a monopoly license for the state's 3,500 poker machines spans half a century and was a policy unanimously supported policy by both major political parties (Boyce 2017). While the history of the deal is murky—with details of the inducements used to leverage support for the policy only now emerging (Boyce 2017)—the ongoing social effects of the Tasmanian gambling monopoly are clear: over AU$110 million in poker machine losses per annum that come disproportionately from problem gamblers in Tasmania's poorest communities (Livingston 2017). So, when the new Tasmanian Labor leader, Rebecca White, proposed a phase-out of all pokies from pubs and clubs—limiting them to casinos and removing them from suburbs—the announcement broke decades' long bipartisan support for the Farrell family. The response from the gaming industry during the election campaign was an unmissable flood of campaign funding and a saturation of political advertisements, both through the Liberal Party (who advocated for a twenty-five-year extension of the poker machine license) and through direct campaigns from the hospitality and gambling industry. Tasmania has the least transparent political donation regulations of any Australian state or territory with parties only required to disclose the source of donations over AU$13,500, and even this partial disclosure can be postponed until after the election is held (Eccleston and Jay 2019). So it was not until February 2019, nearly a year after their comprehensive election victory, that The Tasmania Liberal Party declared AU$400,000 in donations from the gambling industry; "equal to nearly 90% of the party's declared donations, and a tenfold increasing on the amount gambling groups gave in the previous election" (Wood et al. 2019). Thus, despite the rhetoric "New Tasmania"—its spirit of entrepreneurial courage, bipartisanship and diversification, and its idealization of a Tasmania freed from decades of rancorous development conflict—the 2018 election delivered a newly divisive political reality with the old Tasmanian themes of monopolization and corruption newly salient.

SOLUTIONS JOURNALISM

The scenario that this book presented—the over-reliance on political and business spokespeople for solutions, the framing of leadership according to masculine and entrepreneurial ideals, the marginalization of expertise and direct experience, and the consequently narrow range of perceived options in the public domain—is familiar globally, including in places where solutions journalism has emerged as a formalized reporting practice. The election of Donald Trump in 2016 and the subsequent revelations of external influence and corruption have shaken public confidence in the democratic process in ways that are familiar for Tasmanians. In the *New York Times*, solutions journalists read his surprise election victory—which featured strident condemnation of political failure, crime and disorder—as an affirmation of their normative mission: to tell the untold stories of progress, successes, and solutions, and to counteract the false perception of intractability, incompetence, and disorder promoted by traditional news values (Bornstein and Rosenberg 2016). Accordingly, they saw in Trump's victory a parable of how "a steady diet of news about violence, corruption and incompetence leads to increased fear, learned helplessness, hopelessness, cynicism, depression, isolation, hostility, contempt and anxiety" (Bornstein and Rosenberg 2016). However, the lesson for solutions journalists in this episode, as from this book's study of "New Tasmania," is more complex.

For Martin Seligman, the cofounder of the learned helplessness model of optimism, the victory of Donald Trump could be attributed, on the contrary, to a glut of hopeful utterances in American political discourse. In a column for the *Washington Post*, a month before the election, Seligman presented the results of his regular content analysis of both Nominees' convention speeches. Their explanatory style and rumination was used to benchmark their relative optimism, a measure that Zullow and Seligman had used to predict each presidential candidate's election victory nine times out of ten, as well as the margin of their victory from 1900 to 1984 (Zullow and Seligman 1990). However, in 2016, Seligman declined to accompany his conclusion—that Clinton was by far the more optimistic candidate—with a prediction that she would win the General Election. Instead, he conceded that the predictive power of optimism was waning. The reason he gave for this striking shift, paradoxically, was his own theory of learned helplessness. It was now so widely known and adopted by political candidates that "authentic optimism has gotten hard to hear" (2016). Noting that pundits, staffers, and candidates alike both regularly cite his theory of optimism, even asking him to write their speeches, he suggested that "when everyone is doing their best to sound like Reagan, it's hard for any candidate to gain an optimism advantage. And it's hard for voters, and sometimes researchers, to filter the authentic from the contrived" (2016). Trump's campaign was not short on optimistic solutions, despite anchoring them in negative rumination. Solutions were deployed to great political effect with his slogans, "we will build the wall" and "we will make America Great again" (in Kellner 2017, 123), which, despite stretching credulity, drew enormous support and served to construct Trump's political legitimacy on an ability to make the impossible possible through sheer entrepreneurial willpower.

Accordingly, hope is something of a saturated market in presidential campaigns, and arguably journalism more generally. As was seen in Tasmanian reportage, optimistic solutions were pervasive in even the most traditional forms of journalism, as well as opinion pieces and editorials. More generally, a solution-focus is increasingly found in feature-length stories, uplifting documentaries and advertisements. Michael Moore's typically scathing documentaries have lately adopted a pragmatic solutions-orientation with *Where to Invade Next?* (Moore 2015). Meanwhile, documentaries such as *Tomorrow* (Laurent and Dion 2015) typify a new style of uplifting documentary profiling sustainability solutions, supplanting more pessimistic sustainability documentaries such as *Gaslands*, *An Inconvenient Truth*, and *Food Inc.* Likewise, Intel's high-budget documentary series, *Meet the Makers*, aimed to profile "how Intel Edison micro-computing technology is being used by entrepreneurs, musicians, scientists and other 'makers' in unique ways to solve problems for businesses and society at large" (Maddox 2016). In one instance, Tasmanian scientists were profiled fixing microchips to backs of honey bees to cure a disease threatening their survival and our food supply (Maddox 2016).

The pervasiveness of optimistic solutions has led to a new suspicion that hope is being deployed inauthentically to placate and sooth, to popularize technical fixes to structural issues and to acclimatize audiences to unhappy compromises. The charge was leveled most directly by Swedish Climate Activist Greta Thunberg in a series of fiery speeches delivered at Davos and the UN Climate Action Summit (Thunberg 2019a, 2019b):

> Adults keep saying: "We owe it to the young people to give them hope." But I don't want your hope. I don't want you to be hopeful. I want you to panic. I want you to feel the fear I feel every day. And then I want you to act. I want you to act as you would in a crisis. I want you to act as if our house is on fire. Because it is. (Thunberg 2019a)

However, the climate movement itself is hardly immune to the instrumentalization of hope. In the midst of Australia's worst-ever bushfire season, indigenous Australian climate campaigner, Philip Marrii Winzer, railed against the climate movement's "toxic hope" (Winzer 2020). To fundraise and grow its volunteer base, he argued, "the movement reminds us relentlessly why we should still have hope. Every small win—governments taking action, corporations acknowledging climate change, new technology—is another reason for hope, another reason to believe we can beat this thing" (Winzer 2020). The hope offered, he argued, was akin to the toxic hope that makes someone endure an abusive relationship, a hope that stalls a necessary schism with colonialism, racism, and ecocide. Instead, "Real hope can be found in the opportunity this crisis presents to end these toxic, dysfunctional and imbalanced relationships once and for all" (Winzer 2020).

The surplus of hope today, and its frequent misuse and instrumentalization, presents a different normative mission for solutions journalists. The problem is not that there is a surfeit of solutions and optimistic discourse in the public sphere—only to be found "in the food sections, in local columns, in 'feel-good stories,' and in what used to be called the 'women's pages' " (Seligman 2019, 491). Rather, the problem *is* the reporting of solutions. The instrumentalization of public hope for private gain; the overreliance on political and business spokespeople; and the masculine and entrepreneurial leadership ideals embedded in the very language used to describe solutions—these pervasive aspects of solutions journalism erode audience's stocks of hope. As such, the mission of solutions journalism goes beyond reporting responses. The job of solutions journalism is to distribute realistic hope to audiences by extending the governmental field and scrutinizing the goals and pathways of leaders while also autonomously platforming those sources who are best placed to evaluate goals, pathways, and inspire a sense of agency: sources with direct experience, expertise, and practical wisdom.

EXPANDING THE GOVERNMENTAL FIELD

This book's argument is in agreement with Benson's characterization of media power as, ultimately, "the power to 'consecrate', that is, name an event, person, or idea as worthy of wider consideration" (Benson 1998, 469). Solutions journalism brings to this responsibility a more autonomous, standardized, and rigorous practice of reporting—consecrating only scalable solutions that have empirical evidence to substantiate their claims. Solutions journalism is premised on the belief that there are other ideas, solutions, initiatives, goals, pathways, leaders and experts that are worthy of wider consideration—yet many of the ideas with real transformative potential and realistic hope are missed by news values that prioritize power, celebrity, and consequence. While solutions journalists already appear to see leadership and expertise in places that are often overlooked, this book recommends solutions journalists *expand* the governmental field rather than complement it.

In contrast to the globally connected entrepreneurs, corporations, and political leaders (Lippman 1922, 35), solutions journalists looked to a governmental field constituted, especially, by global networks of social entrepreneurs, changemakers, and community leaders. In practice, this means that the solutions of politicians and entrepreneurs are seldom profiled in solutions journalism since they are not readily implemented by communities and are, in any case, often widely reported elsewhere. Rather than creating a parallel community of power, whether in agonistic or supplementary relation to the dominant field, *expanding* the governmental field means subjecting a plurality of solutions, leadership types and expertise to solutions journalism's characteristic rigor. Safeguarding public stocks of hope and trust requires both reactive scrutiny of large consequential solutions offered by prominent politicians and entrepreneurs (where hope is frequently invested), as well as a proactive search for effective innovations and success stories from smaller players. Thus, solutions reporting may also involve a traditional watchdog role, holding power accountable to their stated goals, triangulating their claims with expert sources and contrasting goals and solutions. Thus, the normative mission of solutions journalism is holding power to account for its instrumentalization of hopeful utterances in the public interest—distributing hope by restoring confidence in hopeful utterances and helping audiences distinguish between authentic and inauthentic hope.

A TAXONOMY OF SOLUTIONS JOURNALISM

For this task, I have proposed Snyder's "hope theory" as the most relevant framework for adjudicating, sourcing, and investigating solutions (Snyder 2002; Snyder, Shane, et al. 2002). Hope is not, as solutions journalists sometimes worry, a feel-good emotion and not a proper journalistic concern (Bornstein 2012). Rather, hope is "primarily a way of thinking, with feelings playing an important albeit contributory role" (Snyder 2002, 249). Indeed, Snyder's model of hope has much to recommend it compared to comparable theories such as Seligman's more famous theory of learned optimism as explanatory style (1991). It constructs hope as diametrically opposed to excuse making (Snyder 1989) with solutions journalism likewise interested in combating equivocating leadership (Solutions Journalism Network 2020); it provides a lens for combating "false hope" (Snyder, Rand, et al. 2002) and promoting "realistic optimism" (Schneider 2001); and it is scalable from individual to social hope (Jin and Kim 2019; Snyder and Feldman 2000). I also argued that, rather than standardizing solutions journalism as a monolithic practice, hope theory provides a useful taxonomy of different types of solutions journalism, targeted to each of its three foundational concepts: goals, pathways, and agency. As Schneider argued, "Realistic optimism relies on regular reality checks to update assessments of progress, fine-tune one's understanding of potential opportunities, refine causal models of situations, and re-evaluate planned next steps" (2001, 257). Journalism is well placed to provide these reality checks at each of the goal formation, pathway evaluation and agency stages of the hope process.

Since all action in Snyder's view is in some way goal-directed, a journalist might firstly intervene with lines of questioning that encourage powerful sources to state their goal and state it clearly. Abstract, ill-defined or vague goals, Snyder found, are less likely to be achieved or pursued (Snyder 2002, 250). Such goal commitments might then form the basis of solutions stories, with journalists operationalizing the norms of balance and verification to triangulate these goals with the values and priorities of other sources or with expert comment. Likewise, in relation to agency evaluation, journalists have a role in profiling success stories, noting progress, and contextualizing present challenges in the context of past achievements. Success stories serve to restore confidence that collective action in pursuing shared goals is possible and rewarding while proving the necessary reality checks that moderate this self-belief, acknowledging the benefit of "a slight positive self-referential bias, but not an extreme illusion that is counterproductive" (Snyder, Rand, et al. 2002, 1007).

SOLUTION ENSEMBLES

This thesis was motivated by a concern that too few voices and options are considered in the construction of future potentiality and in "framing the shape of the new" (Beers 2010, 121). The constriction of the governmental field does a disservice to the full range of skills, experiences, and ideas that could be taken seriously and form the basis of solutions journalism. Indeed, pluralism is a central recommendation for a solutions journalism built on hope theory. A high hope society with a powerful sense of agency in pursuing ambitious goals is proficient at generating a plurality of goals and pathways (Snyder and Feldman 2000). As Snyder and Feldman surmise, "There presently are not enough valued goals in our society [beyond] money making, physical appearance, intellectual achievement, and athletic accomplishments" (2000, 391). Instead, they recommend promoting a plurality of goals that, in comparison, "offer benefits for the majority rather than the select few" (2000, 392). Societies such as Tasmania that have been subjected to long periods of economic precarity and instability appear more willing to lock in behind a strong leader with a limited repertoire of goals, journalism has an interest in offering people a diversified investment portfolio of goals and pathways (Snyder, Rand, et al. 2002, 1010).

Solutions journalists seem attuned to this requirement with the *Solutions Journalism Network* now encouraging anxious, self-isolating audiences to "discover our rich selection of solutions stories on COVD-19" with hundreds of stories listed across three subtopics: containment, coping and adapting, and care and compassion ("Solutions Story Tracker" 2020). Indeed, the network's recent shift toward aggregating content under broader issues and topics is significant. Overwhelmingly, solutions journalism pieces, as advised in several iterations of their educational toolkit (Bansal and Martin 2015; The Solutions Journalism Network 2020), have tended to center on a character confronting a challenging solutions with a novel approach, documenting the pitfalls, setbacks, and limitations of their endeavor. This fits within what Benson (2009) has termed a personalized narrative format, which, in his analysis of immigration reporting, tends not to produce a plurality of perspectives and frames. Rather, to make news more multi-perspectival, according to Benson, journalism should adopt a multi-format, opinion ensemble style that is typical of the French press (Benson 2009). This involves, collecting a range of opinion, editorial, and straight news pieces and assembling them in relation to one pressing challenge or current event. Solutions stories, as in the *New York Times* and the *Huffington Post*, are typically segregated from traditional reporting, appearing in dedicated solution columns. In this format, the platforms do not showcase an abundance of pathways or goals pertinent to an issue of current concern. This formatting decision also potentially encourages solutions journalism to draw from a distinct governmental field by encouraging solutions journalists to report stories that are not covered elsewhere. Instead, what might be termed a solution ensemble format might usefully pluralize goals, pathways, and perspectives. Indeed, just as the *Solutions Journalism Network* explores the value of aggregating solutions stories, so too *Quartz* has lately published "What Happens Next": a series of solution ensembles regarding the future of aging, college, water, gaming, home, work, food, cities, money, and fact ("What Happens Next" 2019). These new formats may serve as a model for future reporting, based on a hope theory framework, with future research in this area able to test the effectiveness solution ensembles as a means of augmenting social hope.

METAPHOR ADAPTATION

An important way that hope is made inauthentic (Seligman 2016), I have argued, is through the pervasive use of conceptual metaphor. Pervasively, navigation metaphors were deployed to dramatize leadership virtues of determination and strength, and expert virtues of effectiveness and specialist knowledge. As I argued, the risks, virtues and vices implied by navigational and construction metaphors, in particular, were deployed to justify a myopic focus on the leaders' preferred vision while marginalizing alternative voices. Metaphors tended to valorize a unified leader and protagonist (whether as navigator, engineer, or carer) while highlighting the dangers of alternatives as distracting, reckless, or unrealistic. Likewise, as chapter 6 noted, the incongruous prevalence of expertise metaphors while actual experts were rarely interviewed or were supplanted by "industry experts." Often metaphors were not merely linguistic but also enacted, as in the case of the performative visit of the president of China. In this case, acts of care and parental wisdom were performed liberally, constructing the visit as an expression of parental care—conscientiously correcting the spelling of Tasmanian primary school students—when in fact, the visit was a precursor to a trade deal and investment talks with Tasmanian exporters.

Navigation, construction, and nurturance are "source domains" of hope. In our everyday lives, we are familiar with the act of navigating in hope of reaching our destination; of building something in hope that it will last; of caring for someone in hope that they will grow and get better. The pervasiveness of these metaphors in solutions journalism, at an average of 3.13 per news story, routinely engages our hope cognitions with less necessity for sources to rigorously defend or articulate their goals or furnish their pathways with evidence or expertise demonstrating its likely effectiveness. Thus, with the surplus of inauthentic hope in the public sphere, solutions journalism increasingly reads as a series of governmental clichés—with "moving forward together" perhaps the worst culprit—without providing audiences with real hope, which I have argued is a critical, reflexive, and cognitive process (rather than an emotion).

However, this argument regarding metaphors does not present a straightforward recommendation for solutions journalists. Metaphors are unavoidable tools in cognition and discourse. Our ability to discuss and evaluate such abstract concepts as the future, hope, leadership, or expertise would be greatly impoverished without recourse to metaphor: without "understanding and experiencing one thing in terms of another" (Lakoff and Johnson 2008, 5). Indeed, the nature of metaphor is in its imperfect appropriation of previous embodied experience to navigate present dilemmas and decisions (Lakoff and Johnson 1999, 20). Thus, all metaphor is, to an extent, a mental simulation of the phenomena in question. However, these qualifications should not mitigate the responsibility of journalists to reflect upon their use of metaphor and their incorporation of leaders' preferred metaphors in their own writing.

Indeed, the sample also proved that metaphors are flexible and adaptable structures that could be deliberately revised by journalists. The sample period captured a time of metaphorical innovation, adaptation, and reframing: nation-building metaphors were largely replaced by references to the importance of foundations and structural integrity, while ecological concern for future generations was redirected to concern for inheritance, prosperity, and international debt. While some of these innovations appeared to be motivated by strategic political considerations and ideology, such metaphorical innovation serves a reminder that present schemas are adaptable by journalists themselves, acting autonomously in the public interest. Revaluating this metaphorical schema conducted by solutions journalists might be motivated by a concern for social hope and expanding the governmental field—an endeavor that could be valuably supported by journalism scholarship. As an autonomous journalistic practice, solutions journalism should take metaphors seriously as cognitive tools in hope psychology and seek to implement their own schemas for describing solutions and evaluating leadership and expertise rather than import the metaphors of powerful sources. Indeed, autonomous journalists should exercise discretion in broadcasting the preferred metaphors of powerful sources by, at the very least, placing their preferred figures of speech between apostrophes, especially when those metaphorical constructions originate from the social control apparatus of the Communist Party of China. However, metaphorical language is so pervasive as to be often inconspicuous, and the commonality in the source domains and their links with ideological positions is often not obvious. As such, this book has aimed to raise the profile of the most common metaphorical constructions so that journalists and others might exercise greater caution and reflexivity.

CONCLUSION

For me, solutions journalism is a source of hope, a pathway that could pluralize pathways, and an agent that could augment agency. As an object of hope, writing this book about solutions journalism presented me with similar dilemmas, frustrations, and exhilarations as those that confront solutions journalists: How to report a solution with hope but without bias? How to subject the practice to fair scrutiny and critique without disregarding the perspectives of practitioners implementing change? How to make solutions journalism scalable, without underplaying its embeddedness in local practices? In one sense at least, I would not recommend my chosen strategy. Rather than profiling a best-practice alternative, as solutions journalists do, this book looked to the journalists of a mountainous island to the South of mainland Australia; a heart-shaped jewel in the Southern Ocean; an "open and accessible island imaginary of international desire" (Stratford 2008, 577). I proposed that "New Tasmania," an island re-imagining itself, would hold lessons for a profession re-imagining itself. Just as Tasmania has the cleanest air in the world making it the best location to sample atmospheric carbon, likewise, its journalism has been undisturbed by solution-focused practices that have gained a foothold in the Northern Hemisphere. As such, Tasmania provided a sample of solution reporting in splendid isolation, and a counterpoint to studies of standardized autonomous solutions journalism. Nonetheless, Tasmania was buffeted by the same global winds of change and adversity, raised expectations and dashed hopes. How did Tasmanian journalists, without an agreed blueprint, seek to address the erosion of hope and public engagement? How was the interdisciplinary governmental field mobilized to sandbag collective hopes and revive confidence that Tasmania could weather the storm? Even though their responses to these challenges were imperfect, studying them enriches global understandings of solution reporting, a practice as pervasive as hope itself.

Appendices

SAMPLE COLLECTION

Overall, 1,172 articles were collected from three Tasmanian news outlets over a six-month period in 2014. The three news outlets chosen, The Mercury, The Examiner, and ABC Tasmania, were selected because they represent a diversity of ownership models, regional locations, and broadcast mediums.

First published in 1858, the *Mercury* is now the largest-selling daily newspaper in Tasmania with a yearly Monday to Friday readership of 51,000 in 2017 ("Australian Newspaper Readership, 12 Months to December 2016" 2016). The paper services the state capital of Hobart and the South of Tasmania. In the early 1880s, the paper was an outspoken supporter of large state infrastructure projects, such as the controversial Franklin dam and a vocal critic of conservationists (Lester 2005, 127). Formerly owned by the Davie Brothers, the *Mercury* was purchased by News Limited in 1986 and became a tabloid in 1993 (Lester and Hutchins 2009, 284). The *Mercury* continues to occupy a relatively pro-development editorial position in debates over conservation and the economy. However, in interviews with the editor, Matt Deighton, presented in chapter 6, it appears the paper has sought to appeal to a more diverse political audience in recent years by, for instance, providing a platform for a wide range of political views in its opinion pages. In addition, the paper also appears to have recently tended to favor the tourism industry over large-scale extractive industries. In addition to its weekend supplement, the *Sunday Tasmanian*, the paper also provides online news and video content on its website (themercury.com.au) to paid subscribers.

The second outlet chosen for inclusion in the sample was the Examiner. Founded by three Congregationalists in 1842, the *Examiner* is Tasmania's oldest newspaper. The newspaper services the city of Launceston and the north of Tasmania with a Monday to Friday readership of 36,000 ("Australian Newspaper Readership, 12 Months to December 2016" 2016), almost half the *Mercury*'s current readership. Just as the *Mercury* is mindful of its comparatively progressive Hobart readership, likewise, the *Examiner* reports and editorializes for a diverse Northern Tasmanian and rural audience. Like the *Mercury*, the *Examiner* has also developed an online platform (examiner.com .au) to supplement its newspaper distribution business.

The third outlet chosen for inclusion in the sample was ABC Tasmania. With a 25 percent prime-time share, the national broadcaster is more popular in Tasmania than anywhere else in Australia (Spiegelman 2015). It provides local, national, and international content through nightly news bulletins on television and also through its online platform (http://www.abc.net.au/news /tas). The charter of the ABC is legislated in section 6 of the Australian Broadcasting Corporation Act 1983 (Cth) and commits the corporation to broadcast "programs that contribute to a sense of national identity, inform and entertain, and reflect the cultural diversity of, the Australian community." This duty is partly discharged through an independent daily news bulletin where the duty to inform involves a commitment to impartiality and accuracy.

DATA COLLECTION

The articles were collected over three, two-month sample periods in 2014: April–May, August–September, and November–December. The division of the sample period was designed to capture a variety of propositions and proponents over one entire year. The last sample period, November–December, was chosen to collect summary articles and editorials, which typically surmise the state's progress for the year and its hopes for the future.

Newspaper articles were collected using NewsBank. This service provides a full text electronic database of newspaper articles including the *Examiner* and the *Mercury*. In a recent study of the utility and liability of these archives, Ridout et al. (2012, 451) recommend text archive services, such as NewsBank because "they isolate articles of interest via keyword searches, as opposed to scanning manually through pages of text or, for those newspapers that had them, consulting a periodical index." However, the authors caution that some differences may exist between the printed newspaper copy and the electronic text. In particular, they found that international and national stories purchased through wire services were less likely to be included in electronic databases (2012, 453). The sample for this research did not include any international stories but did cover some national stories where there was a local Tasmania angle.

Accordingly, to confirm there was no serious discrepancy between the paper copy and the digital data, a week-long test case was conducted comparing hand-selected propositional articles from the *Mercury* and the *Examiner* with articles sourced from NewsBank using targeted keyword searches. The manual scanning for propositional journalism in the *Examiner* and the *Mercury* proceeded with the following definition of Tasmanian solutions journalism: *Any news, opinion or editorial article (excluding sport and real estate sections) that was centrally concerned with, and took as its cue, a recommendation for a given proposition where that proposition was considered consequential for Tasmania.* Such propositions could be articulated by any source, including editors or journalists, and could be from editorials, opinion pieces, and standard journalistic reporting. The sport and real estate sections were excluded because, despite discussing propositions and optimistic hopes for the future, they were not consequential for the state of Tasmania. That is to say, using a term discussed in chapter 3, sport and real estate articles did not pertain to a "collective future" (Bain et al. 2013) or "social hopes" (Snyder and Feldman 2000), but to private, short-term futures and hopes.

This weeklong sample of the *Mercury* and the *Examiner* conducted in the first week of April 2014 (Tuesday April 1 to Monday April 7) produced twenty propositional articles. Using word frequency calculation tools, a list of key propositional terms was identified. Recurrent and generic words from these articles were recorded and formed the basis of a keyword list. These were: future, opportunity, proposal, idea, bid, plan, push, vision, Tasmania, Burnie, Hobart, and Launceston. Using search coding terms OR and AND, the search was made in NewsBank for any articles from April 1 to 7, 2014, with the words: "future" OR "opportunity" OR "proposal" OR "idea" OR "bid" OR "plan" OR "push" OR "vision" AND "Tasmania" OR "Burnie" OR "Hobart" OR "Launceston." This search returned all the articles from the sample plus eight extra articles, which were not deemed propositional. While this confirmed that propositional articles tended to be included in both the paper text and the digital copy, it did suggest that additional manual exclusion on non-propositional articles would be required.

The ABC does not provide a comparable keyword searching tool for their online archive. Stories can, however, be searched according to location using the "Google Advance" tool for searching within a nominated URL (Universal Resource Locator). This enabled searching of thc ABC's online database (http://www.abc.net.au/news/archive) for Tasmanian-specific articles. Non-propositional articles were then manually excluded using the same definition outlined earlier. All together this data collection produced an overall sample of 1,172 propositional articles.

METAPHOR ANALYSIS

Content analysis seeks to make inferences based on the measurement of variables in a specific communication text in order to draw inferences about the text's meaning (Riffe et al. 2014, 18). In particular, this study employed a "metaphor analysis" methodology (Hellsten et al. 2014) to locate and organize key "framing devices" (Gamson and Modigliani 1989) into coherent news frames. Following this approach, inspired by Lakoff (2016) and Bourdieu (1996), all instances of metaphorical language were collected and grouped into conceptually related categories to determine the most prevalent evaluative metaphors used to describe the act of proposing.

Metaphors were defined as figurative (rather than literal) language where concepts from a "source domain" are used to talk about subjective of objective phenomena in a "target domain" (Lakoff and Johnson 2003, 48). This employed Lakoff and Johnson's (1999, 60) theory of "complex metaphor" where primary metaphors coherently form parts of more complex metaphors. Accordingly, metaphorical language can be expected to correspond with broader categories corresponding to common fields of meaning and experience.

Following John Sonnett's semantic analysis (2010, 703), this research employed a "snowball sampling with multiple points of entry" procedure in order to identify key metaphorical frames and exclude ephemeral metaphors and idioms. Idiomatic and figurative language was collected uncategorized then a secondary reading of this material was conducted that sought to order the collected language into conceptually related categories. A thesaurus was used to identify semantically related words and determine whether these words formed part of the same "source domain." Because metaphors are pervasive in news texts and speech generally, one challenge associated with this methodology was deciding which metaphorical expressions to include in the content analysis. For instance, common economic language such as "price rise" is metaphorical, relating to the concept of "more is up, less is down" (Lakoff and Johnson 2003, 22). However, bearing in mind this study's research questions and the centrality of leadership, metaphors were only included when the "target domain" was relevant to conceptualizing the subjective concepts of the future, propositionality, and leadership. Accordingly, metaphorical expressions used to reason, evaluate, or describe propositions or proponents were collected while numerical metaphors such as "more is up" were not included. Extraneous metaphors and idioms that did not cohere with broader conceptual categories were excluded. This method resulted in a small number of metaphorical concepts, which contained numerous metaphorical expressions.

Source Analysis

The research also sought to determine who the most prominent news sources were in the sample. A news source was defined as anyone quoted directly in stories. Typically, a news article's most important source, or "primary definer" (Hall et al. 2013, 57), is quoted early in the text, often in the lead or, less commonly, in attributive headlines. Accordingly, rather than include all quoted sources from the articles, only the first three quoted sources were quantified, forming an overall tally of the most important and prevalent sources. This list was further narrowed to include only the top-twenty most quoted sources from each news outlet. Because opinion articles were also included in the sample, the authors of these articles were considered as important sources and included in the tally as a one quote.

BASELINE INTERVIEW QUESTIONS

Two interviews were conducted. One with the then-editor of the *Mercury*, Matthew Deighton, on September 9, 2015, and another with the editor of the *Examiner*, Simon Tennant, on October 27, 2015. The baseline questions that formed the structure of the semi-structured interviews are as follows.

1. Where do you see leadership coming from in Tasmania? Who is leading the debate about Tasmania's future?
2. Are you conscious of particular voices or industries trying to dominate debate at the expense of a more diverse range of voices?
3. How do you go about identifying good leaders and quality ideas for Tasmania's future?
4. From your experience working in the community over a period of time, do you detect a change, a sense of optimism or frustration?
5. When reporting propositions for the future does your organization try to differentiate its reporting for its competitors?

The selection and invitation of interviewees and the recording and transcription of interviews were subject to ethics approval by the University of Tasmania's Social Sciences Human Research Ethics Committee (SSHREC).

References

ABC Tasmania. 2012. "Timber Company Gunns in Administration." September 25, 2012. https://www.abc.net.au/news/2012-09-25/timber-company-gunns-in-ad ministration/4279136.

———. 2014. "Chinese President Xi Jinping Moved by Handwritten Letter from Launceston Primary School Students." November 18, 2014.

Abey, D. 2014a. "Acres of Options on Jobs Horizon." *The Mercury*, April 13, 2014.

———. 2014b. "Godfather of the Tasmanian Whisky Industry." *The Mercury*, May 11, 2014.

———. 2014c. "World of Opportunity in Tasmania's Bottled Gold." *The Mercury*, May 11, 2014.

Abramson, Lyn Y., Martin E. Seligman, and John D. Teasdale. 1978. "Learned Helplessness in Humans: Critique and Reformulation." *Journal of Abnormal Psychology* 87(1): 49.

Aitamurto, Tanja, and Anita Varma. 2018. "The Constructive Role of Journalism: Contentious Metadiscourse on Constructive Journalism and Solutions Journalism." *Journalism Practice* 12(6): 695–713. https://doi.org/10.1080/17512786.2018.14 73041.

Albanese, Anthony. 2014. "Mob with No Agenda on Road to Nowhere." *The Mercury*, August 18, 2014.

Alessandrini, M. 2012. "Political Chronicles-Tasmania January to July 2012." *Australian Journal of Politics and History* 58(4): 656–661.

Altman, C. 2003. "The New Tasmania—A Special Report." *The Australian*, April 5, 2003.

Amiel, Pauline, and Matthew Powers. 2019. "A Trojan Horse for Marketing? Solutions Journalism in the French Regional Press." *European Journal of Communication* 34(3): 233–247. https://doi.org/10.1177/0267323119830054.

Anderson, C. W., Emily Bell, and Clay Shirky. 2014. *Post-Industrial Journalism.* New York: Tow Center for Digital Journalism. https://academiccommons.columb ia.edu/doi/10.7916/D8N01JS7.

Andrews, A. 2012. "Tasmania in Recession: Eslake." *The Examiner*, August 28, 2012.

Ardern, Jacinda, and Nigel Latta. 2020. "Conversations on COVID-19: Nigel Latta." *Facebook*, 2020. https://www.facebook.com/watch/?ref=external&v=21461089 9823257.

Arendt, H. 2013. *The Human Condition*. 2nd ed. Chicago: University of Chicago Press.

Aristotle. 1999. *Nicomachean Ethics*. Edited by W. D. Ross. Kitchener, ON: Batoche Books. https://doi.org/10.4324/9781912281848.

Associated Press. 2004. "Hope Magazine to Cease Publication Because of Financial Woes." *AP*, September 10, 2004. https://archive.commondreams.org/scriptfiles/headlines04/0910-03.htm.

Australian Associated Press. 2011. "It's Time to Act on Climate: Gillard." September 13, 2011.

Australian Institute of Health and Welfare. 2019. "Deaths in Australia." *Canberra*. https://www.aihw.gov.au/reports/life-expectancy-death/deaths-in-australia/contents/leading-causes-of-death.

"Australian Newspaper Readership, 12 Months to December 2016." 2016. *Melbourne*. http://www.roymorgan.com/industries/media/readership/newspaper-readership.

Avelino, Flor, Julia M. Wittmayer, René Kemp, and Alex Haxeltine. 2017. "Game-Changers and Transformative Social Innovation." *Ecology and Society* 22(4). https://doi.org/10.5751/ES-09897-220441.

Bain, Paul G., Matthew J. Hornsey, Renata Bongiorno, Yoshihisa Kashima, and Daniel Crimston. 2013. "Collective Futures: How Projections about the Future of Society Are Related to Actions and Attitudes Supporting Social Change." *Personality and Social Psychology Bulletin* 39(4): 523–539. https://doi.org/10.1177/0146167213478200.

Baird, B. 2006. "Sexual Citizenship in 'The New Tasmania.'" *Political Geography* 25(8): 964–987.

Baker, M. 2014. "Interest Groups Not Speaking for Majority." *The Examiner*, April 13, 2014.

Bansal, S., and C. Martin. 2015. "The Solutions Journalism Toolkit." *The New York Times*.

Barns, Greg. 2013. "Noxious Myth of 'Old' and 'New.'" *The Mercury*, December 2, 2013.

———. 2014a. "Hodgman Has to Sell off Assets." *The Mercury*, April 7, 2014.

———. 2014b. "Why We Should Not Get Too Excited at Not-So-Free Trade Deals." *The Mercury2*, November 24, 2014.

Beck, U. 2009. *World at Risk*. Cambridge: Polity.

Beers, David. 2010. "The Public Sphere and Online, Independent Journalism." *Canadian Journal of Education/Revue Canadienne de l'éducation*. https://doi.org/10.2307/20054149.

Benesch, Susan. 1998. "The Rise of Solutions Journalism." *Columbia Journalism Review* 36: 36–39.

Benson, Rodney. 1998. "Field Theory in Comparative Context: A New Paradigm for Media Studies." *Theory and Society* 28(3): 463–498.

———. 2006. "News Media as a 'Journalistic Field': What Bourdieu Adds to New Institutionalism, and Vice Versa." *Political Communication.* https://doi.org/10.1080/10584600600629802.

———. 2009. "What Makes News Multiperspectival? A Field Analysis." *Poetics* 37: 402–418.

———. 2013. *Shaping Immigration News: A French-American Comparison.* New York: Cambridge University Press.

Benson, Rodney, and Erik Neveu. 2005. *Bourdieu and the Journalistic Field.* New York: Polity.

Benton, Joshua. 2019. "Why Do Some People Avoid News? Because They Don't Trust Us — or Because They Don't Think We Add Value to Their Lives?" *Nieman Lab*, 2019. https://www.niemanlab.org/2019/06/why-do-some-people-avoid-news-because-they-dont-trust-us-or-because-they-dont-think-we-add-value-to-their-lives/.

Beresford, Q. 2015. *The Rise and Fall of Gunns Ltd.* Sydney: NewSouth Press.

Bevilaqua, S. 2014. "Timber Resource 'at Risk'." *The Mercury*, May 10, 2014.

Bibby, W. 2013. "The Cost of Hubris: Due Process, Democracy and Respect." In *Tasmania: The Tipping Point*, edited by J. Schultz, 66–73. Brisbane: Griffith Review.

Billings, P. 2014. "Push to Decriminalise Pot." *The Examiner*, May 12, 2014.

Bloch, Ernst. 1995. *The Principle of Hope: Volume One.* Cambridge: MIT Press.

Bolger, R. 2014. "Tasmanian Budget 2014: Liberals to Axe 700 Jobs in Bid to Balance Books." *ABC Tasmania*, August 28, 2014.

Boltanski, Luc, and Eve Chiapello. 2005. *The New Spirit of Capitalism.* Edited by Gregory Elliot. London: Verso.

Boorstin, Daniel J. 1992. *The Image: A Guide to Pseudo-Events in America.* New York: Vintage Books.

Booth, K., J. O'Connor, A. Franklin, and N. Papastergiadis. 2017. "It's a Museum, but Not as We Know It: Issues for Local Residents Accessing the Museum of Old and New Art." *Visitor Studies* 20(1): 10–32.

Borden, Sandra L. 2008. "The Moral Justification for Journalism."

Borden, Sandra L., and Chad Tew. 2007. "The Role of Journalist and the Performance of Journalism: Ethical Lessons From "' Fake '" News (Seriously)." *Journal of Mass Media Ethics* 22(4): 300–314.

Bornstein, D. 1998. "Changing the World on a Shoestring." *The Atlantic*, January 1998.

———. 2004. *How to Change the World: Social Entrepreneurs and the Power of New Ideas.* New York: Oxford University Press.

———. 2011. "Why 'Solutions Journalism' Matters, Too." *The New York Times*, December 20, 2011.

———. 2012. "Up for Debate: Why We Need Solutions Journalism." *Forbes*, November 29, 2012. https://www.forbes.com/sites/skollworldforum/2012/11/29/up-for-debate-why-we-need-solutions-journalism/#2b02a9745b75.

Bornstein, D., and S. Davis. 2010. *Social Entrepreneurship: What Everyone Needs to Know*. Oxford: Oxford University Press.

Bornstein, D., and T. Rosenberg. 2016. "When Reportage Turns to Cynicism." *New York Times*, November 14, 2016. https://www.nytimes.com/2016/11/15/opinion/when-reportage-turns-to-cynicism.html.

Bourdieu, Pierre. 1984. *Distinction: A Social Critique of the Judgement of Taste*. Cambridge: Harvard University Press.

———. 1986. "The Forms of Capital." In *Handbook of Theory and Research for the Sociology of Education*, edited by J. Richardson, 241–258. Westport: Routledge. https://doi.org/10.4324/9780429494338.

———. 1991a. *Language and Symbolic Power*. Edited by J. B. Thompson. Cambridge: Polity Press.

———. 1991b. "Sport and Social Class." In *Rethinking Popular Culture: Contempory Perspectives in Cultural Studies*, edited by Chandra Mukerji and Michael Schudson, 357–373. Berkeley: University of California Press.

———. 1993. *The Field of Cultural Production: Essays on Art and Literature*. New York: Polity Press.

———. 1996a. *The Rules of Art: Genesis and Structure of the Literary Field*. https://doi.org/10.4324/9780203131527.

———. 1996b. *The State Nobility: Elite Schools in the Field of Power. The British Journal of Sociology*. Cambridge: Polity Press.

———. 1998. *On Television*. New York: The New Press.

———. 2005. "The Political Field, the Social Science Field and the Journalistic Field." In *Bourdieu and the Journalistic Field*, edited by Rodney Benson and Erik Neveu, 29–47. Cambridge: Polity.

Boyce, J. 1996. "Journeying Home." *Island*, 1996.

———. 2008. *Van Diemaen's Land: A History*. Melbourne: Black Inc.

———. 2017. *Losing Streak: How Tasmania Was Gamed By The Gambling Industry*. Melbourne: Black Inc.

Boykoff, Maxwell T., and J. Timmons Roberts. 2007. "Media Coverage of Climate Change: Current Trends, Strengths, Weaknesses." *Human Development Report 2007/2008*. Geneva. https://doi.org/10.1016/j.jenvp.2013.07.003.

Boykoff, Maxwell T., and Jules M. Boykoff. 2004. "Balance as Bias: Global Warming and the US Prestige Press." *Global Environmental Change* 14(2): 125–136. https://doi.org/10.1016/j.gloenvcha.2003.10.001.

Brett, Judith. 2011. "Fair Share: Country and City in Australia." *The Quarterly* 42.

Browne, Tess, Michael Evangeli, and Neil Greenberg. 2012. "Trauma-Related Guilt and Posttraumatic Stress Among Journalists." *Journal of Traumatic Stress* 25(2): 207–210. https://doi.org/10.1002/jts.21678.

Burgers, Christian, Elly A. Konijn, and Gerard J. Steen. 2016. "Figurative Framing: Shaping Public Discourse Through Metaphor, Hyperbole, and Irony." *Communication Theory* 26(4): 410–430. https://doi.org/10.1111/comt.12096.

Carlson, Matt. 2016. "Metajournalistic Discourse and the Meanings of Journalism: Definitional Control, Boundary Work, and Legitimation." *Communication Theory* 26(4): 349–368. https://doi.org/10.1111/comt.12088.

Champagne, Patrick. 2005. "The Double Dependency." In *Bourdieu and the Journalistic Field*, edited by Rodney Benson and Erik Neveu, 48–63. Cambridge: Polity Press.

Christians, C. G. 1999. "The Common Good as First Principle." In *The Idea of Public Journalism*, edited by T. L. Glaser, 67–84. New York: Guilford Press.

Cica, N. 2005. "Turbo Tassie." *Island* 101: 6–16.

———. 2013. "The Cracks Are How the Light Gets In: Does Tasmania Need an Intervention?" In *Tasmania: The Tipping Point*, edited by J. Schultz, 9–19. Brisbane: Griffith Review.

Clark, C. 2014c. "State Seen as 'Environmental Capital.'" *The Examiner*, September 25, 2014.

Clark, N. 2014a. "Learning Will Not Stop Leaving." *The Mercury*, May 25, 2014.

———. 2014b. "Oriental Feast for Primary Producers." *The Mercury*, November 19, 2014.

Clements, N. P. 2013. *Frontier Conflict in Van Diemen's Land*. Hobart: University of Tasmania.

Conboy, M. 2004. *Journalism: A Critical History*. London: SAGE Publications. https ://books.google.com.au/books?hl=en&lr=&id=K62tSZJgZyIC&oi=fnd&pg=PP2 &dq=Journalism:+a+critical+history:&ots=Yf7-kweqSj&sig=a4oNjb5Yf6KgbQ eaVa3MHZ2aFBo.

Croome, Rodney. 1997. "Does Tasmania Have a Future?" *Island* 116: 116–158.

———. 2013. "Churning the Mud: The Battle for the Tasmanian Soul." In *Tasmania: The Tipping Point*, edited by J Schultz, 30–38. Brisbane: Griffith Review.

Curry, Alexander L., Natalie Jomini Stroud, and Shannon McGregor. 2016. "Solutions Journalism and News Engagement." *Center for Media Engagement*. Austin. https://engagingnewsproject.org/wp-content/uploads/2016/03/ENP-Solutio ns-Journalism-News-Engagement.pdf.

Dam, Philippe. 2020. "Hungary's Authoritarian Takeover Puts European Union at Risk." *Human Rights Watch*, 2020. https://www.hrw.org/news/2020/04/01/hung arys-authoritarian-takeover-puts-european-union-risk.

Deighton, Matt. 2015. "Interview with Deighton Matthew." *Hobart*, September 9: Interview by Author.

Denholm, M. 2013. "One Almighty Crash." *The Australian*, May 4, 2013.

Denny, Lisa. 2013. "The Aspirational Tasmanian: Ready for the Right Kind of Change." *The Conversation*, 2013.

Denny, Lisa, and Eugene Polkan. 2015. "Measuring Mendicancy: Identifying Capacity for Future Economic Sustainability by Developing a Measure of Government Dependency." *Australian Economic Review* 48(3): 273–287. https:// doi.org/10.1111/1467-8462.12119.

Department of Economic and Social Affairs. 2020. *World Social Report 2020: Inequality in a Rapidly Changing World*. Geneva: Department of Economic and Social Affairs.

Dewey, John. 1922. *Human Nature and Conduct*. New York: Henry Holt and Company.

Dodd, Bill. 2020. "A Feel for the Frame: Towards a Bourdieusian Frame Analysis." *Poetics* In press: 1–11. https://doi.org/10.1016/j.poetic.2020.101482.

Doyle, R. 2005. *America and Australia: Writings and Observations from the "Empire" and "Van Diemen's Land."* Maryland: University Press of America.

———. 2014. "Feeding, Not Taming, the Dragon." *The Mercury*, 2014.

Drayton, B. 2005. "Where the Real Power Lies." *Alliance* 10(1): 1–2.

Dunmire, Patricia L. 2005. "Preempting the Future: Rhetoric and Ideology of the Future in Political Discourse." *Discourse and Society* 16(4): 481–513. https://doi .org/10.1177/0957926505053052.

Eagly, Alice H., Mona G. Makhijani, and Bruce G. Klonsky. 1992. "Gender and the Evaluation of Leaders." *Psychological Bulletin* 111(1): 3–22.

Easthope, Hazel, and Michelle Gabriel. 2008. "Turbulent Lives: Exploring the Cultural Meaning of Regional Youth Migration." *Geographical Research* 46(2): 172–182. https://doi.org/10.1111/j.1745-5871.2008.00508.x.

Eccleston, Richard, and Zoë Jay. 2019. "Insight Ten Campaign Finance Reform in Tasmania: Issues and Options." *Hobart.*

Editorial Board. 2020. "The America We Need." *The New York Times*, April 9, 2020. https://www.nytimes.com/2020/04/09/opinion/coronavirus-inequality-amer ica.html.

Edwards, Z. 2014. "Tasmania's Peace Deal Dismantled." *ABC Tasmania*, April 8, 2014.

Entman, Robert M. 1993. "Framing: Towards Clarification of a Fractured Paradigm." *Journal of Communication* 43(4): 51–58.

Ettema, J. S., and T. L. Glasser. 1998. *Custodians of Conscience: Investigative Journalism and Public Virtue.* New York: Columbia University Press.

Firmstone, J., and S. Coleman. 2015. "Rethinking Local Communicative Spaces: Implications of Digital Media and Citize Journalism for the Role of Local Journalism in Engaging Citizens." In *Local Journalism: The Decline of Newspapers and the Rise of Digital Media*, edited by Rasmus Kleis Nielsen, 19–43. London: I.B Tauris.

Fisher, Caroline, Sora Park, Jee Young Lee, Glen Fuller, and Yoonmo Sang. 2019. "Digital News Report: Australia 2019." *Canberra.* https://doi.org/10.25916 /5cff18510a051.

Flanagan, Richard. 2012. "Gunn's Demise Lifts a Darkness over Tasmania." *Crikey*, September 26, 2012.

Florida, Richard. 2006. "The Flight of the Creative Class: The New Global Competition for Talent." *Liberal Education* 92(3): 22–29.

Franklin, A. 2014. *The Making of MONA.* London: Penguin.

Fraser, Nancy. 1990. "Rethinking the Public Sphere: A Contribution to the Critique of Actually Existing Democracy." *Social Text* 26(25/26): 56–80. https://doi.org/10 .2307/466240.

———. 2007. "Transnationalizing the Public Sphere: On the Legitimacy and Efficacy of Public Opinion in a Post-Westphalian World." *Theory* 24(4): 7–30. https://doi.org/10.1177/0263276407080090.

Fraser, Nancy, and A. Honneth. 2003. *Redistribution or Recognition? A Political-Philosophical Exchange.* New York: Verso.

Gale, Fred. 2013. "No Basket-Case: Tasmania on the Bumpy Road to Economic Sustainability." *The Conversation*. Melbourne, February 2013. https://theconversat ion.com/no-basket-case-tasmania-on-the-bumpy-road-to-economic-sustainability -11293.

Gamson, W. 1992. "Media Images and the Social Construction of Reality." *Annual Review of Sociology* 18(1): 373–393. https://doi.org/10.1146/annurev.soc.18.1.373.

Gamson, W., and Andre Modigliani. 1989. "Media Discourse and Public Opinion on Nuclear Power: A Constructionist Approach." *American Journal of Sociology* 95(1): 1–37. https://doi.org/10.1086/229213.

Gans, H. 1979. *Deciding What's News*. Evanston: Northwestern University Press.

Garfin, Dana Rose, Roxane Cohen Silver, and E. Alison Holman. 2020. "The Novel Coronavirus (COVID-2019) Outbreak: Amplification of Public Health Consequences by Media Exposure." *Health Psychology*. https://doi.org/10.1037/hea0000875.

Gerrits, Bailey, Linda Trimble, Angelia Wagner, Daisy Raphael, and Shannon Sampert. 2017. "Political Battlefield: Aggressive Metaphors, Gender, and Power in News Coverage of Canadian Party Leadership Contests." *Feminist Media Studies* 17(6): 1088–1103. https://doi.org/10.1080/14680777.2017.1315734.

Gitlin, Todd. 1981. *The Whole World Is Watching: Mass Media in the Making and Unmaking of the New Left*. Berkeley: University of California Press.

Glasser, T. L. 1999. *The Idea of Public Journalism*. New York: Guilford Press.

"Global News and Insights for a New Generation of Business Leaders." 2020. *Quartz*, 2020. https://qz.com/about/#about.

Green, Melanie C., and Timothy C. Brock. 2000. "The Role of Transportation in the Persuasiveness of Public Narratives." *Journal of Personality and Social Psychology* 79(5): 701–721. https://doi.org/10.1037/0022-3514.79.5.701.

Greste, Peter. 2020. "Coronavirus Underscores the of the Free Press in a Crisis." *The Sydeny Morning Herald*, March 30, 2020. https://www.smh.com.au/business/com panies/coronavirus-underscores-the-crucial-role-and-responsibility-of-the-free-p ress-in-a-crisis-20200329-p54f03.html.

Grube, Dennis. 2011. "What the Secretary Said Next: 'Public Rhetorical Leadership' in the Australian Public Service." *Australian Journal of Public Administration* 70(2): 115–130. https://doi.org/10.1111/j.1467-8500.2011.00724.x.

Gutwein, P. 2014. "2014–15 Budget Speech—'Keeping Our Promises. Laying the Foundations for the Future.'" http://www.parliament.tas.gov.au/bills/Bills2014/pdf /notes/20_of_2014-SRS.pdf.

Gyldensted, Cathrine. 2011. "Innovating News Journalism Through Positive Psychology." http://goo.gl/cLDj9f.

———. 2015. *From Mirrors to Movers: Five Elements of Positive Psychology in Constructive Journalism*. Copenhagen: GGroup Publishers. https://issuu.com/ca thrincgyldenstcd1/docs/from_mirrors_to_movers_pdf._full__.

Haagerup, Ulrik. 2017. *Constructive News: How to Save the Media and Democracy with Journalism of Tomorrow*. Aarhus: Aarhus University Press.

Haas, Tanni. 2005. "From 'Public Journalism' to the 'Public's Journalism'? Rhetoric and Reality in the Discourse on Weblogs." *Journalism Studies* 6(3): 387–396. https ://doi.org/10.1080/14616700500132073.

Haas, Tanni, and Linda Steiner. 2006. "Public Journalism: A Reply to Critics." *Journalism* 7(2): 238–254. https://doi.org/10.1177/1464884906062607.

Habermas, J. 1991. *The Structural Transformation of the Public Sphere: An Inquiry into a Category of Bourgeois Society.* Cambridge: MIT Press.

Hage. 2000. *White Nation.* New York: Routledge.

Hage, Ghassan. 1996. "The Spatial Imaginary of National Practices: Dwelling—D omesticating/Being—Exterminating." *Environment and Planning D: Society and Space* 14(4): 463–485. https://doi.org/10.1068/d140463.

———. 2003. *Paranoid Nationalism: Searching for Hope in a Shrinking Society.* Annandale: Pluto Press. http://hdl.handle.net/1885/144694.

———. 2016. "Questions Concerning a Future-Politics." *History and Anthropology* 27(4): 465–467. https://doi.org/10.1080/02757206.2016.1206896.

Hage, Ghassan, and D. Papadopoulos. 2004. "Migration, Hope and the Making of Subjectivity in Transnational Capitalism." *Critical Psychology* 12: 107–121. https ://www2.le.ac.uk/departments/management/research/units/cppe/archiveactivities/ texts/2004-Hage-Papadopoulos-IJCP.pdf.

Hall, Bianca. 2015. "Australia in the Middle of 'Mental Health Crisis' with Unnecessary Deaths Escalating." *The Age*, September 16, 2015. https://www.the age.com.au/national/victoria/australia-in-the-middle-of-mental-health-crisis-with -unnecessary-deaths-escalating-20150916-gjnqpd.html.

Hall, Stuart, Chas Critchter, Tony Jefferson, John Clarke, and Brian Roberts. 2013. *Policing the Crisis: Mugging, the State and Law and Order.* 3rd ed. London: Palgrave Macmillan.

Hallin, D. 1994. *We Keep America on Top of the World: Television Journalism and the Public Sphere.* London: Psychology Press.

Harvey, D. 2007. *A Brief History of Neoliberalism.* New York: Oxford University Press.

Hayek, F. 1976. *The Road to Serfdom.* London: Routlege and Kegan Paul.

Heifetz, Ronald A. 1994. *Leadership Without Easy Answers.* Cambridge: Harvard University Press.

Heller, Scott. 1996. "Harvard Professor Examines America's Fading Sense of Community." *The Chronicle of Higher Education* 42(25): 10–12. https://www.chr onicle.com/article/Harvard-Professor-Examines/97142.

Hellsten, Iina, Amanda J. Porter, and Brigitte Nerlich. 2014. "Imagining the Future at the Global and National Scale: A Comparative Study of British and Dutch Press Coverage of Rio 1992 and Rio 2012." *Environmental Communication* 8(4): 468–488. https://doi.org/10.1080/17524032.2014.911197.

Hermans, Liesbeth, and Cathrine Gyldensted. 2019. "Elements of Constructive Journalism: Characteristics, Practical Application and Audience Valuation." *Journalism* 20(4): 535–551. https://doi.org/10.1177/1464884918770537.

Hockey, J. 2014. "Joe Hockey's Full Budget Speech." *ABC*, May 13, 2014. http:// www.abc.net.au/news/2014-05-13/hockes-full-budget-speech/5450984.

Holman, E. Alison, Dana Rose Garfin, Pauline Lubens, and Roxane Cohen Silver. 2020. "Media Exposure to Collective Trauma, Mental Health, and Functioning: Does It Matter What You See?" *Clinical Psychological Science.* https://doi.org/10 .1177/2167702619858300.

Holmstrom, David. 1998. "'Hope' Has Hard Sell in the Magazine Market." *The Christian Science Monitor*, March 11, 1998. https://www.csmonitor.com/1998 /0311/031198.feat.feat.1.html.

Honneth, A. 1995. *The Fragmented World of the Social: Essays in Social and Political Philosophy.* New York: State University of New York Press.

Hope, E. 2014. "Chinese Students Raise Bar." *The Mercury*, August 7, 2014.

Horne, Donald. 1968. *The Lucky Country.* London: Penguin Books.

Huffington, Arianna. 2015. "What's Working: All the News That's Fit to Print." *The Huffington Post*, 2015. https://www.huffpost.com/entry/whats-working-all-the-ne ws_b_6603924.

Ihlebk, Karoline Andrea, and Arne H. Krumsvik. 2015. "Editorial Power and Public Participation in Online Newspapers." *Journalism* 16(4): 470–487. https://doi.org /10.1177/1464884913520200.

Ikin, S., and T. Nightingale. 2014. "Tasmania Repeals the Forestry Peace Deal Between Conservationists and Loggers, Opening Up 400,000 Hectares." *ABC Tasmania*, September 3, 2014.

Jackson, N., and R. Kippen. 2001. "Whither Tasmania?: A Note on Tasmania's Population Problem." *People and Place* 9(1): 27–37.

James, Ethan. 2020. "Tasmania Shuts Small Airstrips to Flights." *The Advocate*, March 25, 2020. https://www.theadvocate.com.au/story/6697486/tasmania-shuts-small-airstrips-to-flights/?cs=7.

Jin, Borae, and Yong Chan Kim. 2019. "Rainbows in the Society: A Measure of Hope for Society." *Asian Journal of Social Psychology* 22(1): 18–27. https://doi.org/10 .1111/ajsp.12339.

Jones, Michael D. 2014. "Cultural Characters and Climate Change: How Heroes Shape Our Perception of Climate Science." *Social Science Quarterly* 95(1): 1–39. https://doi.org/10.1111/ssqu.12043.

Jones, Michael D., and Mark K. McBeth. 2010. "A Narrative Policy Framework: Clear Enough to Be Wrong?" *Policy Studies Journal* 38(2): 329–353. https://doi .org/10.1111/j.1541-0072.2010.00364.x.

"June Key Figures." 2016. *Canberra.* http://www.abs.gov.au/ausstats.

Kahan, Dan. 2012. "Why We Are Poles Apart on Climate Change." *Nature* 488(7411): 255. https://doi.org/10.1038/488255a.

Keane, John. 2018. *Power and Humility: The Future of Monitory Democracy.* Cambridge: Cambridge University Press.

Kefford, Glenn, and D. McDonnell. 2015. "With Her Network, Lambie Sets Herself Up as a Tasmanian Pauline Hanson." *The Guardian*, April 1, 2015. https://www .theguardian.com/commentisfree/2015/apr/01/with-her-network-lambie-sets- herse lf-up-as-a-tasmanian-pauline-hanson.

Kellner, D. 2017. *American Horror Show: Election 2016 and the Ascent of Donald J. Trump.* Berlin: Springer.

Kempton, H. 2014a. "Farmers Get Help to Lift Milk Output." *The Mercury*, April 21, 2014.

———. 2014b. "Young Bear the Brunt." *The Mercury*, May 15, 2014.

Kerr, Ron. 2008. "Discourse and Leadership: Using the Paradigm of the Permanent State of Emergency." *Critical Discourse Studies*. https://doi.org/10.1080/174059 00802131702.

Kleist, Nauja, and Stef Jansen. 2016. "Introduction: Hope over Time—Crisis, Immobility and Future-Making." *History and Anthropology* 27(4): 373–392. https ://doi.org/10.1080/02757206.2016.1207636.

Krien, A. 2012. *Into the Woods: The Battle for Tasmania's Forests*. Melbourne: Black Inc.

Lakoff, George. 1987. *Women, Fire, and Dangerous Things: What Categories Reveal About the Mind*. Chicago: University of Chicago Press. https://doi.org/10.2307 /1422958.

———. 2008. *Don't Think of an Elephant!* Hartford: Chelsea Freen Publishing.

———. 2010. "Why It Matters How We Frame the Environment." *Environmental Communication* 4(1): 70–81. https://doi.org/10.1080/17524030903529749.

———. 2014. "Mapping the Brain's Metaphor Circuitry: Metaphorical Thought in Everyday Reason." *Frontiers in Human Neuroscience* 8(December): 1–14. https:// doi.org/https://doi.org/10.3389/fnhum.2014.00958.

———. 2016. *Moral Politics: What Conservatives Know That Liberals Don't*. 3rd ed. Chicago: University of Chicago Press.

Lakoff, George, and Mark Johnson. 1999. *Philosophy in the Flesh: The Embodied Mind and Its Challenge to Western Thought*. New York: Basic Books.

———. 2003. *Metaphors We Live By*. London: University of Chicago Press.

Lakoff, George, and S. Ferguson. 2016. *The Framing of Immigration*. Berkeley: The Rockridge Institute.

Landry, C. 2008. *The Creative City: A Toolkit for Urban Innovators*. Chicago: University of Chicago Press.

Laurent, Melanie, and Cyril Dion. 2015. *Tomorrow*. France: Mars Distribution.

Leonard, T. 1999. "Making Readers into Citizens–The Old-Fashioned Way." In *The Idea of Public Journalism*, edited by T. L. Glasser, 85–98. New York: Guilford Press.

Lester, Libby. 2010. *Media and Environment: Conflict, Politics and the News*. Cambridge: Polity.

———. 2019. *Global Trade and Mediatised Environmental Protest the View From Here*. Cham: Palgrave Macmillan.

Lester, Libby, and Brett Hutchins. 2009. "Power Games: Environmental Protest, News Media and the Internet." *Media, Culture and Society* 31(4): 579–595. https:// doi.org/10.1177/0163443709335201.

Lester, Libby, and Simon Cottle. 2009. "Visualizing Climate Change: Television News and Ecological Citizenship University of Tasmania." *International Journal of Communication* 3: 920–936.

Lippmann, Walter. 1922. *Public Opinion*. 3rd ed. New York: The Free Press.

Livingston, Charles. 2017. "Tasmania's Pokie Problem: Stress and Disadvantage Exploited More than Anywhere Else in Australia." *The Conversation*, March 2017. https://theconversation.com/tasmanias-pokie-problem-stress-and-disadva ntage-exploited-more-than-anywhere-else-in-australia-73525.

Lock, Andrew, and Phil Harris. 1996. " Political Marketing—Vive La Différence!" *European Journal of Marketing* 30(10/11): 14–24. https://doi.org/10.1108/030905 69610149764.

Lopez, Shane J., and C. R. Snyder. 2016. *The Oxford Handbook of Positive Psychology*. Edited by Shane J. Lopez and C. R. Snyder. 3rd ed. New York: Oxford University Press. https://doi.org/10.1093/oxfordhb/9780195187243.001.0001.

MacIntyre, Alasdair. 2007. *After Virtue*. 3rd ed. Notre Dame, IA: University of Notre Dame Press. https://doi.org/10.4324/9781912281954.

Maddox, Kate. 2016. "Bees Wearing Backpacks (for Real) Show off Intel's Sophisticated Technology." *AdAge*, May 2016.

Maloney, M. 2014a. "Turning Hell into a Crown Jewel Won't Be Easy." *The Examiner*, April 11, 2014.

———. 2014b. "Long Struggle to Redevelop City Eyesore." *The Examiner*, April 21, 2014.

Marr, Andrew. 2004. *My Trade: A Short History of British Journalism*. London: Macmillan.

Marwick, Alice E. 2015. "Instafame: Luxury Selfies in the Attention Economy." *Public Culture* 27(1): 137–160. https://doi.org/10.1215/08992363-2798379.

Matza, Tomas. 2018. *Shock Therapy: Psychology, Precarity, and Well-Being in Postsocialist Russia*. Durham: Duke University Press.

McCulloch, D. 2014. "Bobbie the Bear to Greet President." *The Examiner*, November 18, 2014.

Mcgaurr, Lyn, Bruce Tranter, and Libby Lester. 2015. "Wilderness and the Media Politics of Place Branding." *Environmental Communication* 9(3): 269–287. https://doi.org/10.1080/17524032.2014.919947.

McGaurr, Lyn, and Libby Lester. 2017. "Environmental Groups Treading the Discursive Tightrope of Social License: Australian and Canadian Cases Compared." *International Journal of Communication* 11: 3476–3496.

McInerney, Lea. 2013. "More than Two Stories: Stretching the Metaphor Mcinery." In *Tasmania: The Tipping Point*, edited by J Schultz. Brisbane: Griffith Review.

McIntyre, Karen, and Cathrine Gyldensted. 2017. "Constructive Journalism: An Introduction and Practical Guide for Applying Positive Psychology Techniques to News Production." *The Journal of Media Innovations* 4(2): 20–34.

———. 2018. "Positive Psychology as a Theoretical Foundation for Constructive Journalism." *Journalism Practice* 12(6): 662–678. https://doi.org/10.1080/175127 86.2018.1472527.

McIntyre, Karen, and Kyser Lough. 2019. "Toward a Clearer Conceptualization and Operationalization of Solutions Journalism." *Journalism*. https://doi.org/10.1177 /1464884918820756.

McIntyre, Karen Elizabeth, and Kyser Lough. 2019. "Toward a Clearer Conceptualization and Operationalization of Solutions Journalism." *Journalism*. https://doi.org/10.1177/1464884918820756.

McKim, N. 2014. "Xi Visit a Time to Talk Straight." *The Mercury*, 2014.

McNair, Brian. 2006. *Cultural Chaos: Journalism and Power in a Globalised World*. Abingdon: Routledge.

Merritt, Davis Buzz. 1996. "Beyond Telling the News." *National Civic Review* 85(1): 22–25. https://doi.org/10.1002/ncr.4100850107.

Milbank, Dana. 1997. "Spreaders of Hope Are Finding Good News Faces a Sad Future." *Wall Street Journal*, March 31, 1997. https://www.wsj.com/articles/S B859764243743759000%0ASpreaders.

Miyazaki, Hirokazu. 2006. "Economy of Dreams: Hope in Global Capitalism and Its Critiques." *Cultural Anthropology* 21(2): 147–172.

Moore, Michael. 2015. *Where to Invade Next*. United States: Neon.

Murphy, K. 2016. "Truth and The New Politics." *Meanjin*, 2016. https://meanjin .com.au/essays/truth-and-the-new-politics/.

Newman, Nic, R. Fletcher, Antonis Kalogeropoulos, and Rasmus Kleis Nielsen. 2019. *Digital News Report 2019*. Oxford, UK.

Nip, Joyce Y. M. 2008. "The Last Days of Civic Journalism: The Case of the Savannah Morning News." *Journalism Practice* 2(2): 179–196. https://doi.org/10 .1080/17512780801999352.

Nisbet, Matthew C. 2009. "Knowledge Into Action: Framing the Debates Over Climate Change and Poverty." In *Doing News Framing Analysis: Empirical and Theoretical Perspectives*, edited by Paul D'Angelo and Jim A. Kuypers, 43–83. New York: Routledge.

———. 2018. "Framing the Debates Over Climate Change and Poverty." In *Doing News Framing Analysis: Empirical and Theoretical Perspectives*, 2009.

Nussbaum, Martha C. 2006. *Frontiers of Justice: Disability, Nationality, Species Membership*. Cambridge, MA: Harvard University Press.

———. 2007. "Non-Relative Virtues: An Aristotelian Approach." In *Ethical Theory: An Anthology*, edited by Russ Shafer-Landau. Malden: Blackwell Publishing.

Oettingen, Gabriele, and Martin E. P. Seligman. 1990. "Pessimism and Behavioural Signs of Depression in East Versus West Berlin." *European Journal of Social Psychology* 20(3): 207–220. https://doi.org/10.1002/ejsp.2420200303.

Our Watch. 2015. "Change the Story: A Shared Framework for the Prevention of Violence Against Women." *Melbourne*. https://www.ourwatch.org.au/getmedia/ c81eceab-c8a0-4f3a-a6fb-2202334b398b/Change-the-story-framework-prevent-v iolence-women-children-AA-new.pdf.aspx.

Park, Sora, Caroline Fisher, Jee Young Lee, and Kieran McGuinness. 2020. "COVID-19: Australian News and Misinformation." *Canberra*. https://www.canberra.edu. au/research/faculty-research-centres/nmrc/publications/documents/COVID-19-A ustralian-news-and-misinformation.pdf.

Paterson, Peter. 1993. *Tired and Emotional: The Life of Lord George-Brown*. London: Chatto & Windus.

Peterson, Christopher, Lester Luborsky, and Martin E. Seligman. 1983. "Attributions and Depressive Mood Shifts: A Case Study Using the Symptom-Context Model." *Journal of Abnormal Psychology* 92(1): 96–103. https://doi.org/10.1037/0021-8 43X.92.1.96.

Polakovic, Gary. 2020. "To Manage COVID-19 Stress, Develop Healthy New Habits and Consume News in Moderation." *USC News*, 2020. https://news.usc.edu/1675 12/covid-19-stress-coping-healthy-habits-usc-social-science-experts/.

Powers, Elia, and Alex Curry. 2019. "NO QUICK FIX: How Journalists Assess the Impact and Define the Boundaries of Solutions Journalism." *Journalism Studies*. https://doi.org/10.1080/1461670X.2019.1586565.

Prismall, B. 2014a. "Time to Act on Future Eyesore." *The Examiner*, April 21, 2014.

———. 2014b. "Creating Jobs Must Be Top Priority." *The Examiner*, August 19, 2014.

———. 2014c. "Focus on State's Potential." *The Examiner*, December 9, 2014.

Putnam, Robert D. 1995. "Bowling Alone: America's Declining Social Capital." *Journal of Democracy* 6(1): 223–234.

———. 2000. *Bowling Alone: The Collapse and Revival of American Community*. New York: Simon & Schuster Paperbacks.

Rand, K. L., and K. K. Touza. 2016. "Hope Theory." In *The Oxford Handbook of Positive Psychology*, edited by C. R. Snyder, S. J. Lopez, L. M. Edwards, and S. C. Marques. 3rd ed., 291–300. New York: Oxford University Press. https://doi.org/10.1093/oxfordhb/9780199396511.013.25.

Rani, Rikha. 2016. "Study: Solutions-Oriented Headlines Got More Clicks." *Solutions Journalism Network*. New York. http://solutionsjournalism.org/solutions?journalism?click?bait?solutions?oriented?headlines?outperform?problem?ones?study/.

"Regional Population Growth, Australia, 2014–15." 2015. *Canberra*. https://www.abs.gov.au/ausstats.

Reynolds, H. 2013. *Forgotten War*. Kensington: NewSouth Press.

Richards, B. 2014a. "Accusations Fly at Woodchip Inquiry." *The Mercury*, August 16, 2014.

———. 2014b. "Vow to Keep Promises." *The Mercury*, August 29, 2014.

Ridout, Travis N., Erika Franklin Fowler, and Kathleen Searles. 2012. "Exploring the Validity of Electronic Newspaper Databases." *International Journal of Social Research Methodology* 15(6): 451–466. https://doi.org/10.1080/13645579.2011.638221.

Riffe, Daniel, Stephan Lacy, and Frederick Fico. 2014. *Analyzing Media Messages: Using Quantitative Content Analysis in Research*. 3rd ed. New York: Routledge.

Rosen, Jay. 1999. *What Are Journalists For?* New Haven: Yale University Press.

———. 2011. "Why Political Coverage Is Broken." *PressThink*. http://pressthink.org/2011/08/why-political-coverage-is-broken/.

Scaptura, Maria N., and Kaitlin M. Boyle. 2019. "Masculinity Threat, 'Incel' Traits, and Violent Fantasies Among Heterosexual Men in the United States." *Feminist Criminology*. https://doi.org/10.1177/1557085119896415.

Schneider, Sandra L. 2001. "In Search of Realistic Optimism: Meaning, Knowledge, and Warm Fuzziness." *American Psychologist*.

Schudson, Michael. 2006. "The Trouble with Experts—And Why Democracies Need Them." *Theory and Society* 35(5–6): 491–506. https://doi.org/10.1007/s11186-006-9012-y.

———. 2008. "The 'Lippmann-Dewey Debate' and the Invention of Walter Lippmann as an Anti-Democrat 1986–1996." *International Journal of Communication* 2: 12.

Schultz, Ida. 2007. "The Journalistic Gut Feeling: Journalistic Doxa, News Habitus and Orthodox News Values." *Journalism Practice* 1(2). https://doi.org/10.1080/1 7512780701275507.

Schultz, J. 2013. "Oscillating Wildly: Learning from the Past to Create the Future." In *Tasmania: The Tipping Point*, edited by J. Schultz, 7–8. Brisbane: Griffith Review.

Searle, B. 2002. "Federal Fiscal Relations in Australia-2001." *Canberra*.

Seligman. 1991. *Learned Optimism*. New York: Alfred A. Knopf.

Seligman, Martin. 1999. "President Address." *American Psychlogist*. https://doi.org /10.1007/bf03262405.

———. 2002. "Positive Psychology, Positive Prevention, and Positive Therapy." In *Handbook of Positive Psychology*, edited by C. R. Sneider and S. J. Lopez, 3–9. New York: Oxford University Press. https://doi.org/10.1017/CBO9781107415324 .004.

———. 2016. "Clinton Is More Optimistic than Trump. But Optimism Doesn't Predict Winners." *The Washington Post*, August 6, 2016. https://www.washingt onpost.com/posteverything/wp/2016/08/05/optimism-clinton-trump/.

———. 2019. "Constructive Journalism and Moyers' Dictum*." *Journalism*, April 1, 2019. https://doi.org/10.1177/1464884918770933.

Seligman, Martin, and Mihaly Csikszentmihalyi. 2012. "Positive Psychology: An Introduction." *Indian Journal of Positive Psychology* 55(1): 5–14.

Shanahan, Elizabeth A., Michael D. Jones, Mark K. Mcbeth, and Ross R. Lane. 2013. "An Angel on the Wind: How Heroic Policy Narratives Shape Policy Realities." *Policy Studies Journal* 41(3): 453–483. https://doi.org/10.1111/psj.12025.

Shannon, L. 2014. "Chinese President Xi Jinping 'Considering Visit to Tasmania' After G20." *ABC Tasmania*, September 2, 2014.

Shipway, J. 2005. "Scars on the Archive, Visions of Place: Genocide and Modernity in Tasmania." *The University of Tasmania*.

Sifton, Sam. 2020. "At Home." *The New York Times*, April 18, 2020. https://www.nyt imes.com/spotlight/at-home?action=click&module=Top Stories&pgtype=Homep age&contentCollection=AtHome.

Simons, M., and E. Khan. 2018. "Working with Media to Prevent Violence Against Women: The Uncovered Intervention." *Australian Journalism Review* 40(1): 51–63.

Singer, Peter. 1980. "Utilitarianism and Vegetarianism." *Philosophy & Public Affairs* 9(4): 325–337.

Smart, John Jamieson Carswell, and Bernard Williams. 1973. *Utilitarianism: For and Against*. Cambridge: Cambridge University Press.

Smart, R. N. 1958. "Negative Utilitarianism." *Mind* LXVII(268): 542–543. https://do i.org/10.1093/mind/LXVII.268.542.

Smiley, S. 2014. "Tasmanian Cabinet Set to Review Report on Royal Hobart Hospital's Redevelopment." *ABC Tasmania*, December 8, 2014.

Smith, L. 2014. "Our Time to Shine." *The Mercury*, April 6, 2014.

Smith, M. 2014a. "Cascade's Wildcard Role with Cable Car." *The Mercury*, April 16, 2014.

———. 2014b. "Twiggy's TasInvest Visit." *The Mercury*, November 9, 2014.

Snow, Nancy E. 2018. "Hope as a Democratic Civic Virtue Nancy e. Snow." *Metaphilosophy* 49(3): 407–427. https://doi.org/10.1111/meta.12299.

Snyder, C. R. 1989. "Reality Negotiation: From Excuses to Hope and Beyond." *Journal of Social and Clinical Psychology* 8.

———. 2002. "Hope Theory: Rainbows in the Mind." *Psychological Inquiry* 13(4): 249–275.

Snyder, C. R., and D. B. Feldman. 2000. "Hope for the Many." In *The Handbook of Hope*, edited by C. R. Snyder. 1st ed., 389–412. Oxford: Oxford University Press.

Snyder, C. R., J. L. Shane, L. M. Edwards, and S. C. Marques. 2002. "Hope Theory A Member of the Positive Psychology Family." In *Handbook of Positive Psychology*, edited by C. R. Sneider, J. L. Shane, L. M. Edwards, and S. C. Marques. 1st ed., 257–276. New York: Oxford University Press.

Snyder, C. R., Kevin L. Rand, Elisa A. King, David B. Feldman, and Julia T. Woodward. 2002. "'False' Hope." *Journal of Clinical Psychology* 58(9): 1003–1022. https://doi.org/10.1002/jclp.10096.

Solutions Journalism Network. 2020. "Who We Are." *Solutions Journalism Network*, 2020. https://www.solutionsjournalism.org/who-we-are/mission.

"Solutions Story Tracker." 2020. *Solutions Journalism Network*, 2020. https://storytracker.solutionsjournalism.org.

Sonnett, John. 2010. "Climates of Risk: A Field Analysis of Global Climate Change in US Media Discourse, 1997–2004." *Public Understanding of Science*. https://doi.org/10.1177/0963662509346368.

Sontag, Susan. 2003. *Regarding the Pain of Others*. New York: Picador.

Spiegelman, James. 2015. "All About Audiences: Annual Report 2015." *Sydney*. https://about.abc.net.au/wp-content/uploads/2015/10/2014-15_Annual_Report.pdf.

Spreitzer, Gretchen M., and Scott Sonenshein. 2004. "Toward the Construct Definition of Positive Deviance." *American Behavioral Scientist* 47(6): 828–847. https://doi.org/10.1177/0002764203260212.

Stephens, P., J. Barry, and A. Dobson. 2006. *Contemporary Environmental Politics: From Margins to Mainstream*. Abingdon: Routledge.

Stevenson, M. 2014. "Road Linking Tassie and Victoria Part of Dreamland." *The Examiner*, September 18, 2014.

Stratford, Elaine. 2007. "Isolation as Disability and Resource: Considering Sub-National Island Status in the Constitution of the ' New Tasmania .'" *The Round Table* 95(386): 575–588. https://doi.org/10.1080/00358530600929933.

———. 2008. "Islandness and Struggles Over Development: A Tasmanian Case Study." *Political Geography* 27(2): 160–175.

Sutherland, Georgina, Angus McCormack, Jane Pirkis, Patricia Easteal, Kate Holland, and Cathy Vaughan. 2015. *Media Representations of Violence Against Women and Their Children: State of Knowledge. ANROWS Landscapes*. Melbourne: ANROWS & Our Watch. http://apo.org.au/node/58986.

Tennant, Simon. 2015. "Interview with Simon Tennant." *Lauceston*, 27 October: interview by Author.

The Examiner. 2014. "Time for Action on Isolation." November 29, 2014.

The Mercury. 2013. "It's Time to Play Ball." August 14, 2013.

———. 2014a. "Broadband Schemozzle." April 13, 2014.

———. 2014b. "Broadband Blues." April 16, 2014.

———. 2014c. "She's Comin' Round the Mountain." April 16, 2014.

———. 2014d. "Keep Eyes on the Ball." April 17, 2014.

———. 2014e. "State Left $1.1b Black Hole." April 28, 2014.

———. 2014f. "Prosperity a State of Mind." April 30, 2014.

———. 2014g. "Fix Hole in City's Heart." May 3, 2014.

———. 2014h. "Hodgman on the Ball." May 20, 2014.

———. 2014i. "Wonderful Waterfront." May 24, 2014.

———. 2014j. "Dream the Achievable." May 26, 2014.

———. 2014k. "Fists Fly but No Jobs." August 14, 2014.

———. 2014l. "Connected to the World." August 15, 2014.

———. 2014m. "Time to Seal the Deal." August 23, 2014.

———. 2014n. "Embrace Our Diversity." September 15, 2014.

———. 2014o. "The Long and Winding Road." September 16, 2014.

———. 2014p. "Remarkable Success Story." September 26, 2014.

———. 2014q. "It's Time for People Power." September 29, 2014.

———. 2014r. "The Great Call of China." November 10, 2014.

———. 2014s. "In Search of Wild." November 12, 2014.

———. 2014t. "Tasmania Ready to Go." November 18, 2014.

———. 2014u. "Rolling up the Sleeves." November 24, 2014.

———. 2014v. "Devil in the Detail of RHH Plan." December 8, 2014.

———. 2014w. "Tough Call on Domain." December 13, 2014.

———. 2014x. "Our Chance to Shine." December 29, 2014.

The Solutions Journalism Network. 2020. "Basic Toolkit." 2020. https://learninglab. solutionsjournalism.org/en/courses/basic-toolkit/print.

Thier, Kathryn, Jesse Abdenour, Brent Walth, and Nicole Smith Dahmen. 2019. "A Narrative Solution: The Relationship Between Solutions Journalism, Narrative Transportation, and News Trust." *Journalism* In press (September): 146488491987636. https://doi.org/10.1177/1464884919876369.

Thompson, John B. 1990. *Ideology and Modern Culture: Critical Social Theory in the Era of Mass Communication.* Cambridge: Polity.

———. 1991. "Editor's Introduction." In *Language and Symbolic Power*, edited by John B. Thompson, 1–31. Cambridge: Polity Press.

———. 1995. *Media and Modernity: A Social Theory of the Media.* Stanford: Stanford University Press.

———. 2005. "The New Visibility." *Theory, Culture & Society* 22(6): 31–51. https:// doi.org/10.1177/0263276405059413.

Thunberg, Greta. 2019a. "'Our House Is on Fire': Greta Thunberg, 16, Urges Leaders to Act on Climate." *The Guardian*, January 26, 2019. https://www.theguardian.c om/environment/2019/jan/25/our-house-is-on-fire-greta-thunberg16-urges-leaders -to-act-on-climate.

———. 2019b. "Transcript: Greta Thunberg's Speech At The U.N. Climate Action Summit." *NPR*, September 23, 2019. https://www.npr.org/2019/09/23/763452863/ transcript-greta-thunbergs-speech-at-the-u-n-climate-action-summit.

Tierney, Kathleen, Christine Bevc, and Erica Kuligowski. 2006. "Metaphors Matter: Disaster Myths, Media Frames and Their Concequences in Hurricane Katrina." *The Annals of the American Academy of Political and Social Science* 604(March): 57–81. https://doi.org/10.1177/0002716205285589.

"Trends in Net Overseas Migration: Tasmania." 2011. *Canberra*. http://www.abs.gov.au/ausstats.

Truss, W. 2015. "Ministerial Directions for the Operation of the Tasmanian Freight Equalisation Scheme." *Canberra*. https://infrastructure.gov.au/transport/programs/maritime/tasmanian/files/TFES_Ministeri al_Directions.pdf.

Verdich, Madeleine. 2010. "Creative Migration? The Attraction and Retention of the 'Creative Class' in Launceston, Tasmania." *Australian Geographer* 41(11): 129–140. https://doi.org/10.1080/00049180903535642.

Vowles, G. 2014. "Letters to Melt a President's Heart." *The Mercury*, November 22, 2014.

Wahl-Jorgensen, Karin, Mike Berry, Iñaki Garcia-Blanco, Lucy Bennett, and Jonathan Cable. 2017. "Rethinking Balance and Impartiality in Journalism? How the BBC Attempted and Failed to Change the Paradigm." *Journalism* 18(7): 781–800. https://doi.org/10.1177/1464884916648094.

Webb, M. 2014. "Get a Job or Dig up a Begging Bowl." *The Mercury*, August 21, 2014.

Weinstein, Neil D., Judith E. Lyon, Peter M. Sandman, and Cara L. Cuite. 1998. "Experimental Evidence for Stages of Health Behavior Change: The Precaution Adoption Process Model Applied to Home Radon Testing." *Health Psychology* 17(5): 445–453. https://doi.org/10.1037/0278-6133.17.5.445.

Wells, G. 2014. "Tasmanian Liberals Steer Clear of Structural Change with 'Nip and Tuck' Budget." *ABC Tasmania*, August 29, 2014.

Wenzel, Andrea, Daniela Gerson, Evelyn Moreno, Minhee Son, and Breanna Morrison Hawkins. 2018. "Engaging Stigmatized Communities Through Solutions Journalism: Residents of South Los Angeles Respond." *Journalism* 19(5): 649–667. https://doi.org/10.1177/1464884917703125.

West, J. 2012. "Report of the Tasmanian Forests Intergovernmental Agreement Independent Verification Group." *Hobart*. https://www.environment.gov.au/resource/independent-verification-group-report.

———. 2013. "Obstacles to Progress: What's Wrong with Tasmania, Really?" In *Tasmania: The Tipping Point*, edited by J Schultz, 50–59. Brisbane: Griffith Review.

"What Happens Next." 2019. *Quartz*. New York, 2019. https://qz.com/is/what-happens-next-2/.

Willig, Ida. 2013. "Newsroom Ethnography in a Field Perspective." *Journalism* 14(3): 372–387. https://doi.org/10.1177/1464884912442638.

Winzer, Philip Marrii. 2020. "I'd Rather Be Called a Climate Pessimist than Cling to Toxic Hope." *Overland*, March 2020. https://overland.org.au/2020/03/id-rather-be-called-a-climate-pessimist-than-cling-to-toxic-hope/.

Wolfe, Tom. 1975. *The Painted Word*. New York: Bantam Books.

Wood, Danielle, Carmela Chivers, and Kate Griffiths. 2019. "Tasmania's Gambling Election Shows Australia Needs Tougher Rules on Money in Politics."

The Conversation, February 2019. https://theconversation.com/tasmanias-gamblin g-election-shows-australia-needs-tougher-rules-on-money-in-politics-110977.

Woodstock, Louise. 2002. "Public Journalism's Talking Cure." *Journalism* 3(1): 37–55.

World Commission on Environment and Development. 1987. *World Commission on Environment and Development*. Edited by Gro Harlem Brundtland. Oxford: Oxford University Press.

World Health Organisation. 2020. "Mental Health and Psychosocial Considerations During COVID-19 Outbreak." *World Health Organization*. Geneva. https://www .who.int/docs/default-source/coronaviruse/mental-health-considerations.pdf.

Wright, Sara. 2014. "Don't Stifle Our Voices." *The Examiner*, April 12, 2014.

Xiaoge, S. 2009. "Development Journalism." In *The Handbook of Journalism Studies*, edited by Karin Wahl-Jorgensen and Thomas Hanitzche, 357–370. New York: Routledge.

Zizek, Slavoj. 1991. *For They Know Not What They Do: Enjoyment as a Political Factor*. London: Verso.

Zullow, Harold M., and Martin E. P. Seligman. 1990. "Pessimistic Rumination Predicts Defeat of Presidential Candidates, 1900 to 1984." *Psychological Inquiry* 1(1): 52–61.

Index

Abbott, Tony, 81
American Psychological Association
 (APA), 1
Ardern, Jacinda, 1
Arendt, Hannah, 47
Aristotle, 137; practical reason, 137. *See*
 virtue ethics
Ashoka, 42–44
attention economy, 2–3
audience analytics, 89

balance, 89, 95. *See also* objectivity
Beck, Ulrich, 26, 46
Beers, David, 4, 8, 31–32
Benesch, Susan, 15
Benson, Rodney, 32, 145
Bornstein, David, 9, 42–45
Bourdieu, Pierre, 5, 8, 50–52, 58, 61,
 99–100, 131, 138
Boyce, James, 67–68
Bridcut Review, 95
Brown, Bob, 72

China: free trade agreement, 80; human
 rights, 80; Tasmania relations, 122–
 23; trade, 79. *See also* Jinping, Xi
cinematic representations of journalism,
 19–20

collective futures, 31
The Constructive Institute, 5, 7
constructive journalism, 5–7, 17, 21–22
constructivism, 6
content analysis, 25
COVID-19, 1, 2, 26
creative class, 74–76
creative migration, 74–75

Davos (World Economic Forum), 49–50
debate ensemble format, 32, 35, 129,
 148; solution ensemble, 32, 147–48
deliberative democracy, 9, 39
development journalism, 43
Drayton, Bill, 42–45

earn or learn policy, 82
editorial practice, 88
engagement journalism, 45
Entman, Robert, 56–57
environmental conflict, 66, 77, 81
expertise: definition, 128; experts as
 news access, 127; industry experts,
 129–30

field theory, 5, 7, 8, 50–53; autonomy
 and heteronomy, 51, 88, 150;
 bodily hexis, 99, 113, 116; capital,

About the Author

Dr. Bill Dodd is a lecturer and researcher at the University of Tasmania's Media School. His research examines how perceived solutions to environmental challenges are constructed at the interdisciplinary intersection of journalism, science, politics, business, and activism, and, in particular, how news values shape whose voices are heard in future-focused discourses. His latest research considers optimism as a vital social good, and explores how emerging solutions and constructive journalism practices might distribute realistic optimism more equitably through communities, re-engaging diverse publics in the political process. Bill is also a freelance journalist and, previously, a political communications and campaign consultant. His writing has appeared in *Agency France-Presse*, *Al Jazeera*, the *Japan Times*, the *Mercury*, and *Forty South*. In 2018, he was invited to judge *Island Magazine*'s essay prize.